D0899138

Studies in Syntactic Typology
and Contrastive Grammar

JANUA
LINGUARUM

Series Maior 89

Studia Memoriae
Nicolai van Wijk Dedicata

edenda curat

C. H. van Schoonefeld

Indiana University

Studies in Syntactic Typology and Contrastive Grammar

László Dezső

Mouton Publishers
The Hague · Paris · New York

Translated by
Imre Gombos and Béla Hollósy

© Akadémiai Kiadó, Budapest 1982
Joint edition with Akadémiai Kiadó, Budapest

ISBN 90 279 3108 9

Printed in Hungary

Contents

Preface

This book is founded on the assumption that typology is an optimum basis for theoretical contrastive studies. This is widely accepted but typology is rarely applied in contrastive research. The first part of the book attempts to demonstrate how the typology of sentence structure and the expression of sentence constituents by various types of case systems can be used in the typological characterization of some nominative languages and in contrasting them. The second part applies the typology of word order and sentence stress in the characterization of Hungarian and in a brief contrastive study with Russian. The presentation of general typology and of the languages characterized and contrasted in brief are both the subjects of several volumes of monographs.

The third part comments on the problems of the theoretical foundations of typology: on the questions of theory and method, on the integration of typology, and on the typological characteristics of individual languages and on contrasting them. These issues are treated in the last part because they require a certain amount of knowledge of typology.

I am afraid that the book's decimal classification and cross references may mislead the reader as far as the character of the book is concerned; it is, in fact, the volume of studies written between 1971 and 1979, but revised and completed in 1980. They were published in languages other than English. In the revision I could not incorporate those results which would have required the rewriting or a considerable extension of the book. The bibliography also contains literature for further reading.

I have benefited from the suggestions of many people in the course of preparing these studies, and would like to thank especially my colleagues at Kossuth University in Debrecen for their comments and to typologists and contrastive linguists in Europe and America for theirs.

I alone, of course, am responsible for the shortcomings of these final versions.

Part 1

Basic Sentence Structure and
its Expression by Case Systems

1.1. General Typology and Basic Sentence Structure

1.1.1. FROM UNIVERSAL INVARIANT STRUCTURE TO THE TYPES OF SENTENCE STRUCTURE

On the Universal Invariant Structure

Up to the middle of the twentieth century morphological investigations were in the centre of the study of typology. In the field of syntax only those investigations were undertaken which had "strong" morphological implications. Such are, for instance, the analyses concerning the expression of parts of sentence by means of case suffixes, prepositions and postpositions. The analysis of the correlations of cases and parts of sentences resulted in the emergence of typological categories which may be brought into correlation with parts of sentence and may also be related to cases, but are not identical with them, being more universal, and independent of the types of case systems as well as of the definition of the grammatical categories which may vary according to grammars (let us recall the different conceptions of object, indirect object and adverbial complement in Hungarian, Russian and English grammars). Such typological categories and features constitute the basis of the following examination. Before going into details, we have to say a few words about the base structure.

The problem of the relationship of universal base structure and of derived structures of various languages is a case of correlation between base and derived structures well-known in Marxist structure theory. We have to point out here that only the most important elements of the derived structure are determined by the base structure and that the latter is controlled by specific laws of its own. (Cf. Svidersky 1962, 146 seq., Dezső.) This is a matter of common knowledge in other sciences. In the realm of grammar the same can be illustrated by the fact that the morphological questions of the surface case system cannot be explained by the base structure only, because the surface case system also possesses specific rules that have to be taken into consideration. This is one of the central questions of the study of case system, and concerns the traditional contradiction between syntactic and morphological approaches.

The linguistic system is a special, secondary, material semantic system (Cf. Solncev 1971, 17 seq.), which is bound to reveal, in addition to its general features, its special character also. The typological examination of linguistic structure, as well as the utilization of universal invariant base structure for linguistic description will not be appropriate unless we have a clear notion of the relation of variant and invariant in the Jakobsonian sense. (The theory of invariant has been expounded in many of Jakobson's works. In the following, we rely on the so far unpublished lecture he gave in Budapest on 21 October 1972.) It is impossible for us to have an insight into the multiplicity of manifestations of the more than three thousand languages of the world if we cannot find the invariant underlying the multiplicity of variants. Mere registration of phenomena results in a complete disintegration of linguistics. The universal categories of base structure are to be regarded as invariants realized in linguistic types. At the same time, type rules are invariants in comparison with individual linguistic rules. Let us take an example from case system. Active and transitive verbs denoting transitive action are complemented by an active and a non-active argument; the agent-subject being the typical representative of the former, and the object of the latter. These are universal categories; still their linguistic expression is governed by two distinct typological principles. In nominative languages, the agent-subject is put in the nominative case and the object in the accusative case. In the latter the morphological expression is based on the following principle: mark the object of the sentence. Accordingly, you will have the subject in the unmarked case: in the nominative, and the object primarily in the accusative: Hung. *A fiú megírta a levelet.* 'The boy has written the letter'. In ergative languages the principle of marking is contrary: the agent-subject is put in the ergative case while the object is in the nominative: Georgian: *Kicma dačera cerili* (meaning the same). These are, however, type rules only, and we need further rules in order to explain, for instance, the omission of the case suffix of Hungarian accusative with a possessive personal suffix: Hung. *Te írod a leveled.* 'You are writing your letter'. Further, in some of the ergative languages, for example in Georgian, the agent is expressed by the ergative case only in connection with verbs of a perfective aspect, but a different rule comes into play in the case of an imperfective verb. In Chuckchee, the ergative construction is used only in the case of an individualized object, and so on. Consequently, type functions as an invariant in relation to further variants, and we have to consider more and more new factors. This view induces a certain kind of system in the description of languages, a degree of generalization, which also serves to illustrate the multifarious nature of languages.

Here we reach a point where a substantial deviation from the traditional typological approach can be observed. Thus far the fundamental method of typology was analytical: it started from individual linguistic phenomena and so arrived at generalizations. Contemporary linguistics, however, is characterized by a claim to synthesis: on the basis of generalizations obtained from analytical results it formulates universal and type structures from which it returns to the facts of individual languages through synthesis. Nevertheless, synthesis presupposes analysis. In the history of linguistics synthesis looks back upon a period of analytical work, and in concrete investigations synthesis presupposes an analytical stage. Synthesis is not a simple reversion of analysis: it reveals new aspects, thus making investigation fuller. At the same time, however, not all linguistic facts are determined by more general rules, and some of the phenomena cannot be generalized, not at least for the present.

It is not so well known, however, that nineteenth-century typologists were acquainted with, and made use of, most of the categories, relations and features applied today. Twentieth-century typology inherited them, they were incorporated into the theory of grammar, and especially the Prague school did much in order to develop them further. It is mainly due to that school that they received acceptance by the exponents of generative grammar, and other trends as well. The study of these categories, relations and features developed gradually and relatively slowly, and since they did not occupy a central position in grammatical investigations, they followed an intermittent course of evolution, until they came into the forefront of interest.

But there is a great difference between the earlier and the present stage of development. Formerly universal categories, relations and features were used only sporadically in addition to surface grammatical categories, especially to the traditional parts of sentence. At present—in a period of synthetic approaches—primary importance has been assigned to them: investigations are aimed at revealing them and their combinations, and the morpholgical and syntactic categories of individual languages are deduced from them. The question of parts of sentence, had lost its central role because it is tied up with individual languages, but its role in the description of individual languages cannot be neglected.

The problems of base structure, as has already been made clear, concern just a part of syntactic examination representing the starting point only; more important is the process that takes us to the type, and to individual languages. The base structure as an invariant must be as flexible and variable as possible. This is why we have broken down into features such categories as the agent, and this is why we regard the agent, and the like as a typical combination of these features.

It follows from the foregoing that we suppose, agreeing with H. Birnbaum, the underlying structure to have several strata: the "deepest" one includes the universal features and categories and the related rules; the next one the features and categories characteristic of types; and the "shallow" one those of individual languages (Cf. Birnbaum 1970). Typological research is aimed at investigating precisely these strata, and their mutual interdependences. The work has only just started, and we have to proceed in this way to explore the features of verbs and the grammatical relations between the constituents of sentences.

The Features in Universal Invariant Structure

In the foregoing I assumed that base structure represents the universal invariant from the viewpoint of typological comparison. This is achieved by an analysis of individual languages and types of languages. Synthesis starts back from here to individual languages through the type. This is the starting point for synthetic grammatical theories as well, thus the problem of base structure stands in the focus of attention in formalized and exact theories. The approach to be expounded briefly below represents a synthetic approach and stands closest to the conception of the Leningrad typologists (Tipologija 1974, 10 ff, Khrakovsky 1980). It is typological research that primarily played a role in its formation, among them my own investigations. It has the impact of two major components of a possible exact theory: grammatical relations and case theory.

My views differ from the Leningrad typologists' approach at several points. The first departure is of terminological character. I do not think that my base component is of semantic nature. It is a universal invariant structure of "deep" syntax. A semantic component can be added to it. It can consist either of interpretative rules applied to the surface structure as in generative grammar or of a "generative" semantic component preceding the syntactic base as in Keenan's variant of universal grammar. The Leningrad group applies a dependency tree when formalizing both "semantic" and "syntactic" components. Since I do not aim at formalization at present, I leave the question of "tree" open. Case theory is a necessary component of "deep" or universal syntax, because the types of base structure (ergative, active, nominative) cannot be derived without them but they are not relevant to all sub-systems of syntax. Case theory can be applied in the form of assigning "functional" features to the predicate and to its arguments resulting in categories like "agent", "deep object" or "patient" etc. The terms deep or universal "subject", "object" are also relevant to syntactic typology, especially for diatheses, i.e. the interrelation of active, passive sentences. The latter can be considered as primes, or as nodes in the hierarchy of a tree. As the reader can conclude, I feel sympathy to relational grammar using the latter terms in an explicit way and ready to adopt the results of case theory. Anyway, the Leningrad approach and relational grammar are close to each other. At present, neither of them is elaborated to a degree that an outsider grammarian could have a clear picture of them and define his relationship to them. In no case can a grammarian neglect the recent development of other grammatical theories either.

As far as the formulation of the general structure of the base component is concerned, there are several procedures available. In one of these features acquire a significant role. Unfortunately, there is no consensus of opinion as to the universally relevant features or structure they form, therefore, the factual results of investigations are formulated in different ways.

The primary elements of the base are the predicate and its arguments. These terms have already been accepted, nevertheless, because of their identity with logical terms and it would be more correct to use other labels like *explicans* and *explicandum*, as was suggested by Katsnel'son (1972, 133—138). The argument may be obligatory or optional labelled as "actants" and "circumstants" by the Leningrad approach following the tradition of Russian structuralist approach. The actants figure as the subject and objects of the predicate in individual languages, while circumstants represent various adverbials. Valence necessarily plays a significant role in this approach.

The actants figure in "pure" grammatical relations following the terminology of relational grammar, the circumstants represent "impure"

2

relations (Cf. Johnson 1977, 153 ff.). Subject and direct object are nuclear terms and have the feature "nuclear".

A subject is irrelevant from the point of view of the "direction" of a predicate, an object has the positive feature "direction". Indirect object has the feature "non-nuclear", but both are primary terms in comparison to secondary object and have the feature "primary", e.g. *The linguist* (subject) *reads a paper* (direct object) *to the students* (indirect object) *about the features* (secondary object). The status of secondary object is not clear, it may not belong to the universal base structure. The use of relational terms can and often must be complemented by the terms of "deep" cases because of the types of sentence structure. The subject may be an agent or an experiencer, in the first case it has an "active" feature, in the latter it is "non-active" and this fact results in various structures in ergative and active languages. The direct object is the typical expression of "deep object" and the indirect object is an "addressee" in a broad sense of this term including the beneficiary.

In primary diathesis, i.e. in active complete sentences, the relational and case feature show the following correspondence:

Subject [+ nuclear, + primary, ± direction] if [+ action] = agent, if
    [— action] = experiencer

Direct Object [+ nuclear, + primary, + direction]

Indirect Object [— nuclear, + primary, + direction]

Secondary Object [— nuclear, — primary, + direction]

Object has a "non-active" feature. The feature "animate" implied by the first version of deep cases is frequently associated with an agent and an addressee but is not compulsory.

The terms and features in universal base structure must be separated from those of individual languages because the subject, direct and indirect objects of base structure will appear as various parts of sentence in individual languages even in primary diathesis, i.e. in complete, active sentences. Nevertheless, their relationship must be clarified from the point of view of typology.

The parts of sentence of individual languages may be marked by case suffixes or may be marked only by other devices (verbal affixes, ordering). If sentence constituents are marked by case suffixes one must take into consideration the types of case systems and the features of various cases. The features of cases in various case systems have common features, e.g. the accusative in Russian and in Hungarian represent various types. There is some correspondence between the features of relational terms and those of cases typically expressing one of the relational terms, nevertheless, the case features must differ from those of relational terms, at least, as long as their correspondence can be established. Let us compare the features of subject, direct and indirect objects of base structure with those of nominative, accusative and dative typically expressing them in Russian and Hungarian:

(1) Subject [+ nuclear, + primary, ± direction]
Nominative [± approximation, + central]
(2) Direct Object [+ nuclear, + primary, + direction]
Accusative [+ approximation, + central]
(3) Indirect Object [— nuclear, + primary, + direction]
Dative [+ approximation, — central]

There is an apparent correspondence between features "nuclear" and "central", "direction" and "approximation", but their order is different. These features and their order reflect the present stage of grammatical typology and my knowledge of it and must be considered as temporary and tentative.

Less attention has been devoted to the typological analysis of parts of speech (Cf. Kacnel'son 1972, 126—176). The semantic features of deep predicate, the *explicans* appear primarily as a verb or adjective in the grammatical realization. In certain languages the verb and the adjective form one category, the predicative. The argument, the *explicandum*, on the other hand, is chiefly realized as a noun. The verb and the noun are universal parts of speech, present in all languages. The relationship between the verbs and nouns of individual languages and the universal *explicans* and *explicandum* is a highly interesting typological problem, which has not yet been clarified as far as its details are concerned. Thus, the verb and the noun appear as universal categories in the base component, to be concretized in individual languages.

Of the features of the predicate, it is presumably the "dynamic" feature that has to be mentioned in the first place in the hierarchy, as it distinguishes the bulk of verbs from that of adjectives. The "dynamic" feature of verbs makes possible the emergence of continuous aspectuality, e.g. in English: *John is looking at the picture* vs. *John sees the picture.* Dynamic verbs formed from adjectives denote process, Hung. *beteg* 'ill' and *betegeskedik* 'be in bad health'. The feature "change" adds 'change-that-has-ensued' to this: Hung. *alszik* 'sleep' and *elalszik* 'fall asleep', where *alszik* has the dynamic feature, or *beteg* is non-dynamic, whereas *megbetegszik* 'become ill' has the features "dynamic" and "change". The action may have an "inner causative" or "factive", feature, e.g. Hung. *leül* 'sit down' vs. *ül* 'sit'. "Causation" or "external causation" presupposes the impact of an external person or object: Hung. *beszéltet* 'make speak' vs. *beszél* 'speak' or *leültet* 'make sit down' vs. *ül* 'sit' or *felfrissít* 'make fresh' vs. *friss* 'fresh'. It may also be necessary to mark transitive verbs by means of a separate feature. (On the combinations of features and their variability during word formation see Vědecká 1974, 12—15, on the typology of causation see Tipologija 1969.) The fact that, in spite of the differences, approximately the same features occur and in similar configurations indicates that these features are universal, although their grammatical realization differs from language to language and type to type. In addition to the theoretical context, linguists are also influenced by the properties of languages they study in describing and formulating features and their relations. A feature or combination of features may acquire immediate and systematic expression in a language. In English, for example, the feature "dynamic" makes possible the use of continuous aspect forms, but they may also be marginal, indirect or may belong to the covert part of grammar. Grammatical realization may take place in morphology, syntax or word formation. As has been seen from the above examples, the feature "dynamic", either alone or together with the feature "change", appears in Hungarian in deadjectival verb formation rather than in morphology. Transitivity is irrelevant in English either from the aspect of morphology or word formation, whereas in Hungarian it is important from both aspects.

The characteristic features of states, actions and events that can be observed in reality are also reflected in the non-inherent or role categories of the argument. The usual way of indicating these is by means of "case" labels rather than features: e.g. agent, who/which carries out the action, patient at whom/which the action is levelled; addressee, who does not directly take part in the action. The expression of these roles by means of features is also conceivable: e.g. the agent has the "active" feature, while the experiencer the "non-active" features. The interpretation of these roles is usually evident. Since, however, neither the set nor the exact definition of roles have, as yet, been clarified, they had better be resorted to only if necessary. But they could fairly often be put to good account, for example, the agent is the primary subject, the patient the primary object, and the ergative and nominative types differ in their expression.

Of the features of the noun, "countability" is essential, for only nouns marked by this feature may have the grammatical number. The universality of the features "animate" and "person" cannot be questioned either, for there is an essential rule referring to them in some grammatical sub-system of every language. Presumably, it is also universally important to distinguish between concrete and mass nouns (Cf. Katsnel'son 1972, 136—139). A number of features, however, become grammatically significant only in some languages (e.g. the size and shape of objects in some languages with nominal classes).

The subject and object are universal categories. The establishment of parts of the sentence ultimately depends on the individual properties of languages. Moreover, grammatical tradition is not to be neglected either, although this reflects individual properties of languages. Grammatical types also come into play here: the categories subject and object in nominative languages are treated fairly unanimously in various grammars. Various case systems allow for a great diversity in the morphological realization of the subject and object. In nominative languages the subject is usually expressed by the nominative, although it may also be rendered by the partitive in partitive languages. There are several cases available for the expression of the object in Russian, depending on the semantic features of the verb, but the definiteness of the object, negation or some other factor may also interplay. It is the coincidence of various factors that provides the rules for the establishment of case suffixes in individual languages. These, however, also reflect certain typological laws (Cf. 1.3). As has been mentioned, role categories can also be relevant, e.g. the agent is primarily a subject, whereas the patient an object—in the primary linear variant. Czech theme-rheme theory investigated this problem from another aspect, in another theoretical context. According to this, the constituents have differing communicative dynamisms. The dynamism of the object functioning primarily as the rheme or the core of the rheme, exceeds that of the subject, that is why the latter appears as the theme or the core of the theme. In passive sentences and in active sentences differing from the basic word order and stress variants, communicative dynamism changes in accordance with the context or the intention of the speaker, which is reflected in a change of word order and stressing.

In addition to the inherent features and role categories of the constituents, the features of the auxiliary components are also crucial from the viewpoint of grammatical realization. Determination as well as aspect and tense serve for the actualization of nouns and verbs respectively. Approximately the same can be stated about the universal features of determination as was about those of the verb and the noun. A small set of universally relevant features as "determination", "definite" etc. stands out and is expressed by universal pronouns. Further features that are systematically expressed only in languages possessing articles are then added to these. The features of aspect and tense are much more problematic. The three basic tenses (past, present, future) are perhaps universal, or almost universal, whereas aspect or aspectuality is a type phenomenon with non-universal features. Unfortunately, the typological research into the categories of tense and aspect is still in its rudimentary stage.

H. Birnbaum's conception aimed at a typological interpretation of the standard variant of American generative grammar of the late sixties (Birnbaum, 1970), and has interesting implications concerning the typological status of features. In accordance with H. Birnbaum's conception, the syntactic component of synthesis is thought to consist of more than one layer or stratum: a deep universal layer, a typological middle layer, and a 'shallow' language specific layer, labelled as universal, typological and language specific layers. The universal layer is characterized by a restricted number of semantic features, which are further unanalyzable (Cf. Birnbaum 1970, 11 ff). About the interdependence of the features of universal, typological and language specific layers he states: "While many deep structure features, ascertainable at less deep-seated strata (i.e., 'shallow' and 'typological' deep structure) will be lost or, rather, irretrievable at this deepest level, those properties identifiable at the profound or bottom layer must be characterized as truly universal and thus wholly invariant" (Birnbaum 1970, 27—28). The topmost layer is characterized by Birnbaum in the following way: "shallow 'infrastructure' will include all those properties and features which can find their surface expression in the syntactic synonymy of a given language or, in other words, on a complete set of possible, well-formed paraphrases of one and the same message (information-complex), without any semantic loss or addition. Of these deep-seated properties some will be limited to the 'infrastructure' level only, while others will be represented at that level merely as reflections of categories and relations found at a deeper and hence more generalized level (typological or 'profound'), projected as it were, into the 'shallow' level of deep structure." (Birnbaum 1970, 28).

Thus the characteristic features of the universal layer, or some of them, are transposed into the typological, then into the language specific layer, but the latter two layers are characterized by specific characteristics and features which cannot be traced back to the universal stratum; but one of the essential objectives of typological analysis is to analyze them and to clarify whether they are derivable from the universal layer and if they are, in what way, and from where do they enter into the two higher layers. In individual languages and types of languages, beside the formally expressed categories, an important role is played by the categories which are not expressed formally. Some of these are derived from the universal layer, others from the typological layer (Cf. Birnbaum 1970, 39); for instance in Hungarian and in the Slavic languages the perfective aspect is expressed by formal means too, and it is in a more advanced degree in the Slavic languages than in Hungarian. The progressive aspect as a marked aspect, however, is not expressed by form. Thus the typological and language-specific rules of Hungarian and English aspect show fundamental divergence, while the same rules in Russian and Hungarian show that they are only variants within one type. In what way can continuity be formulated in the typological stratum of languages characterized by the perfective aspect? In what way can perfectivity be formulated in the typological layer of languages characterized by the progressive aspect? In what way are these clearly typological phenomena related to profound structure? Such questions can be answered only if one assumes a complex procedure of derivation of grammatical features and categories. However, the layered deep structure suggested by Birnbaum raises numerous problems and in its present form it can only serve as a working hypothesis.

On the Derivation of the Types of Sentence Structure

The universal was the centre of attention in the investigation of the base component. The survey of the important processes of the grammatical derivation, primarily those of the syntactic structure, will shed light on types. The study of individual languages is not pursued here. The grammatical component is shaped by certain universal processes, resulting in types, of which basic sentence structure and communicative organization will be analyzed in detail (Cf. 1.2. and 2). The presentation even of these fragments of syntactic typology will by no means be complete. The relationships between individual processes will only be touched upon. Nor will a few processes be linked with each other, as is done by H. Seiler in the course of the analysis of dimensions, for this would presuppose a more detailed treatment of processes and their interrelations (Cf. Seiler 1980).

The transformation of the base component into derived syntactic structures takes place in accordance with the rules of communicative organization. They fall into two parts, namely the system of rules relating to diathesis and the one concerning word order and stress, or theme and rheme. The initial and derived variants of diathesis are created by the diathesis rules from the base component. These are then acted upon by the rules relating to word order and stress or theme and rheme, which may generate further variants within the same diathesis. These are used by the speaker in different situations and contexts with different aims. The typology of diathesis has been elaborated by the Leningrad group of typologists (Cf. Tipologija 1974), whereas the typology of theme and rheme (word order and stressing) has emerged in the wake of J. H. Greenberg's paper (Cf. Greenberg 1963).

The basic concepts of diathesis can be determined as follows: "Let us call the equivalents of parts of sentence to the participants of a situation diathesis. Then, the equivalence of parts of sentence with the participants of the situation to be fixed in the initial construction can be called initial diathesis. In the process of transition from the initial construction to the derived one, the initial diathesis undergoes a change. The essence of the change consists in the participants no longer being denoted by the same parts of sentence as in the initial construction. Moreover, these participants may not be designated on the lexical level at all." (Tipologija 1974, 13.)

The result of initial diathesis is the primary sentence structure: a complete active sentence in basic word order. Typology has studied the structure of sentences composed of a subject and an intransitive verb, or of subject, transitive verb and object. The types of sentences with adverbials are less known. There are two principles concerning the morphological marking of constituents: subject marking and object marking. Active languages mark with special ergative device the subject of both transitive and intransitive verbs or the verbs themselves. Ergative languages are "less ergative" because they mark only the subject of transitive verbs. Nevertheless, I shall often call both active and ergative languages ergative because this term is generally accepted. Nominative languages mark the object, or the verb is referred to the object. There are languages neutral from the point of marking the subject or the object.

The various possible variants of diathesis can be given by means of calculuses, for example the following variants may emerge in the syntactic component from the participants A and B of the semantic component:

AB, BA, or, after the elimination of the variables, indicated by X, AX, BX, XX, e.g. Russ. AB: *Metrostrojevcy* (A = 1) *postroili metro* (B = 2) 'The builders of the underground have built the underground'; BA: *Metro* (B = 1) *pǫstrojeno metrostrojevcami* (A = 2) 'The underground has been built by the builders', BX: *Metro* (B = 1) *postrojeno* 'The underground has been built' (Cf. Khrakovsky 1975, 39 ff). Further variants can be created by means of rules relating to word order and stressing on the basis of individual diatheses in the course of theme and rheme e.g. A = S and B = O in the initial diathesis, which appears in the basic word order type SVO in Russian: *Metrostrojevcy postroili metro* (see also above). The other five word order variants are also possible, among them VSO, with the stress on the verb: *Postroili metrostrojevcy metro*. In passive diathesis (BA), B becomes S, while A is degraded into à complement (C), the basic word order type being SVC (see above): *Metro postrojeno metrostorjevcami* (see also above). These may serve as a basis for the formation of five further variants. The basic word order in elliptical passive diathesis (BX) is SV: *Metro postrojeno* but the variant VS is also possible: *Postrojeno metro*, with a stress on S. The diathesis and word order calculi determine the possible variants, but their emergence is restricted by type rules. In some groups of languages it is not possible to form passive sentences, whereas it is possible in others. Two subtypes can be found in the latter: in most languages only elliptical passive sentences can be formed (BX), whereas in the remainder both the full (BA) and the elliptical (BX) variants exist. The formation of the word order variants of initial and derived diatheses are restricted by the rules of word order typology, which have been elaborated only for active initial sentences with two actants (S, O). The rules of four word order types impose constraints on the formation of the variants of such sentences with S, O and V. It is customary to call these SVO, SOV, VSO and VOS word order types, in accordance with the basic word order. The quoted Russian examples represent the type SVO, more exactly one of its free word order sub-types. The principles of sentence stressing are also necessary for a proper understanding of the function of word order variants. The typological questions of this are not yet elaborated. In the case of fixed word order, in addition to SVO the variants OVS and VSO are also possible, while the further possible variants of SOV are OSV or perhaps VSO, and those of VSO are VOS or SVO.

The types and surface realizations of the constituents of the base must also be taken into account in the detailed elaboration of diathesis as well as word order typology. The addressee can figure as the subject of a passive construction in relatively few languages: it is impossible to form sentences of the type *Peter was given a book* in Russian. Nor can a circumstance figure in subject position in a passive sentence, that is why there is no construction like *The bed was slept in* in Russian. In the course of surface realization, the problems connected with ergative and partitive sentences as well as the questions of definiteness and aspectuality must be taken into account in the system of rules of both diathesis and functional perspective.

Theme-rheme rules determine the place and communicative role of constituents. It is the categories tense and aspect of the predicate and the determiners of arguments, i.e. the auxiliary components that contain information on actualization or the rules of deixis in the broad sense of the word. Thus, actualization falls into two great processes: the actualization of the predicate and that of the arguments. Together with mood, tense and aspect constitute the verbal paradigm, while the actualization may affect the declination of nouns. Both enter into interactions in the shaping of syntactic structure.

Only the two above-mentioned processes of the formation of simple propositions will be presented. In the course of the creation of complex propositions, a proposition is subordinated to an argument or an argument is replaced by a proposition. In the first case, an attributive construction emerges in the syntactic component. This may be expressed by a construction with a subordinate clause or a participial construction or an attributive noun phrase, e.g. Hung. *János megkapta azt a levelet, amelyet Péter írt.* 'John received the letter that had been written by Peter'; *János megkapta a Péter által írt levelet.* 'John received the letter written by Peter'; *János megkapta Péter levelét.* 'John received Peter's letter'. In the second case, the actants and circumstances of the sentence are replaced by a subordinate clause, non-finite construction or noun phrase, which are analyzed in individual languages as subject, object and adverbial clauses, e.g. Hung. *János látta, hogy Péter megérkezett.* 'John saw that Peter had arrived'; *János látta Pétert megérkezni.* 'John saw Peter arrive'; *János látta Péter megérkezését.* 'John saw Peter's arrival'. Languages are divisible into types according to what ways they can choose for complementing and substituting arguments. The Cologne project unites the determination of arguments and the various ways of its substitution by attributive propositions in the dimension of determination, then it also analyzes the word order of noun phrases emerging in this way. The following German examples illustrate the various types of attributes and their place in the noun phrase (Seiler, 1978, 307): *Alle diese meine erwähnten zehn schönen roten hölzernen Kugeln, die ich dir jetzt gebe.* If one handles the problem in this way, the expression of the argument becomes a central issue. Consequently, the relationship between the argument and the predicate is thrust into the background and the two processes of actualization become separated. It also loses importance that the complementing and substituting of the arguments take place essentially the same way (by means of a subordinate clause, non-finite construction and attributive noun phrase). This indicates that it is possible to group these complicated and involved processes in various ways.

A work on syntactic typology inevitably has to face questions of morphological typology, but it cannot set their detailed examination as an aim, for the major processes investigated in the course of synthesis necessarily affect morphological realization, but the typological rules of the latter cannot be understood only from syntactic factors, as they present special problems. This can be examined in the typology of case systems. The realization of syntactic processes in English, Russian, Hungarian and the Caucasian Tabasaran is influenced by the fact that there is no case system in English, whereas the case systems in the other three, are of a different type. It has not yet been sufficiently proved, but it is likely that there is a certain connection between the agglutinative or inflectional character of languages and the type of case systems; only agglutinative languages have a case system of the second and the third type, illustrated by Hungarian and Tabasaran, respectively. A case system of the first type can also be found in agglutinative languages, but this is the only possible type in the case of inflectional languages. This statement ought to be made more precise by means of an analysis of agglutinative languages having a case system of the first type. Agglutination and inflection are synthetic procedures and both oppose the analytic one, which does not seem to tolerate a case system. Even though these statements need to be made more precise, they illustrate the way syntactic typology is related to traditional morphological typology.

1.1.2. ON THE TYPOLOGICAL PROBLEMS OF DETERMINATION AND ASPECT

Determination and aspectuality belong to a complex process labelled by the term actualization. Actualization takes place in the process of the formation of the sentence. Information concerning actualization is contained in the auxiliary components of arguments and the predicate and receives its typical expression in personal, demonstrative and other pronouns, articles, special suffixes of nouns, adjectives, sometimes of verbs and in the verbal categories of tense and aspect.

Actualization includes two processes of the determination of the arguments and the tense and aspectuality of the predicate.

a) The correlation of arguments with the participants of the speech situation. The typical expression of the participants of the speech situation by the first and second person personal pronouns, whereas non-participants may be replaced by a third person personal pronoun or a demonstrative pronoun, e.g. Russ. *Ja otdam jego tebe.* 'I give it to you', Hung. *Én odaadom ezt/azt neked.* 'I give this/that to you'.

b) If a non-participant is expressed by a noun, it may be referred to by a pronoun, with possible attention to the participants of the speech situation, Russ. *Daj mne tot karandaš.* 'Give me that pencil' Sr.-Cr. *Daj mi tu/onu olovku.* 'Give me that pencil close to you/far from you'.

If the non-participant is expressed by a noun, it may be identified by an article, Bulg. *Kăšta-ta e chubava.* 'The house is nice'.

Personal and demonstrative pronouns are universal means of determination, articles are characteristic of a sub-group of languages.

c) The time of the action, of the event, of the state is correlated with the time of the speech act and is viewed by the speaker from a given aspect, Russ. *Maľčik čital/pročital knigu.* 'The boy read/has read the book.' The action is expressed by the past tense of an imperfective or a perfective verb.

As the processes singled out above are interrelated in reality, the formal expression of various processes may be regulated by general rules and be expressed by the same devices. For example, in Hungarian there is some correlation between determination and aspect. They have their specific formal devices: determination is expressed by articles, aspect by preverbs, but some features of determination of the noun are marked by a special series of affixes of definite conjugation on the verb. In Finnish, the opposition of case suffixes expresses both aspectual òpposition and determination.

Below, some typological questions of the processes of actualization are noted, a detailed analysis of which can be found in the works referred to.

On Determination

On the Correlation of Arguments with the Participants of the Speech Situation. There are universal correlations between the participants of the speech situation and the grammatical persons: the speaker is expressed by the first person, the addressee is represented by the second person personal pronouns, whereas the non-participant is referred to by the third person of personal pronouns, although, besides personal pronouns, demonstrative pronouns may also be used to express the latter. Their interrelationship may be diverse. In Hungarian, for example, the non-participant subject is replaced by a personal pronoun if it represents a person, but by a demonstrative one if it is a non-person. In the expression of the number of participants and non-participants, the opposition of 'one' and 'more than one' (singular and plural) is universally taken into account, while within 'more than one' further oppositions are possible, as between two and more than two, three and more than three, although number may also be unmarked. First person non-singular may include or exclude another person. Therefore, the system of personal pronouns lends itself to classification according to participation in the speech act and to number and serves as a basis for establishing universal rules (Cf. Ingram 1971). If the non-participant is replaced by a demonstrative pronoun, deictic features are also taken into consideration, Hung. *Én neked adom ezt/azt* 'I give you this/that'.

On Deixis and Identification. In the correlation of arguments with the speech situation, the non-participant is characterized only negatively, for it is neither the speaker nor the addressee. If it is substituted by a demonstrative pronoun or, with the noun being preserved, is collocated with it, it is characterized more precisely. Its place is determined in relation to the place of the speaker, 'near to the speaker' or 'non-near to the speaker'. If it is 'non-near to the speaker', it may be 'near to the addressee' or 'non-near to the addressee'. Thus, a dichotomous or trichotomous system of demonstrative pronouns comes into being. (A comparison of Hungarian dichotomous and Serbo-Croatian trichotomous systems can be found in Mikes-Dezső-Vuković 1972.)

The process of deixis, indicated by demonstrative pronouns, is to be distinguished from the process of identification, which is typically expressed by articles. It would, however, be a mistake not to take into account their general features, which serve as a basis for the use of pronouns in one language, but for the use of articles in the other. (The correlations of use between the Hungarian definite article and Serbo-Croatian demonstrative pronouns are analyzed in Mikes-Dezső-Vuković 1972, see also Krámský 1972, 188—190 on English articles and Czech *ten*.) Besides, it is well known that the definite articles of various languages come into being from demonstrative pronouns (Cf. Moravcsik 1969). The article, however, is characterized by an absence of the feature 'deixis', which has an emphatic character and is dependent on the speaker. The same object, for example, may be mentioned either in the company of a pronoun or an article: Hung. *Add ide ezt/azt/az asztalt* or *az asztalt*. 'Give me this/that table' or 'the table'. The given example, however, also shows that if the definite article is employed, the feature of the relationship between the place of the object and that of the speaker is left unspecified. Although this is so in the majority of languages possessing articles, there are languages where the article is distinguished according to this feature as well, e.g. in Macedonian.

Although deixis is expressed by a universal means, nevertheless it is less thoroughly studied (Majtinskaja 1969) than identification with the help of articles (Krámský 1972, Moravcsik 1969). The functions of articles are generally considered jointly, but here I have in mind situational identification. I apply the term identification, but there are others as well: definiteness and familiarity. They also serve to name the basic feature.

For the expression of identification various languages may have 1. a definite or indefinite article, and, parallel with them, a zero article as well with a narrow or wide scope of application, 2. a definite and a zero article, 3. only an indefinite article, with the role of the zero article left unclear. The last variant seldom occurs.

Things that are counted may figure either in isolation or as members of a set, containing more than one element. A set may be designated by grammatical number: plural, dual, trial, of which the plural is universal. The marking of grammatical number, however, is not obligatory: in the Yoruba language where it is rarely expressed it is indicated only if it has communicative significance. In Hungarian, it may not be expressed if it is irrelevant from the viewpoint of communication, whereas in Slavic languages the expression of number is obligatory. In non-singular numbers the rules of identification, elaborated for the identification of isolated things, are modified, especially if the language disposes of an indefinite article as well, which is not employed in the plural.

In the case of grammatical number, exact number is not expressed, with the exception of two, three or four in certain languages. Numerals serve to express exact number, whereas non-exact number and its evaluation are conveyed by indefinite numerals. If things are viewed as members of a set rather than in isolation, noun phrases with numerals are not primarily identified, the identification of the set takes place only secondarily: Hung. *hat szék* 'six chairs', *sok szék* 'many chairs', *a hat szék* 'the six chairs'. The indefinite article is not used here. It is usually resorted to in the case of a thing isolated or, in certain languages, singled out of a set: Hung. *egy szék* 'a chair', 'one of the chairs', although Hungarian possesses a special pronoun for the designation of the indefinite element of a definite set: *egyik* 'one of'. The Hungarian suffix *-ik* has this meaning and it may also be collocated with other pronouns. The definite objective conjugation of verbs in Hungarian is used not only in the case of an identified isolated *thing* but also with an indefinite element of an identified set: *látom* 'I see' *az asztalt* 'the table', *azt az asztalt* 'that table', *az egyik asztalt* 'one of the tables', *valamelyik asztalt* 'some one of the tables', *melyik asztalt* 'which table'. I have adduced these examples in order to draw attention to a broader area of "definiteness" within determination.

The absence of identification with an isolated thing is expressed by the indefinite article. As it is isolated and its number does not exceed one, it is understandable that the indefinite article was formed from the numeral 'one'. The interrelationship of the numeral and the indefinite article is well demonstrated by such English examples as *a chair, one chair, one of the chairs*. Serbo-Croatian *jedan* occupies a transitional position between an article and a numeral (Cf. Ivić 1971): it is not yet an article, but is also used when number is irrelevant. The fact that the indefinite article is employed in the presence of one thing links it with the numeral 'one', while the absence of identification links it with indefinite pronouns. The latter, however, also contains an emphatic element: indefiniteness is emphasized. As emphasis belongs to subjective categories, much depending on the judgement of the speaker, in Hungarian disposing of both the indefinite article and pronoun indefiniteness is expressed by both parts of speech, and both of them have as their equivalents in Serbo-Croatian either *jedan* or an indefinite pronoun or a zero element (Cf. Mikes-Dezső-Vuković 1972).

Similar to the expression of number, identification is not obligatory even in a number of languages having the definite article. It depends on communicative purpose, for if it is irrelevant for communication, it may not be expressed by an article even when the thing in question could be identified: e.g. Hung. *a zsűri eredményt hirdet*, or *a zsűri kihirdeti* **az** *eredményt* 'the panel result announces' (lit.) or 'the panel announces the result'. In English, as a rule, such synonymy is impossible because one of the articles is obligatorily used with countable nouns.

With this, the problems of determination have not been exhausted. I shall leave out of account the correlation of various articles, problems of their formal expression and place (Cf. Krámský 1972, Moravcsik 1969) as well as a number of other questions and I only note the problem of the whole and the part. The action represented by the predicate may encompass either the whole thing or a part of the thing. In both cases one thing or a number of things may be meant. The given question is closely bound up with the question of quantity: part and whole are contrasted, a part being characterized by the absence of identification, while the whole by its presence. In the given case, identification is often tied up with aspect. In Balto-Finnic languages the partitive case, expressing a part of a thing as a subject or object, inherently expresses indefiniteness, which implies imperfective aspect in the verb, while the nominative and accusative are essentially characterized by definiteness, implying perfective aspect in the verb. A similar phenomenon can be observed in Lithuanian, and, though in a less developed form, it may even be witnessed in Slavic languages, e.g. Sr.-Cr. *Petar je popio vino* and *Petar je pio vina* 'Peter has drunk the wine' and 'Peter has drunk some wine'. The opposition in terms of definiteness in Hungarian is expressed by an article or its absence, but the opposition in terms of aspect can be well observed in the translations of the Serbo-Croatian examples: *Péter megitta a bort* 'Peter has drunk the wine', *Péter ivott bort* 'Peter drank (some) wine'.

I have by no means enumerated all the phenomena within the scope of determination yet. Incorporation, according to the evidence of Chuckchee, occurs only if the object of the verb is not identified. The identified object does not become incorporated. Chuckchee is interesting also in another respect: it uses different types of word order with an unidentified, incorporated object and with an identified object: in the former case SOV, in the latter SVO (Cf. Skorik 1965, 232). This corresponds exactly to the rules of Hungarian, in which no incorporation exists but the non-determined object and the verb constitute one tone-group and appear in SOV order: *Péter levelet írt* (lit.) 'Peter was letter writing', while the non-determined object goes with SVO word order: *Péter írta a levelet* 'Peter wrote the letter.'

Determination influences the rules of diathesis, the rules of theme and rheme and those of the case system. That is the reason why one has to take it into account when analyzing the typological problems related to it. What has been said about the question is no more than some basic typological information relevant to our further discussion of the types of sentence structure. I must briefly mention some features and some frequent means of determination necessary for our analyses.

Determination includes several features, of which only three will be treated here. One is that of "determined" which is the most important of them. It is not obligatory to determine the object of the verb; in incorporating languages the incorporated object is not determined. The non-incorporating languages also can manage without determination. For example, in Hungarian:

A fiú levelet ír. 'The boy letter writes.' (lit.)

A fiú kenyeret eszik. 'The boy bread eats.' (lit.)

where *levelet* and *kenyeret* has no article (zero article) because it is irrelevant for the speaker whether the letter or the bread are determined or not, and only the complex action is of importance: that is, letter writes and bread eates. If the letter is "determined" it may receive a "definite" feature; but it may remain "non-definite" or indefinite as well, and the alternative choices are expressed by definite or indefinite articles, respectively:

Hung.

A fiú írja a levelet. 'The boy is writing the letter.'

A fiú ír egy levelet. 'The boy is writing a letter.'

Kenyér, 'bread', being a mass noun, may only take the definite article, if any:

Hung.

A fiú eszi a kenyeret. 'The boy is eating the bread.'

Definiteness may imply that the thing meant by the noun is given in the situation or mentioned in the previous text. The noun with a "non-definite" feature may refer to one or another element of a definite group in which case the group is identifiable while the individual representative of the group is not. For instance:

Hung.

Melyik levelet írja a fiú? 'Which one of the letters does the boy write?' These make necessary a feature "element of a definite group" expressed by non-definite pronouns with suffixe -*ik* in Hungarian. These are the features we are going to need to establish what features characterize the determiner of the noun. It is also interesting how these features influence the selection of the case in sentences with an object.

3

The various formal devices expressing determination can best be demonstrated on the object because it displays the most varied representations of determination, being the primary element of the comment. Determination primarily comes into play in the form of the object as stated by E. Moravcsik on the evidence of a hundred languages (Cf. Moravcsik 1969). The various features of determination may find expression in the following manner:

1. Through the object

(a) by the opposition of the absolute and accusative cases when definiteness is expressed by the latter (for example, in the Altaic languages).

Turkish:

Ali kitap ariyor. 'Ali reads (a) book.'

Ali kitabı ariyor. 'Ali reads (the) book.'

(b) by the opposition of Accusative and Partitive (in Balto-Finnic languages), and here belong also the instances of partially opposed Accusative and Genitive in Baltic and Slavic languages.

Sr.-Cr.:

Petar moli vode. 'Peter asks for water.'

Petar moli vodu. 'Peter asks for (the) water.'

2. Through the verb with reference to the object:

(a) opposed to indefinite conjugation definite or objective conjugation can express the features "definite" and "element of a definite group":

Hung.

Péter könyvet olvas 'Peter reads (a) book.'

Péter olvassa a könyvet. 'Peter reads the book.'

Péter olvassa valamelyik könyvet. 'Peter reads one of the books.'

(b) when an indefinite object is unmarked but the definite one is being referred to by class infix *(-ki-)* in the verb:

Swahili:

Ali anasoma kitabu 'Ali is reading a book.'

Ali anakisoma kitabuhiki. 'Ali is reading the book.'

Aspectuality

The question of actualization includes the problems of aspect and tense
as well. They have been thoroughly examined in many individual
languages. There are interesting studies in contrastive aspectology (Cf.
Voprosy sopostavitel'noj aspektologii). Comrie's book outlines the
typological problems of aspect with special regard to perfective aspect (Cf.
Comrie 1976). The relationship between aspect and tenses in many
languages has been studied by Serebrennikov (Serebrennikov 1974), and
formulated in the form of implicational frequentals which, however, need
typological interpretation. I shall examine the questions of aspectuality to
a degree necessary for sentence typology.

Before the examination of the types of aspect and aspectuality, of
their relationship to tenses and of their impact on sentence structure the
definitions of aspectuality and aspect must be given. Aspectuality can be
represented in the verb, in a verbal group, in a simple sentence or in a
complex sentence. Later we shall meet aspectuality expressed by the verb
(as in Slavic, Lithuanian or Hungarian) and by a verbal group (as in
Estonian). The major form of aspectuality is the one expressed in the verb:
"the aspectual meaning can be expressed by overt opposition of grammatical forms of the same verb, both synthetic or analytic, and then one
can speak of the grammatical category of aspect. Besides this aspectual
meanings are also expressed by the opposition of aspectual classes of verbs
(such as verbs of action—verbs of state, or terminative—non-terminative
verbs etc.) and with the help of smaller sub-classes of these verbs (i.e. with
the help of *Aktionsarten*). Aspectual classes and their sub-classes—
Aktionsarten—have no compulsory marking by morphemes. In numerous
cases, however, such marking exists; nevertheless, in principle, they must
be considered as phenomena of covert grammar" (Maslov 1978, 21). This
definition of aspectuality also included that of aspect. Maslov highlights
the systematic formal representation of aspect "one can speak of aspect, if,
and only if, some aspectual meanings have regular expression by help of
paradigmatic opposition of grammatical forms of the same verb in the
majority of verbs if not in all verbs of the lexicon" (Maslov 1978, 24). The
opposition of aspectuality and aspect is important for both the theory of
aspect and its impact on syntax. I must emphasize, however, the
connections between aspectuality and aspect of the same type, e.g.
between perfective aspectuality in Lithuanian, Hungarian, Estonian and
aspect in Russian.

3*

Languages in which the perfective aspect is the marked category and in which "totality" is presumably the general feature obviously represent a separate type; in Slavic linguistics this question has been greatly studied both from the synchronic and diachronic aspect. Also, the type of aspect based on the feature of "continuous", to which English also belongs, has often been investigated.

In the sub-system of temporality there is a differentiation between present and past, or present and future, in other words the temporal actualization has to express if the event, action, etc. takes place in the present or not in the present.

A tense system may be shaped according to two features of aspectuality: "perfect" and "continuous". When added to temporal features they result in various combinations of present and past tenses in English, in Swahili and in very many other languages. Continuous aspectuality shapes the whole system of tense forms but as far as I know, it does not affect word formation and *Aktionsart*.

Aspect is a highly abstract category relevant to the tense system, word formation and *Aktionsart* (the latter two are closely connected). The best known type of aspect is demonstrated by Slavic languages. Its marked pole is the perfective aspect having a very abstract feature "totality". It involves pairs of verbs; one member of the pair represents the imperfective, the other the perfective aspect: e.g. Russ. *pisat'* (imp.), **na**pisat' (perf.) 'write' and **pere**pisat' (perf.) **pere**pisyvat' (imp.) 'rewrite'. The one of the perfective aspect is formed by a prefix, that of the imperfective aspect is shaped without or with a suffix. In Russian both perfectivization and imperfectivization are expressed by morphological means. In a less "developed" sub-type in perfective aspectuality, only perfectivization is expressed by morphological means, e.g. Hung. *ir* (imp.) *megir* (perf.) 'write', *átír* (imp.) 'rewrite' and there is no special variant for imperfectivization corresponding to **pere**pisyvat' in Hungarian (Cf. Deže 1982a).

The pairs of verbs double the number of tense variants: e.g. there will be two past, and two future tenses. If the present tense of a perfective verb indicates a concrete action etc., it refers to the future, or also to the future, because "totality" presupposes completion or "result" which refers to the future. Thus the present tense form with a prefix is usually interpreted as a future tense. This is the explanation of the first frequental: "If in a language perfective aspect is expressed by means of preverbs then it is highly probable that in that language there will alsø be a future tense formed by means of preverbs" (Serebrennikov 1974, 305).

Now what happens to a more complicated tense system having e.g. three past tenses: perfect, aorist, and imperfect. Either the three tenses must be doubled, or there will be a compromise between aspect and temporality in order to avoid an oversophisticated and little differentiated tense system. The latter happened in the history of the majority of the Slavic languages and it is testified by the two variants of the Serbo-Croatian literary language: both verbs have the perfect, only the perfective one has aorist and only the imperfective one has the imperfect in the Bosnian variant, the latter two tenses are out of use in the Voivodina variant and there is only one past form formed from both perfective and imperfective verbs. The formation of the perfective aspect has led to the restriction of the tense system in a great majority of Slavic languages. In Hungarian a less developed type of this aspect has led to the reduction of its tense system. These facts explain the second frequental: "A great number of tenses in a language often indicates the lack of aspect differentiation" (Serebrennikov 1974, 303). But there are other factors contributing to the explanation of this and other frequentals.

Thus far I have considered only one type of tense system having "perfective" aspectuality that can easily be absorbed into perfective aspect because of the intersection of their semantics. This is not the case with continuous aspectuality because its semantic feature "continuous" (or a similar one) is incompatible with "totality". Their semantic opposition is basic, they cannot mingle. This supports the third frequental stating the impossibility of the mixture of various aspect systems: "Various aspect systems usually do not mingle" (Serebrennikov 1974, 302). The terms "aspect" and "aspectuality" have no relevance here, they show only the difference in the impact on the grammatical system: perfective aspect involves both tense system and word formation, continuous aspectuality influences only the tense system, as far as I know. But this difference is rather relative and depends on the degree of development of the perfective aspect.

Since perfective aspect requires the subordination of the tense system, a tense system dominated by continuous aspectuality is not compatible with it. Serebrennikov's last frequental is supported by typological considerations: "Continuous forms most usually develop in languages having no aspect opposition" (Serebrennikov 1974, 304). It can be formulated in a different way: "No perfective vs. imperfective opposition can develop in languages having continuous tense forms."

Any tense system has a minimum of two tenses: present and past, the perfective aspect tends to keep the number of tenses near to this minimum because the pairs of verbs differentiate the use of past tenses, and the "perfective present" expresses future temporality. As opposed to this minimum number of tenses, continuous aspectuality renders a rich system of tenses because in addition to continuous and simple tenses it admits also another kind of aspectuality leading to a further increase of tense forms. It is to be pointed out that aspect may exert an important influence on word order types: in some languages the different types of word order are attached to different types of aspect, even though these observations have not yet been generalized. Let us illustrate this by a simple example: in Hungarian a verb having perfective aspect can only be followed by the object, it cannot be preceded by it, SVO: *Péter megírta a levelet* (Peter has written the letter). The object has to be determined as well, that is, it has to have either a definite or an indefinite article. The latter refers also to the relation of aspect and identification. In the case of an imperfective verb, if the object is supplied with an article, it follows the verb, SVO: *Péter írta a levelet*, while the object without an article precedes it, SOV: *Péter levelet írt*. Let us not increase the number of examples, but refer to other phenomena instead. The first one was mentioned above and concerns the relation of the aspect and case system. In Finnish and Estonian, definiteness, aspect and the rules of the use of cases are interrelated: while identified subjects and objects are in the nominative and accusative and go with verbs having perfective aspect, unidentified subjects and objects are in the partitive and take imperfective verbs. The other phenomenon concerns the relation of aspect and ergative sentence construction: in Georgian, ergative sentences are used only if the verb is perfective, otherwise nominative sentences are used.

Aspectuality and temporality is most consistently expressed by the indicative mood according to a universal established by Uspensky (1968, 11). On the basis of Slavic languages a further universal may be surmised: aspectual opposition can be best expressed in affirmative sentences while the opposition may be somewhat modified, "suppressed", in negative, interrogative and imperative sentences.

1.2. Types of Sentence Structure with Objects

Types of Sentence Structure: Klimov's Proposal

G. A. Klimov studied the ergative and active types in detail (Klimov 1973 and 1977). He accepted the thesis, on the priority of lexicon, of word classes over grammar: over sentence structure and over the the morphological representation of the constituents of sentence. In an article (Klimov 1976) he proposes a complex, in his term, a "contensive" typology of word classes, sentence structure consisting of a subject, predicate, objects and their morphological representation.

Besides the ergative, active languages described earlier in detail, his typology also consists of the characteristics of nominative, neutral and class types. Thus his proposal is supposed to give a complete description of the given sub-systems. He formulated the contensive types into a table which will be presented here with a brief explanation. Then the active and ergative types will be presented briefly and be compared with a more detailed description of the sub-types of nominative languages based on my research in some nominative languages (Estonian, Hungarian, Russian and Lithuanian) and their contrastive studies. General typology (1.2. 1) will be followed by a brief contrastive analysis of two nominative languages: Russian and Hungarian, complemented by observations concerning other languages (1.2. 2.).

Klimov proposed five contensive types connecting the phenomena of lexicon, syntax and morphology (Klimov 1976, 141—142).

The typical representatives of the neutral type are the Mande languages in West Africa, the Bantu languages belong to the class type, the active type is represented by the Na-Dene, the Sioux and other Amero-Indian languages, the ergative type by the Nahv-Daghestan and by the Abhaz-Adig groups and by various other languages in Asia, Australia and America. The nominative languages are familiar to the reader (Cf. Klimov 1976, 130 ff.)

		Neutral	Class	Active	Ergative	Nominative
Lexicon	Noun	?	set of classes	active ~ inactive classes	∅	∅
	Verb	?	situation ~ quality	active ~ stative	transitive ~ intransitive	transitive ~ intransitive
Syntax	sentence structure	neutral	?	active ~ inactive	ergative ~ absolute	nominative
	objects	unified	?	close ~ distant	direct ~ indirect	direct ~ indirect
Morphology	declension	∅	∅	active ~ inactive cases	ergative ~ absolute cases	nominative ~ accusative cases
	conjugation	∅	set of affixes of classes and persons	active ~ inactive series of personal affixes	ergative ~ absolute series of personal affixes	subjective ~ (objective) series of personal affixes

Klimov's proposal, summarized in the table, also attempts at an explanation of mixed types. Languages of transitive typology reveal only structural criteria of types closest to the left or to the right, e.g. the Abhaz-Adig languages can be characterized as ergative languages with some criteria of active structure, the group Na-Dene as active with some features of class type. The only exception is the active type because it may have the criteria of the nominative type (Cf. Klimov 1976, 143 ff.)

In the brief presentation of the active and ergative types I shall use the results of Klimov's books (1973, 1977) which will also help me in the comparison of these two types with the nominative type.

Active Type

The active type has the following criteria: active vs. inactive classes of nouns, and active vs. stative classes of verbs in the lexicon. In morphology either the nouns have active and inactive cases, or the verbs have active and inactive series of personal affixes or both. The syntax of the active type displays two major structures, obligatory to all active languages: the active and inactive constructions consisting of a subject, a predicate and a possible object (omitted in the following scheme). Both can be marked in three ways:

1. only the predicate, 2. both the subject and the predicate, 3. only the subject is marked.

Active structure
1. N — V active
2. N active — V active
3. N active — V
Inactive structure
1. N — V stative
2. N inactive — V stative
3. N inactive — V

In various active sentences with verbs denoting involuntary action or state: *(verba affectuum* and *verba sentiendi)* demonstrate an affective structure in which 1. the predicate, 2. the subject and the predicate, 3. only the subject is marked. Thus, the principles and possibilities of marking are identical with those of the active and inactive structure.

Affective structure
1. N — V affect.
2. N affect. — V affect.
3. N affect. — V

A brief summary of the syntax of the active type is given by Klimov (1977, 315—316): "The synchronic dominant of any model of the active sentence typology is the verbal predicate. This is reflected in the incorporation of the subject with the stative verb-predicate or the nearest object with the active verb-predicate, the process being widespread in languages of active typology. Here, too, the subject and the predicate form two grammatical nuclei of the sentence. At the same time both objects are included in the set of secondary parts, as well as the affective one, occuring in the construction with involuntary action and state verbs. The nearest object is used only in sentences with active verb-predicate and denotes an object to which the action refers, as it is represented in sentences like 'a bear breaks a tree', 'a serpent crawls to the river'. The distant object is similar in its function to adverbials. The typical word order for active languages depends on the syntactic relations in a sentence. It may be represented by the pattern S—(O′)—(O″)—V for the active constructions (O′ designating the distant object, O″— the nearest one) and by the pattern S—(O′)—V for inactive constructions."

The active verbs instead of distinguishing between active and passive forms have a diathesis of centrifugal and non-centrifugal versions, cf. 'to put— to lie down'. The verb has highly expressed domination of aspectual meaning over temporal ones (Cf. Klimov 1977, 316).

In active languages "there is a process of strengthening the opposition of subjective and objective principles. The two schematic lines of this process obviously denote the ergativization or the nominativization of the linguistic structures correspondingly." (Klimov 1977, 318).

There are no instances of transition from the ergative or the nominative type to the active one.

I gave a brief but relatively full characterization of active type because it displays a clear opposition to the nominative type which is our main concern here. For our further analysis it will be relevant to have a closer look at the active, stative and affective verb classes of active languages.

"Active verbs or the so-called 'verbs of action' denote various actions, motions, events produced by the *significata* of the active noun class" (Klimov 1977, 85). Transitivity is not a relevant feature of the active verbs. "Stative verbs or the so-called verbs of state (the terms: middle, neuter verbs are used in American descriptive works) denote state, characteristics or quality mostly connected with the *significata* of the nouns of inactive class" (Klimov 1977, 85). Stative verbs can be divided into the following groups: state of emotion: 'feel shame', 'be angry', 'be happy', 'weep'; state of intellect: 'know', 'forget', 'remember', 'understand'; physical state: 'be suspended', 'blow' (about wind), 'roll', 'lie', 'stick out', 'limp', 'tremble', 'contract', 'be dissipated', 'bloom', 'stink', 'be tired', 'be hungry', 'be thirsty', 'be drunk'; quality: 'be high', 'be long', 'be heavy', 'be clean', 'be big', 'be black', 'be old'; state of possession; 'to possess'.

The so-called affective verbs denote involuntary action or state and consist of *verba sentiendi and verba affectuum*. The former group includes the verbs of perception: 'see', 'hear', and the verbs of knowing and thinking: 'know', 'think', 'understand', 'realize'. *Verba affectuum* can be classified into the verbs of physical and spiritual state: 'be awake', 'wear out', 'break', 'be tired', 'sleep', 'smile' and into the verbs of affection: 'love', 'like'.

The set of stative verbs has a significant intersection with the verbs governing the Partitive in Estonian and genitive in Lithuanian. All subgroups of stative verbs are represented in the given verb group of these nominative languages except those of physical state. A number of the verbs of the latter group corresponds to the adjectives in Estonian and Lithuanian (as well as in English).

There is a small set of affective verbs in ergative languages corresponding to both the stative verbs and the affective verbs of active type. They consist of *verba sentiendi*, *verba affectuum* and *verba habendi*.

Ergative type

Verbs in ergative languages can be divided in two classes: transitive and intransitive verbs. This implies the opposition of transitive and absolute sentence structures. Transitive verbs are used in ergative sentences. There are the possibilities of marking: 1. predicate marking, 2. subject and predicate marking, 3. subject marking.

1. $N - N - V_{erg.abs.}$
2. $N_{erg.} - N_{abs.} - V_{erg.abs.}$
3. $N_{erg.} - N_{abs.} - V$

Absolute structures consist of an intransitive verb and a subject and a possible noun in oblique case. The possibilities of marking are identical with those of the ergative structure:

1. $N - (N_{obl.}) - V_{abs.}$
2. $N_{abs.} - (N_{obl.}) - V_{abs.}$
3. $N_{abs.} - (N_{obl.}) - V$

Verbs have series of personal affixes referring either to an ergative subject and absolute object or to an absolute object. Nouns have ergative or absolute affixes (for details see Klimov 1973, 42 ff.). Languages without synthetic devices will not be considered here.

"Ergative and absolute constructions are two compulsory models of sentence, their opposition determines the essence of ergative structure" (Klimov 1973, 55). In numerous languages there are other models corresponding to the ergative scheme. I shall mention affective (or dative or inverse) and possessive constructions. Affective constructions consist of one of the *verba sentiendi* or *verba affectuum* and a subject with a case suffix different from that of ergative or of absolute, usually with the suffix of dative and an unmarked object. The possessive construction is shaped in a similar way with a possessive verb. The principles of morphological marking are identical with those of ergative structures (Cf. Klimov 1973, 54 ff.). Thus, affective and possessive sentences follow the structural principles of the ergative type.

As it was noted, the affective verbs of ergative languages correspond to a subset of stative verbs and to the verbs of involuntary action or state of active languages. There are about 20 verbs belonging to this set. They consist of *verba sentiendi* including verbs of perception: 'see', 'hear', verbs of knowing and thinking: 'know', 'remember', 'forget', 'think', and verbs of emotion: 'love' 'like', 'hate', 'pity for', 'be envious', verbs of judgement: 'suit', 'fit', 'seem', verbs denoting volition, necessity, possibility: 'want', 'wish', 'need', 'be necessary', 'be possible' (Cf. Klimov 1973, 71—72).

On Class Type

I cannot give even a brief characterization of this type. Only two remarks concerning Bantu languages will be made. Since there is no declension, the definiteness of the deep direct object is expressed by a class infix in the verb which refers to the definite object and is identical with the class of the direct object:

Swahili:
Ali amesoma kitabu.
'Ali has read a book.'
Swahili:
Ali amekisoma kitabu.
'Ali has read the book.'
Infix *ki-* shows the definiteness of the object. But the construction is the same in both sentences. Deep indirect object is referred to by an infix *(-i-)* making the verb capable of accepting an indirect object (or locative of direction) and an infix of class, identical with the class of the indirect object:
Swahili:
Ali alimwandikia Edgar barua.
'Ali wrote Edgar a letter.'
Thus, the constructions with intransitive or transitive verbs do not display structures similar to active or ergative languages.

W. A. Whiteley, an outstanding expert in Bantu languages, classified the objects expressing deep direct object, deep indirect object and locatives according to the possibility of them being referred to by class infixes in the verb. According to his classification "a primary object is an object which may occur in a controlled relationship with a verb, the exponent of this being a pre-radical infix" (Whiteley 1966, 110). There are radicals with which such an infix occurs permissively, with others it occurs regularly, with some radicals such an infix never occurs. The Swahili examples demonstrated primary objects referred to by class infixes in the verb. "A secondary object is one which cannot occur in that controlled relationship with a verb the exponent of which is an object infix. The secondary object may occur alone, or in association with other objects. . . . A large number of simple radicals only co-occur with secondary objects: to give a full list of these would be to embark on a piece of lexicography" (Whiteley 1966, 118—119). The primary or secondary objects may represent deep direct object or deep indirect object. "Tertiary objects differ from other objects in the rarity with which *any* may occur in a controlled relationship with a verb as examplified by an object infix" (Whiteley 1966, 122). Tertiary objects typically express deep locatives and are marked by local prefixes:
Yao:
Mbúsi jiwiile kumusi.
'A goat has died at home.'

Mitééla jimesíle paasí.
'Trees grow in the ground.'
The verbal predicate, however, can agree with the local adverbial and
be marked by its prefix (or pre-prefix). In the resulting sentence the local
adverbial becomes a surface quasi-subject:
Yao:
Kumusi kuwiilé mbusi.
'At home there has died a goat.'
Paasí pámesílé mítééla.
'Trees grow in the ground.'
(lit: 'In the ground grow trees.')
The subject and the object do not exhaust the parts of the sentence in
Yao. There is an adjunct—class, the relationships of which "are never
characterized by control" (Whiteley 1966, 166). There is certain relational
hierarchy between the various parts of sentence (Cf. Whiteley 1966, 167).

Whiteley's approach to Yao syntax can be applied to any Bantu
language despite their differences, especially in the use of tertiary objects
(e.g. in Swahili and Yao). From the point of view of Klimov's types it is
important to note the impact of noun classes on various sentence
structures, on the classification of the parts of sentence. The local prefixes
or pre-prefixes form special sentence structures which are characteristic of
class type. Whiteley paid much attention to groups of verbal radicals
which are or can be used with various kinds of objects but I could not
examine them because this would go beyond the scope of my study.

The class type has criteria which are not treated in Klimov's proposal
because they are relevant to the formation of complex sentences. The
"subordinate" clauses are formed by the help of the relative variants of
class prefixes infixed in the verb (Whiteley 1966, 113).
Lisimba **li***twálíweeni lila lyékúlúngwa.*
'The lion which we saw was large.'
This raises the problem of the possibility of including compound
sentences and non-finite constructions in the classification. They figure
among the criteria of Skalička's complex types (Cf. Skalička 1974) and
would complete Klimov's proposal.

Nominative Type: General Characteristics

The derivation of sentence structures from a base structure consisting of a verbal predicate, a subject and an object is governed by two principles of morphological marking. 1. The features of the predicate are reflected in the form of the subject in active languages and ergative languages by case suffixes or verbal affixes. They can be considered as subject-marking languages. 2. An opposite principle is at work in nominative languages, they do not mark the subject but they do mark the object instead. Since morphological marking is not universal, there are languages neutral from this point of view. They belong to the neutral type in Klimov's classification.

The ergative and nominative types can be classified into sub-types according to the impact of determination and aspectuality. The ergative languages are not our concern here (Cf. Kibrik 1979), the role of determination and aspectuality will be analyzed only in nominative languages.

Before the examination of the sub-types of nominative languages, I must mention some other basic criteria of the nominative type as well. In lexicon the differentiation of transitive and intransitive verbs is relevant. This implies the differentiation of direct and indirect objects in syntax and the opposition of nominative and accusative cases in the declension and that subjective and objective personal affixes in the conjugation are also possible. A detailed analysis, however, must refine these criteria proposed by Klimov. First, I shall examine a negative criterion of nominative sentence structure: the lack of marking of the agent, a subject with "active" feature. Ergative and active languages mark the agent, differing only in the structures in which it occurs: active languages mark any agent, ergative languages mark only the agents of the transitive verbs.

Non-active subjects also reflect the features of the predicate in stative, absolute and affective construction. Nominative languages can mark the non-active subject of some verbs in a way similar to the active and ergative languages and leave the object in the unmarked nominative if the predicate is a verb of possession or some other affective verb, e.g.

Hung.
Nekem van kalapom.
'I have a hat.'
'To-me is hat-my.' (lit.)

Hung.

Nekem kell a kalap.

'I need the hat.'

'To-me needs the hat.' (lit.)

Russian sentences corresponding to the first example can be formed in two ways: either by marking the subject, similar to the Hungarian and then the subject is expressed by a Genitive with the preposition *u* and the object is in the nominative:

Russ.

U menja jest' šljapa.

or in a nominative way: with the subject in the nominative and with the object in the accusative:

Ja imeju šljapu.

The second Hungarian example has a corresponding Russian sentence consisting of a nominal predicate, a non-active subject in the dative and an object in the nominative:

Russ.

Mne nužna šljapa.

Despite such constructions both Hungarian and Russian are characterized by sentences with subjects in the nominative. The case of the object reflects the features of the verb and the impact of determination and of other factors and is expressed by the accusative, genitive, dative or instrumental in Russian. Here the paradigmatic structure of the case system must also be accounted for. Hungarian marks the object with the accusative far more consistently than Russian does, but Russian reflects the semantics of the predicate more precisely; e.g.

Russ.

Petr želajet sčast'ja. (gen.)

Hung.

Péter boldogságot (acc.) *kíván.*

'Peter wishes happiness.'

Russ.

Učenyj zavedujet sektorom. (instr.)

Hung.

A tudós vezeti az osztályt. (acc.)

'The scholar directs the department.'

The use of different cases in Russian is to be explained by the semantics of the verb which differs, in both examples, from that of concrete transitive verbs governing the accusative (for details see 1.2. 2.).

The sub-types of the examined Finno-Ugric and Indo-European languages of nominative type reflect the phenomena of syntax, of morphological categories and of morphological paradigms. The partitive sub-type is represented by Estonian, the total one by Hungarian and the semi-partitive one by Russian and Lithuanian. There is no specific overt means for the categories of determination and aspect in the partitive type. Both are expressed by the opposition of the partitive and non-partitive cases (nominative, accusative) of the subject and of the object. (I am concerned only with the latter.) In total sub-type, determination is expressed by articles, a specific overt system of marking and perfective aspectuality is expressed by preverbs. The semi-partitive sub-type does not have overt, specific means for the category of determination, but it displays a system of means for the perfective type of aspect in Russian.

There is only perfective aspectuality marked by prefixes in Lithuanian. (It is very close to that of Hungarian.) The difference in the overt expression of aspect is reflected in the individual characteristics of Russian and Lithuanian: the latter has the opposition of the nominative and the genitive similar to that of Estonian. The case system of Russian and Lithuanian is of the same type (i.e. type 2, see 1.2.), Estonian and Hungarian have the case systems of type 2, but they belong to different sub-types: Estonian has the partitive case as opposed to the nominative and the accusative, in Hungarian this opposition is lacking.

The characteristic sentence structures of the three sub-types of the nominative type can be represented by sentences consisting of a deep subject, a verbal predicate and a deep direct object. The variants of the subject are not considered.

Partitive Sub-type

A) The opposition of total and partitive objects.

total: $N - V_{term.} - N_{acc.}$

partitive: $N - V_{curs.} - N_{part.}$

$V_{term.}$ is a terminative verb implying, with the noun in the accusative, perfective aspectuality and definiteness. $V_{curs.}$ is a cursive verb implying, with the noun in partitive, non-perfective aspectuality and indefiniteness.

B) Partitive object without the opposition of a total object

$N - V - N_{part.}$

Semi-Partitive Sub-type

(A) The opposition of total and partitive direct objects
total: $N - V_{perf.} - N_{acc.}$
partitive: $N - V - N_{gen.}$
In the total construction a perfective verb corresponds to the terminative verb of the total construction in the partitive sub-type. In the partitive construction the aspect of the verb is not indicated because it depends on the construction, on the language. Definiteness is not overtly expressed. The accusative, however, frequently implies definiteness and genitive indefiniteness.

(B) Indirect objects
$N - V - N_{gen. \ (instr.) \ dat.}$
The noun is assigned the suffix of the genitive, instrumental or, less frequently, that of the dative.

Total Sub-type

(A) The opposition of definite and indefinite objects
definite: $N - (Prev.) + V - Art. + N$
indefinite: $N - V - N$
Art usually is the definite article, the lack of article refers to zero-article. In constructions with a definite object the verbs often have a preverb, implying perfective aspectuality.

(B) The constructions corresponding to partitive or indirect objects in the two other sub-types typically consist of an object expressed by a noun in the accusative, with or without an article but a noun in another case is also possible. The latter is considered an adverbial by grammars. This also holds for the relationship between the partitive object in the partitive sub-type and the indirect object in the semi-partitive sub-type: an indirect object in Russian can be rendered by a case other than the partitive and is considered as an adverbial in the grammar of Estonian.

The construction corresponding to B) is
$N - V - (Art.) + N_{acc.}$ or (N_x)
where N_x signals an "adverbial" case.

The examples illustrating the different constructions will be given below.

Partitive Sub-type: Estonian

The opposition of total and partitive constructions with terminative and cursive verbs, respectively, was examined above:

(A) (1) (N) — $V_{term.}$ [+ pert.] + $N_{acc.}$ [+ def.]
    (2) (N) — $V_{cursiv.}$ [— perf.] — $N_{part.}$ [— def.]

(1) "In Estonian total object can be used only in affirmative sentences. It denotes object (or the sum of objects) totally involved by a finished action expressed by direct-transitive verb" (Pjall et al. 246). In the singular its regular expression is a noun in the genitive used as an accusative and a noun with a nominative used in specific constructions. In the plural the nominative is the case of the total object. In order to simplify and generalize the case of total direct object I shall denote it by the accusative by which I mean the accusative, genitive and nominative depending on the conditions of its use. The Estonian construction with a total object, as a rule, corresponds to a Russian sentence with a direct object expressed by a noun in the accusative and a predicate which is a perfective verb.

(2) "In Estonian a construction with a partitive object usually denotes an object (or a sum of objects) not totally involved by the action or reflects a non-finished or iterative action expressed by direct-transitive verb" (Pjall et al 247). Partitive object is expressed by the partitive both in the plural and singular.

Estonian construction with a total object and its Russian and Hungarian equivalents:
Est.
    Ma ostis raamatu.
Russ.
    Ja kupil knigu.
Hung.
    Én megvettem a könyvet.
    'I have bought the book.'
In Estonian the accusative expresses both finished or to be finished action and the definite object, in Russian finished action is overtly expressed by perfective verb and the noun is in the accusative. In Hungarian the preverb refers to the finished action, and the definite article is an overt expression of determination. The Estonian construction with a partitive object and its equivalents in Russian and Hungarian:

4*

Est.
>   *Ma ostan raamatud.*

Russ.
>   *Ja pokupaju knigu.*

Hung.
>   *Én könyvet veszek.*
>   'I buy a book.'

In Estonian the partitive expresses a non-finished or iterative action and an indefinite object. In Russian the non-finished action is overtly expressed by imperfective verb and the noun is in the accusative. In Hungarian the non-determined action is expressed through the lack of article.

In Slavic languages the use of the genitive or the accusative with a noun-object denoting not totally involved object, varies from language to language. In a construction denoting an action involving some part or the whole of the object the object in the accusative and the imperfective verb are opposed to an object in the genitive and a perfective verb in Serbo-Croatian:

Sr.—Cr.:
>   *Ja sam pio vode.*
>   'I drank some water'.
>   *Ja sam popio vodu.*
>   'I drank all the water'.

This pair of constructions corresponds to the opposition of the accusative and partitive in Estonian. In Russian, however, the opposition of the genitive and accusative is only used with perfective verbs:

Russ.:
>   *Ja vypil vody.*
>   'I drank some water.'
>   *Ja vypil vodu.*
>   'I drank (all) the water.'

These constructions differ from those of Serbo-Croatian in the use of a perfective verb in both cases and reflect the peculiarities of Russian aspect.

In negative sentences the partitive construction is used consistently in Estonian, its use is less consistent in Slavic because determination plays an important role in it: the definite object usually prefers the accusative and a non-definite one is expressed by the genitive. The use of the two constructions depends on other factors as well, and their influence is different in Russian and Serbo-Croatian (Grammatika II. 1: 122—124, Gortan—Premk 1971, 73 ff., Menac 1978).

In Estonian the opposition of the accusative and partitive objects is reduced to partitive constructions if the predicate is expressed by the following groups of verbs (Pjall et al. 248—249).

1. Verbs of intellectual life, e.g. *teadma* 'know', *mõistma* 'understand', *mäletama* 'remember', *manitsema* 'teach', *huvitama* 'interest' etc.

2. Verbs of perception and feeling: *nägema* 'see', *vaatama* 'look', *kuulma* 'hear', *kuulama* 'listen', *nuusutama* 'smell', *tundma* 'feel' etc.

3. Verbs expressing relationship to the object, positive relationship: *armastama* 'love', *austama* 'honour', *kaitsma* 'defend', *toetama* 'support', *kiitma* 'praise', *veetlema* 'attract', *soovima* 'wish', *tahtma* 'want', etc., negative relationship: *vihkama* 'hate', *süüdistama* 'accuse', *needima* 'curse', *kiruma* 'abuse', *karistama* 'punish', *kiusama* 'make angry'; *kartma* 'be afraid', etc.

This list is far from being complete and will be complemented further (e.g. it includes the verbs of possession and other smaller groups). Even so, it is apparent that the major groups partially coincide with the groups of verbs used with the genitive in Lithuanian (Frankel 66 ff) and the group of verbs in both languages has a considerable overlap with the stative and affective verbs in active languages. The latter includes the major groups of verbs: governing the partitive or genitive in nominative languages.

Nominative — partitive languages	Active languages
1. verbs of mental life	*vs.* verbs of mental state, knowing
2. verbs of perception and feeling	*vs.* stative verbs of perception and emotion
3. verbs of positive and negative relationship	*vs.* verbs of affection

But the stative verbs of the active type also consist of verbs of physical state which are not among the verbs requiring the partitive or genitive in the nominative type. Most of the verbs of physical state correspond to intransitive verbs or to adjectives in nominative languages. Most of the affective verbs of active and ergative languages have equivalents among the verbs used with the partitive or genitive in the nominative type. The fact of the considerable correspondence of groups of verbs in ergative, active and nominative languages shows an inter-type regularity: a set of features are reflected in the form of the subject in active and nominative languages and in the form of the object in nominative-partitive languages depending on the subject or the object marking principles, respectively. The means of marking are different in the various pártitive or semi-partitive languages (e.g. in Estonian, in Lithuanian or Russian) and are lacking in total sub-type (in Hungarian).

The next step will be the examination of this group of verbs in Estonian, Hungarian, Russian and Lithuanian because it determines the sub-types of nominative languages to a high degree.

Partitive and Total Sub-types: Estonian and Hungarian

Estonian, as a partitive language, has no specific means of expressing determination: the opposition of the accusative and partitive implies both aspectuality and definiteness. A total language, like Hungarian, has specific means for expressing determination and, therefore, it does not need the opposition of cases for this purpose, and the accusative in Hungarian corresponds to both the accusative and partitive in Estonian. The accusative is a generalized case of the direct object in Hungarian and is used also with verbs requiring the partitive in Estonian. The cross-type tendency of the three groups of verbs to form special constructions in active, ergative and nominative–partitive languages does not work in Hungarian in which most verbs of these three groups require the accusative, even if some of them admit alternative cases as can be seen from the comparison of Estonian and Hungarian verbs of the three groups presented above. All Estonian verbs govern a noun in the partitive, all Hungarian verbs require the accusative except those with different section.

1. Verbs of mental life, e.g.

Est.	Hung.		
teadma	*tud*	'know'	
mõistma	*ért*	'understand'	
mäletama	*emlékszik*	'remember' sublative	
manitsema	*tanít*	'teach' accusative/sublative	
huvitama	*érdekel*	'interest'	

2. Verbs of perception and feeling:

nägema	*lát*	'see'
vaatama	*néz*	'look' accusative/sublative
kuulma	*hall*	'hear'
kuulama	*hallgaι*	'listen'
nuusutama	*szagol*	'smell'
tundma	*érez*	'feel'

3. Verbs expressing relationship with the object:

armastama	*szeret*	'love'
austama	*tisztel*	'honour'
kaitsma	*véd*	'defend'
toetama	*támogat*	'support'
kiitma	*dicsér*	'praise'
veetlema	*vonz*	'attract'
soovima	*óhajt*	'wish'
tahtma	*akar*	'want'
vihkama	*gyűlöl*	'hate'
süüdistama	*vádol*	'accuse'
needima	*átkoz*	'curse'
kiruma	*szid*	'abuse'
karistama	*büntet*	'punish'
kiusama	*bosszant*	'bother'
kartma	*fél*	'fear' ablative

As is apparent from this list all verbs govern a direct object in the accusative, two of them with alternative sublative, except one verb requiring the sublative and another one with the ablative.

Semi-Partitive Languages: Russian and Lithuanian

Semi-partitive languages can be compared with both partitive and total languages because they share some features with both sub-types. As we have seen in the analysis of the partitive sub-type represented by Estonian widespread opposition of the total and partitive objects expressed by the accusative and the partitive respectively corresponds to the opposition of the accusative and genitive in Slavic languages. Negation has a similar impact on the sentence structure in both sub-types.

However, the groups of verbs requiring a partitive object in Estonian do not coincide with the verbs governing the genitive in Slavic languages. Most verbs in the three groups examined above have an object in the accusative in Russian, except *učit'* + accusative or dative 'teach', *interesovat'sja* instr. 'interest', *bojat'sja* gen. 'fear'. Thus Russian is very close to Hungarian in this respect and differs from Estonian.

Lithuanian, the other representative of the semi-partitive type, is close to Estonian because most verbs used with the partitive in Estonian govern the genitive in Lithuanian. The major groups of Estonian "partitive" verbs can be found among the verbs governing the genitive in Lithuanian. Thus, most of the verbs of mental life, of perception, govern the genitive but the accusative can also be used if the verb means a completed or resultative action usually expressed by prefixes. The verbs expressing relationship to the object and requiring the partitive or genitive have a considerable overlap in Estonian and Lithuanian. The use of the accusative is more limited here (Frankel 1928, 66 ff).

These facts show that the semi-partitive sub-type must be considered as a heterogeneous mixed sub-type sharing the features of both partitive and total sub-types to a different degree. A brief comparison of Russian with Hungarian and Estonian will shed more light, not only on the semi-partitive, but also on the partitive and the total sub-types.

1.2.2. CONTRASTIVE ANALYSES

Semi-Partitive and Total Sub-types: Russian and Hungarian

Semi-partitive languages are represented by Russian with references to Lithuanian and Serbo-Croatian. Total sub-type will be demonstrated by data from Hungarian. The comparison of Russian with Hungarian will be brief, restricted to the major groups of verbs (for a detailed study see Deže 1982a). The expression of deep direct object and indirect object will be analyzed. Their representation by the accusative, genitive, instrumental and dative in Russian will be compared with their expression in Hungarian cases. Direct and indirect objects are primary objects and case suffixes without prepositions, i.e. primary means, are used for their morphological marking. Secondary objects are usually expressed by secondary means in morphology, by case suffixes and prepositions in Russian. Lithuanian differs from Russian only in the marking of secondary objects: case suffixes without prepositions also mark various secondary objects expressed both by case suffixes and prepositions in Russian.

Both Russian and Lithuanian belong to type 1 of the case systems, with a limited number of cases (in Russian 6, in Lithuanian 7 cases). Hungarian and Estonian represent type 2 of the case systems, with a greater number of cases (Estonian 14, Hungarian about 20).

Verbs which include a volitional feature are *chotet'* 'want', *želat'* 'wish', *prosit'* 'ask for', or *ždat'* 'wait', *dostigat'* 'to reach', but the use of the genitive can be restricted by the semantic features of the object.

There are also those verbs which include a feature referring to a non-total effect on the object. This feature may be accompanied by others showing its degree, e.g. *otlit'* 'to pour of liquid', *nakupit'* 'to buy a lot', *najest'sja* 'to eat too much or as much as possible'.

In Hungarian, verbs including a volitional feature are rendered by the accusative. Verbs with a feature referring to non-total effect on the objects are used with the accusative, if there is no feature indicating the maximum quantity because then a special construction is needed:
Russ.
> *Petr najelsja chleba.*

Hung.
> *Péter teleette magát kenyérrel.*
> 'Peter full-ate himself with bread' (lit.)

with a reflexive pronoun in the accusative and the object in the instrumental-commitative. If one highlights non-totality, more precisely partiality in Hungarian, then the elative can be used:
Hung.
> *Péter önt a borból.*
> 'Peter pours the wine-of' (lit.)

If the perfective verb has no feature indicating obligatory non-totality, then in case of total object the accusative is used and the genitive denotes non-total object in Russian. In Hungarian both objects are in the accusative, the total object is accompanied by the definite article, the non-total object goes with an indefinite article.

(1)
Russ. *Petr vypil vino.* 'Peter drank the wine.'
Hung. *Péter megitta a bort.*

(2)
Russ. *Petr vypil vina.* 'Peter drank some wine.'
Hung. *Péter ivott bort.*

The totality of action is expressed by a verb with a perfective preverb *(meg)* in Hungarian.

The majority of case suffixes, however, are used for the representation of various "adverbial", mostly local, relations and secondary objects in both languages.

Direct Object Expressed by the Accusative and the Genitive in Russian. In Russian, the accusative is the major means of expressing the deep direct object. It is used with verbs denoting concrete action and its object, with the possible features of result, or of partial or complete change. Verbs denoting a change in the position in space also govern the accusative. These two major groups of verbs require the accusative for the expression of the direct object in nominative languages and the active or ergative for the representation of an active subject in active and ergative languages. Verbs denoting perception, speaking, thinking, emotions, moral attitude, and intellectual activities are used with the accusative of the direct object in Russian. As we have noticed above, Russian shares the features of total sub-type in this respect and is opposed to partitive Estonian and, more or less, to Lithuanian.

In Hungarian, the accusative is used whenever the accusative is applied in Russian. This is natural because Hungarian is a representative of the total sub-type. The difference between the two languages will be revealed in the genitive, instrumental and dative, because objects expressed by these cases in Russian are often rendered by the accusative in Hungarian.

In Russian, the genitive is used to express the deep direct object in sentences where the verbal predicate is partitive. The elative can be used in Hungarian, but this is to be done only in rare cases.

There are small groups of verbs governing the genitive in Russian and usually rendered by the accusative in Hungarian:

Russ. *kasat'sja*, Hung. *érint*

Russ. *zasluživat'*, Hung. *kiérdemel*, but

Russ. *stoit'*, Hung. *érdemel* with the illative.

There is only one major group of verbs with the features of deletion which requires the genitive—ablative in Russian and the ablative or accusative in Hungarian. Verbs which are accompanied by a deep direct object in the genitive in Russian and in the ablative in Hungarian are Russ. *bojat'sja*, Hung. *fél* 'be afraid'; Russ. *čuždat'sja*, Hung. *idegenkedik* 'be averse'; Russ. *lišat'*, Hung. *megfoszt* 'deprive'. There are also verbs requiring a deep direct object in the genitive in Russian and one in the accusative in Hungarian: Russ. *izbegat'*, Hung. *kerül* 'avoid', Russ. *stydit'sja*, Hung. *szégyell* 'be ashamed'. Hungarian applies the accusative, if the feature of deletion is less apparent.

If the deep direct object is represented by the genitive in Russian, it is classified as an indirect object in Russian grammars. The fact that such object is expressed by the accusative in Hungarian and is classified as a direct object in Hungarian grammars shows that one is dealing with a deep direct object governed by a verb with a feature of non-totality or partiality. This is marked by a special case, by the genitive, in Russian, but is left unmarked in Hungarian except in specific cases of emphasis, when the elative is used. A deep object can accompany a verb with a feature of deletion. In Hungarian a noun in the ablative corresponding in Russian to one in the genitive—ablative is used when deletion is an important component of the verb, otherwise the accusative also expresses this kind of the deep direct object.

Direct Object Expressed by Instrumental in Russian.

The Russian instrumental serves a secondary means, the representation of a direct object which cannot appear in the accusative for various reasons. One of the reasons is the semantics of the active verb (1). If the verb is neutral, it cannot be accompanied by a direct object in the accusative and the instrumental is used instead of the accusative. This reflects the semantic properties of the verb as well (2). If the indirect object or locative has "total" feature and is expressed by the accusative, the direct object will be rendered by the instrumental, too, because two nouns in the accusative are not permitted (3).

In these cases, the instrumental replaces the accusative. But the instrumental can also be used when the deep direct object and the instrumental coincide and it is up to the individual language to choose the instrumental or accusative to represent such a transitory category (4). The clear instances of deep instrumental will not be examined here.

The use of the Hungarian instrumental-commitative is more restricted but more or less corresponds to that of the Russian instrumental, because such factors as blocking the use of the accusative with neutral **verbs, marking** total indirect object or locative with the accusative, and the choice of the instrumental for the expression of a deep object-instrumental are present in Hungarian, too.

(1) The comparison of two languages starts from the active verbs denoting possession, direction: Russ. *obladat'*, Hung. *bír* 'possess', Russ. *pravit'*, Hung. *kormányoz* 'govern', Russ. *rukovodit'*, Hung. *vezet* 'lead', Russ.

zavedovat', Hung. *irányít* 'direct', 'run'. The Hungarian accusative corresponds to the Russian instrumental, except a neutral verb with suffix *-ik* not permitting the accusative: Russ. *rasporjažat'sja*, Hung. *rendelkezik* 'dispose'.

(2) Russian neutral verbs of positive or negative relationship are usually expressed by neutral verbs with the suffix *-sja* which do not allow the accusative object. If they are rendered by neutral verbs with the suffix *-ik* in Hungarian neither of the languages can express the object with the accusative, and the Russian instrumental often corresponds to the postposition *iránt* in Hungarian: Russ. *voschiščat'sja*, Hung. *lelkesedik* 'be enthusiastic', Russ. *interesovat'sja*, Hung. *érdeklődik* 'be interested', but the Hungarian instrumental: Russ. *gordit'sja*, Hung. *büszkélkedik* 'be proud' or the illative also can be used: Russ. *ljubovat'sja*, Hung. *gyönyörködik* 'take delight'. If the Hungarian verb has no neutral suffix the accusative is applied: Russ. *naslaždat'sja*, Hung. *élvez* 'enjoy', Russ. *prenebregat'*, Hung. *megvet*.

(3) If the deep indirect object has the feature of totality and is expressed by the accusative in both languages, the direct object is in the instrumental in both languages. This happens with the object of the verbs denoting donation, 'supply', 'equipping': Russ. *nagradit'*, Hung. *kitüntet*, 'decorate', Russ. *snabdit'*, Hung. *ellát* 'supply'. It is, however, a question that is still to be clarified, whether such an object can be considered as a direct or as a secondary object. These verbs are related to those of giving, and can be paraphrased by the verbs 'to give', 'to donate', e.g. Hung. *A parancsnok érmet adományozott a katonának.* 'The commander medal donated to the soldier.' (lit.) Hung. *A parancsnok éremmel tüntette ki a katonát.* 'The commander decorated the soldier with a medal.'

The first sentence consists of the verb 'donate', the deep direct object in the accusative and the deep indirect object in the dative. In the second sentence, the verb 'decorate' has the deep direct object in the instrumental and the deep indirect object in the dative. If the two sentences can be correlated, one has to deal with an indirect object in the dative and accusative, respectively.

Such analysis is supported by another type of evidence. There is a group of Russian transitive verbs which have a semantic element 'filling', and govern the instrumental expressing direct object, and the accusative, representing deep indirect object or locative.

In Hungarian there is a construction which corresponds exactly to that of Russian:

Russ.
> *Petr nagruzil gruzovik drovami.*

Hung.
> *Péter megrakta a teherautót fával.*
> 'Peter loaded the truck with wood.'

Russ.
> *Petr gruzil drova na gruzovik.*

Hung.
> *Péter rakta a fát a teherautóra.*
> 'Peter loaded the wood on the truck.'

But it can often be substituted by a sentence consisting of the same verb without a prefix or preverb, a noun in the accusative expressing deep direct object, and a noun in a locative case representing deep locative in both languages (for further analysis see below).

Similar synonymous constructions are possible with the verbs: Russ. *nabit'*, Hung. *töm*, Russ. *napolnit'* and *načinit'*, Hung. *tölt*, 'fill'. There are no synonymous constructions with internal causative verbs: Russ. *nakormit'*, Hung. *jóltart* 'give (enough) food', *napoit'* 'give (enough) to drink'. They can be correlated with constructions where the predicate is a verb of giving accompanied by the infinitive of a non-causative verb and has a noun in the accusative expressing deep direct object and a noun in the dative representing deep indirect object, e.g. a construction with a causative verb.

Russ.
> *Petr napoil rebenka molokom.*

Hung.
> *Péter megitatta a gyereket tejjel.*
> 'Peter gave the child drink with milk.' (lit.)

and the synonymous construction with a verb of giving and a non-causative verb:

Russ.
> *Petr dal pit' moloko mal'čiku.*

Hung.
> *Péter adott inni tejet a fiúnak.* (lit.)
> 'Peter gave to drink milk to the boy.' (lit.)

These constructions correspond to those analyzed in connection with the first group of verbs of (3).

If the Russian verb has the suffix *-sja*, the deep direct object is represented by the instrumental instead of the accusative and the deep locative is expressed by a local preposition. In Hungarian the suffix -*ul* of the verb also blocks the use of the accusative which is replaced by the instrumental: Russ. *Petr povernulsja spinoj k Pavlu*, Hung. *Péter háttal fordult Pál felé* 'Peter turned with back towards Paul' (lit).

(4) In any human language there are borderline cases which can be classified in two ways. One of them is the object-instrumental expressed by nouns denoting parts of the body or object kept in them. They are governed by verbs of motion and are expressed by the instrumental in Russian, but by the instrumental or accusative in Hungarian. The Russian instrumental corresponds to the Hungarian instrumental:

(1)
Russ.
Petr mašet rukami.
'Peter waves (his) hands.'
Hung.
Péter integet a kezével.
(2)
Russ.
Petr stučit kulakami.
'Peter thunders with (his) fists.'
Hung.
Péter dörömböl az öklével.

The Russian instrumental is rendered by the accusative in Hungarian:

(3)
Russ.
Petr skrežeščet zubami.
'Peter grinds (his) teeth.'
Hung.
Péter csikorgatja a fogait.
(4)
Russ.
Petr ševelit gubami.
'Peter moves (his) lips.'
Hung.
Péter mozgatja az ajkait.

Another borderline case is represented by constructions consisting of an abstract verb, a deep indirect object in the accusative and a deep direct object or instrumental in the instrumental in both languages. The abstract verbs denote surprise, conviction, threat, etc.

(5)

Russ.

Marija poražala menja svojej krasotoj.

Hung.

Mária meglepett engem a szépségével.

'Mary surprised me with her beauty.'

(6)

Russ.

Petr ubedil Pavla slovom.

Hung.

Péter meggyőzte Pált szóval.

'Peter convinced Paul with words.'

(7)

Russ.

Bolivija ugrožala Tanzaniju vojnoj.

Hung.

Bolívia (meg)fenyegette Tanzániát háborúval.

'Bolivia threatened Tanzania with war.'

Direct Object Expressed by the Dative in Russian. The dative is the basic means of representing an indirect object, therefore, there is only a small number of verbs governing the direct object in the dative. Most of them can be clustered into small groups; verbs denoting benefaction or malefaction: Russ. *sposobstvovat'*, Hung. *elősegít* 'promote', Russ. *vredit'*, Hung. *megkárosít* 'hinder', correspondence or assimilation: Russ. *sootvetstvovat'* Hung. *megfelel* 'suit', *upodobljat'sja*, 'become assimilated', teaching: Russ. *učit'*, *obučat'* Hung. *tanít, oktat* 'teach' 'instruct'; surprise: Russ. *divit'sja, udivljat'sja*, Hung. *csodál, csodálkozik* 'be surprised'; happiness: Russ. *radovat'sja* Hung. *örül* 'be glad'.

Some of the Hungarian verbs require the dative: *megfelel, örül*, others govern the accusative: *elősegít, megkárosít, csodál*, the accusative or an "adverbial" case: the sublative: *tanít, oktat*, or only "adverbial" cases; the allative: *hasonul*, the superessive: *csodálkozik*.

A number of Russian verbs are neutral and have the suffix *-sja* which blocks the use of the accusative and this implies a choice between the genitive, instrumental or dative. Dative is chosen here because the semantic structure of the verb does not contain an element requiring the genitive or instrumental. The transitive verbs of teaching: *učit', obučat'* 'teach', 'instruct' have a double rection: either the indirect object is expressed by the accusative and the direct one by the dative, or the direct object is represented by the accusative and the indirect one must be left unexpressed. The semantic structure of the verbs of benefaction and malefaction require the use of the dative.

The Expression of Indirect Object. In Russian the indirect object in the dative may be the only primary object required by many verbs which denote internal relationship, emotion or thought. The Hungarian verb governs either of the two cases, and the semantics of the verb does not suggest any cue concerning the choice of the case. Some verbs have their objects in "adverbial" cases: in the sublative, allative or instrumental-commitative. The semantics of these verbs is very heterogeneous. Their only common characteristic is their abstract feature: they denote or imply abstract activity or state. Some examples will be given.

Verbs denoting emotion, raising emotion or the result of emotion:

(1)

Russ.

Petr zavidujet sosedu.

Hung.

Péter irigyli a szomszédot. (acc.)

'Peter envies the neighbour.'

(2)

Russ.

Pavel sočustvujet drugu.

Hung.

Pál együttérez a barátjával. (instr.-commit.)

'Paul sympathizes with his friend.'

(3)

Russ.

Anna l'stit načal'niku.

Hung.

Anna hízeleg a főnöknek. (dat.)

'Ann flatters the boss.'

(4)

Russ.

Orator nadojedajet slušateljam.

Hung.

A szónok untatja a hallgatóságot. (acc.)

'The orator bores the audience.'

(5)
Russ.
Šapka nravitsja Petru.
Hung.
A sapka tetszik Péternek. (dat.)
'The cap pleases Peter.'
(6)
Russ.
Publika applodirujet pevcu.
Hung.
A publikum tapsol az énekesnek. (dat.)
'The audience applauds the singer.'
Verbs denoting help, hindering and various acts:
(7)
Russ.
Petr pomogajet Anne.
Hung.
Péter segít(i) Annának (dat.) or *Annát.* (acc.)
'Peter helps Ann.'
(8)
Russ.
Pavel mešajet Petru.
Hung.
Pál akadályozza Pétert. (acc.)
'Paul hinders Peter.'
(9)
Russ.
Anna klanjajetsja znakomym.
Hung.
Anna üdvözli az ismerősöket. (acc.)
'Ann greets acquaintances.'
(10)
Russ.
Rycar' prisjagajet knjazu.
Hung.
A lovag esküt tesz a hercegnek. (dat.)
'The knight swears to the duke.'

In some cases there is, or can be, a secondary object added to the
indirect one. In Russian, it is expressed by the instrumental, by the

accusative with the preposition *na* or by the prepositive with the preposition *v*. In Hungarian the case of the secondary object "corresponds" to that of the Russian noun. The instrumental is rendered by the instrumental (see above) *na* + accusative by the sublative, *v* + prepositive by the inessive, i.e. by Hungarian cases usually corresponding to Russian case suffixes and prepositions. If the indirect object is represented by the dative in Hungarian, the secondary object may be expressed by the accusative:

(11)

Russ.

Bolivija grozit Tanzanii vojnoj.

Hung.

Bolívia fenyegeti Tanzániát háborúval. (instr.)

'Bolivia threatens Tanzania with war.'

(12)

Russ.

Student žalujetsja direktoru na pitanije.

Hung.

A hallgató panaszkodik az igazgatónak az étkezésre. (subl.)

'The student complains of the meal to the director.'

(13)

Russ.

Petr priznalsja Anne v ošibke.

Hung.

Péter elismerte Annának a hibát. (acc.)

'Peter admitted to Ann the mistake'. (lit.)

The secondary object may be expressed by an infinitive construction in Russian and by a subordinate clause in Hungarian. This usually happens with verbs denoting command, permission, promise:

(14)

Russ.

Petr obeščal Anne prinesti knigu.

Hung.

Péter megígérte Annának, hogy odahozza a könyvet.

'Peter promised Ann to fetch the book.'

Another major group of verbs has both direct and indirect objects. The direct object is expressed by the accusative and the indirect one by the dative, in both languages, except in some instances where the indirect object has the suffix of a different case in Hungarian. This group of verbs is very heterogeneous. The verbs of giving and those of communication are among them.

(15)

Russ.

Anna adresujet pis'mo otcu.

Hung.

Anna címezi a levelet az apjának. (dat.)

'Ann addresses the letter to her father.'

(16)

Russ.

Počtaljon vručajet posylku adresatu.

Hung.

A postás átadja a csomagot a címzettnek. (dat.)

'The postman hands over the parcel to the addressee.'

(17)

Russ.

Direktor soobščil novost' kollegam.

Hung.

Az igazgató közölte az újságot a kollégákkal. (instr.-comm.)

'The director announced the news to the colleagues.'

Most verbs of communication can have a secondary object or a subordinate clause instead of a direct object. The secondary object is expressed by the prepositive in Russian and by the delative in Hungarian. The secondary object denotes a relevant piece of information contained in the subordinate clause.

(18)

Russ.

Anna rasskazyvala Pavlu ob ekskursii.

Hung.

Anna mesélt Pálnak a kirándulásról.

'Ann told Paul about the excursion.'

(19)

Russ.

Anna rasskazyvala Pavlu o tom, kak prošla ekskursija.

Hung.

Anna mesélt Pálnak arról, mi történt a kiránduláson.

'Ann told Paul what had happened on the excursion.'

5*

In Hungarian the subordinate clause is referred to by a surface pronominal indirect object in the delative corresponding to the Russian prepositive with preposition *o*.

If the verb is perfective in both languages, the subordinate clause is referred to by a pronominal direct object which is usually ommitted:

(20)

Russ.

Anna rasskazala Pavlu, kak prošla ekskursija.

Hung.

Anna elmesélte Pálnak (azt), (hogy) mi történt a kiránduláson.

'Ann told Paul what had happened on the excursion.'

If the Hungarian verb has a preverb only having the function of perfectivization, the secondary object, represented by a noun, can only be in the accusative;

(21)

Hung.

Anna elmesélte Pálnak a kirándulást (*a kirándulásról).

'Ann told Paul the excursion.' (lit.)

The problem of secondary object is more complex but I do not want to go into details here. It will suffice to say that in Hungarian the secondary object more often is, or can be, expressed by a pronoun in the accusative than in Russian. Verbs of communication admitting both the accusative and *o* + prepositive in Russian govern only the accusative in Hungarian.

As it was demonstrated in the analysis of both kinds of objects, the deep indirect object can be expressed by the accusative in both languages, but in Hungarian the accusative is used more frequently than in Russian. If the deep indirect object is represented by a noun in the accusative, the deep direct object can only appear as a noun in the instrumental or dative in Russian and by the same or some other cases in Hungarian.

On the Expression of Secondary Object and Locative. When analyzing the deep direct and indirect objects I touched upon the question of the secondary object as well. But the problem of the latter has not been exhausted, it would require a detailed contrastive analysis. I have restricted this brief survey of the expression of the objects to Russian cases without prepositions. It covered nearly all instances of the surface representation of deep direct and indirect objects. The secondary objects are marked by a great variety of prepositions with different case suffixes and imply a complex morpho-syntactic problem as well. In Hungarian secondary objects are rendered by "adverbial" suffixes or postpositions. Thus, in Russian primary objects are represented by cases without prepositions, secondary objects by cases with prepositions. In Hungarian, primary objects are mainly expressed by two "grammatical" cases: accusative and dative, secondary objects by "adverbial" cases.

The expression of deep locative, including direction, is out of the scope of our comparative analysis. I will mention only instances when the locative is represented not only by a locative case but also by the accusative.

In the analysis of the deep direct object expressed by the instrumental in Russian, I paid attention to the fact that both languages can represent deep direct object with the instrumental, and locative with accusative. In a parallel construction the primary correspondence of deep and surface categories can be preserved: the deep direct object is expressed with the accusative, the deep locative by a local preposition in Russian and with a local case in Hungarian. Compare the primary construction with the secondary one:

(22)

Russ.

Rabočije gruzili drova na baržu.

'The workers loaded wood on the bark.'

Russ.

Rabočije gruzili baržu drovami.

'The workers loaded the bark with wood.

The perfective verb will have the prefix *za-* in the first sentence and *na-* in the second. The verbal predicate of the second sentence implies 'filling the bark with wood'. The first one does not have such implication. In Hungarian the corresponding constructions are also possible:

(23)

Hung.

A munkások rakták a fát az uszályra.

Hung.

A munkások (meg)rakták az uszályt fával.

The verb of the second sentence prefers the preverb *meg-*, which makes the verb perfective. In the first sentence the verb would have the prefix *rá-* with local meaning 'onto', but it is not necessary.

In Hungarian, the double expression of deep direct object and locative denoting approximation or deletion is very frequent and follows a similar pattern:

(24)

Hung.

A munkás (rá)keni az olajat (DO) *a tengelyre* (loc.).

'The worker smears oil on the axle.'

Hung.

A munkás (meg)keni a tengelyt (loc.) *olajjal* (DO).

'The worker covers the axle with oil.'

(25)

Hung.

A munkás (le)törli az olajat (DO) *a tengelyről* (loc.).

'The worker wipes oil from the axle.'

Hung.

A munkás (meg)törli a tengelyt (loc.) *az olajtól* (DO).

'The worker wipes the axle from the oil'. (lit.)

The difference between the last two pairs of sentences is to be explained by the two directions. It is apparent that the "local" cases must be different depending on the two direction: approximation expressed by the sublative in (24), and delation expressed by the delative in (25). In the first pair the locative denotes approximation, therefore, the structures of the sentences coincide with those of the previous examples denoting the same direction. In the second pair the locative denotes deletion and this fact is also reflected in the form of the deep direct object: if its surface representation does not correspond to its usual form then the ablative replaces the instrumental. Compare the second sentences in (24) and (25):

(24) loc. = accusative, DO = instrumental

(25) loc. = accusative, DO = ablative

The change in the surface expression in the second sentences is caused by the feature 'total' implied by the use of the accusative and by the preverb *meg-* denoting completed action. The same can be observed in verbs with a locative argument only:

(26)

Hung.

A fiú hozzáér a falhoz.

Hung.

A fiú megérinti a falat. (acc.)

'The boy touches the wall.'

Here the preverb *hozzá* is replaced by *meg-*, and a suffix is added.

The double constructions with a deep direct object and a locative correspond to those with a direct and an indirect object examined above:

the surface expression of the indirect object will change from the more usual dative to the accusative, the verb will have the preverb *meg-:*
(27)
Hung.
Péter ajándékozott egy lovat Annának.
'Peter presented a horse to Ann.'
Hung.
Péter megajándékozta Annát egy lóval.
'Peter presented Ann with a horse'. (lit.)

Semi-Partitive and Partitive Sub-types: Russian and Estonian

This brief analysis of Russian and Estonian proceeds in the same way as the Russian—Hungarian comparison did, it examines Russian cases expressing first direct and then indirect object and compares them with the use of Estonian cases expressing object. The difference in the use of the Estonian partitive and accusative, represented by the genitive and nominative, is not taken into consideration because it was analyzed above. The case of the object in Estonian will be labelled as "partitive" adopting the term of Russian—Estonian contrastive grammar. When comparing Russian with Estonian I shall refer to the Hungarian as well and the comparison of the three languages will be summarized at the end.

The Expression of the Direct Object. Russian concrete verbs requiring a direct object in the accusative will not be examined. The opposition of the constructions consisting of a perfective verb and a definite object and those with a non-perfective verb and an indefinite object is not our concern here because they were analyzed above. The first topic of our comparison is constructions with a verb requiring a deep direct object in the genitive in Russian and the partitive in Estonian (Pjall et al. 252—254).

The first group includes verbs with the feature 'volition' governing nouns in the genitive with or without restrictions connected with the features of the noun: Russ. *chotet'*, Est. *tahtma* 'want'; Russ. *želat'*, Est. *soovima* 'wish'; Russ. *dostigat'*, Est. *saavutama* 'reach'; Russ. *ždat'*, Est. *ootama* 'wait'; Russ. *prosit'*, Est. *paluma.*

The second group consists of the verbs with a feature referring to a non-total effect on the object. This feature is accompanied by another one indicating maximum quantity, e.g. Russ. *najest'sja, nakušat'sja* Est. *kõhtu täis sööma* (the Estonian verb has an adverb with an affix).

There are small groups of verbs governing the genitive in Russian, and the partitive in Estonian: Russ. *kasat'sja*, Est. *puudutama, puutuma, riivama* 'to touch'; Russ. *zaslušat'sja*, Est. *kuulama jääma* 'listen (with attention)'.

The third group includes verbs with the feature of deletion requiring the genitive—ablative in Russian and the partitive in Estonian: Russ. *bojat'sja*, Est. *kartma* 'be afraid'; Russ. *stydit'sja*, Est. *häbenema* 'be ashamed'; Russ. *izbegat'*, Est. *vältima* 'avoid'; Russ. *lišat'sja*, Est. *kaotama* 'be deprived'.

In Hungarian, the Russian genitive was rendered by the accusative except for some verbs with the feature of deletion which require the ablative. The groups of verbs governing the instrumental in Russian and the partitive in Estonian are more or less identical with those examined in the Russian—Hungarian constrastive analysis (Pjall et al. 257—262).

The first group consists of verbs denoting possession, direction: Russ. *vladet'*, Est. *valdama* 'possess', 'have', Russ. *upravljat'*, *pravit'*, Est. *valitsema, juhtima*, 'govern'; Russ. *zavedovat'*, Est. *juhatama* 'direct', 'run'; Russ. *rasporjažat'sja*, Est. *korraldama* 'give orders'.

In Hungarian the accusative is used, except with neutral verbs not admitting the accusative.

The second group includes verbs denoting a positive or negative relationship to the object:

Russ. *voschiščat'sja*, Est. *imetlema* 'be enthusiastic', Russ. *ljubovat'sja*, Est. *imestama* 'take pleasure'; Russ. *naslaždat'sja*, Est. *nautima* 'enjoy'; Russ. *prenebregat'*, Est. *põlgama*. Most of the Russian verbs have the neutral suffix -*sja* which does not admit the accusative. If the Hungarian verb has the neutral suffix -*ik*, it does not admit the accusative and the postpositive *iránt* is used, otherwise it requires the accusative.

The next group of Russian neutral verbs with the suffix -*sja* requires the instrumental instead of the accusative for the expression of a direct object and a local case representing deep locative. In Estonian, the deep direct object is expressed by the partitive, the deep locative by *vastu* + partitive (or ablative):

Russ. *prižimat'sja ščekoj k steklu*, Est. *suruma põske vastu klaasi*. This group consists of more verbs and with greater variety of constructions in Russian—Hungarian constrastive analysis. They are not among the constructions examined in the Estonian—Russian contrastive grammars, except some verbs denoting 'filling' (Pjall et al. 261).

The verbs of motion require a borderline category: direct object—instrumental if they are complemented with a noun denoting a part of the body or an object kept in it. This borderline category is expressed by the instrumental in Russian and by the partitive in Estonian: Russ. *machat' platkom*, Est. *lehvitama rätikut*, Russ. *skrežetat' zubami*, Est. *kiristama hambaid*. The second of these two verbs denotes 'giving sound' as well. In Hungarian, either the instrumental or the accusative of the noun is used for the expression of the direct object—instrumental. The accusative is the typical case of the deep direct object, the instrumental is the typical representative of the deep instrumental. Our analysis of the verbs governing the instrumental in Russian and the partitive in Estonian will not consider a few small groups of verbs connected with their object in a way that requires further analysis (Pjall et al. 260—262).

In Russian, the dative representing a deep direct object is used with a couple of small groups of verbs. Such a dative can be rendered as an object in Estonian (Pjall et al. 254—257). Verbs requiring the dative can denote benefaction or malefaction: Russ. *sposobstvovat'*, Est. *soodustama*, 'promote'; Russ. *prepjatstvovat'*, Est. *takistama* 'hinder'; teaching: Russ. *učit'*, Est. *õpetama* 'teach'; surprise: Russ. *udivljat'sja*, Est. *imestama* 'be surprised'. In Hungarian, the deep direct objects of these verbs are also rendered by the accusative except the last one which is a medial verb.

The Expression of the Indirect Object. In Russian, deep indirect object is typically expressed by the dative. In Estonian it can be expressed as an object, symbolized by the partitive besides the allative corresponding more or less to the dative in Russian and in Hungarian. In this respect Estonian and Hungarian are close because the latter also uses both the accusative and the dative where only the dative is applied in Russian (see above). I shall give some Russian and Estonian examples of the various groups of verbs governing the dative in Russian and the partitive in Estonian. Verbs denoting emotion, raising emotion, the result of emotion: Russ. *zavidovat'*, Est. *kadestama* 'envy'; Russ. *grozit'*, Est. *ähvardama* 'threaten'; Russ. *nadojest'*, Est. *tüütama* 'bore'; Russ. *dosaždat'*, Est. *kiusama* 'irritate'; verbs expressing help, hindering and similar acts: Russ. *pomagat'*, Est. *aitama*, 'help'; Russ. *mešat'*, Est. *segama* 'hinder'; Russ. *prisluživat'*, Est. *teenindama* 'assist'; Russ. *akkompanirovat'*, Est. *muusik-ariistal saatma* 'accompany' (as a musical term); verbs of command: Russ. *velet'*, Est. *käskima* 'command'; Russ. *zaprešcat'*, Est. *keelama* 'forbid'; Russ. *pozvoljat'*, Est. *lubama* 'permit'; verbs with various meanings

including an emotional component: Russ. *verit'*, Est. *uskuma* 'believe';
Russ. *doverjat'*, Est. *usaldama* 'to have confidence'.

On Secondary Objects. Since the examination of secondary objects is
beyond the scope of my study, I shall make only a brief comment on the
expression of this relationship in Russian and Estonian. In Russian,
secondary objects are represented by prepositions and case suffixes. In
Estonian, nouns with case suffixes, postpositions and prepositions usually
correspond to Russian nouns with prepositions (Pjall et al. 207 ff.). There
are, however, various groups of verbs requiring a deep secondary object
expressed by nouns with prepositions in Russian rendered by the partitive
in Estonian (Pjall et al. 262—273), in some cases, Hungarian uses the
accusative, the case of the object, as well: e.g. Russ. *uderživat'sja ot slez, ot
smecha* with preposition *ot* + genitive, Est. *(tagasi) hoidma (pisaraid,
naeru)*, Hung. *visszatartja könnyeit, nevetését* 'hold back tears, laugh'; or
Russ. *klast'sja drugu v vernosti* Est. *vanduma sobrale truudust*, Hung.
esküszik barátjának hűséget. In the second example the indirect object is
expressed by the dative in Russian and in Hungarian, by the allative in
Estonian, the secondary object is represented by the cases of the object in
Hungarian and in Estonian and by preposition *v* + prepositive in
Russian.

The cases of the object (accusative, partitive) are used more
frequently in these Finno-Ugric languages than in Russian. I have the
impression that Estonian applies the case of object more often than
Hungarian does but I have no comparative study at my disposal and can
judge only on the contrastive study of Russian and Estonian.

The correspondence between Hungarian and Estonian and their
opposition to Russian concerning the representation of various objects
can be explained to some degree by the fact that these Finno-Ugric
languages belong to type 2 of case systems, and Russian belongs to type 1.
The fact that Russian uses case suffixes without prepositions for the
representation of primary objects and cases with prepositions for the
expression of secondary objects is specific to Russian or to a sub-type of
type 1 with a sophisticated system of prepositions. Then the other sub-type
would be represented by Lithuanian with a limited set of prepositions and
postpositions (Fraenkel 1928, 64 ff).

1.3. Sentence Structure and Case Systems in Russian and in Hungarian

In chapter 1.2. the types of sentence structure were analyzed on the basis of relational terms: the surface representation of the deep subject, direct object and indirect object were examined but some questions of secondary objects and locatives were also considered. In the surface representation the cases of individual languages were our heroes. The parts of a sentence (or members of a sentence) were only indicated because they can easily be determined by surface cases. In chapter 1.3.1. some questions of sentence structure will be discussed on the base of "deep cases" instead of relational terms as done in chapter 1.2. The relational terms and "deep cases" can be correlated: the deep subject is typically an agent or an experiencer in primary diathesis, the deep direct object is a patient (or objective), the deep indirect object is an addressee. It would, therefore, be unneccessary to give a systematic analysis of the surface representation of the types of sentence structure relating "deep cases" to surface cases and to parts of a sentence. I shall be interested in those phenomena when the direct, simple relationship between deep and surface categories does not exist, their relationship varies in one language or from one language to another. I shall restrict my analysis to some problems of nominative languages which were in the centre of attention in chapter 1.2.

In chapter 1.2. only the individual cases were considered. I mentioned that Russian and Lithuanian belong to type 1, Estonian and Hungarian to type 2 of case-system typology, but the latter requiring a paradigmatic analysis could not have been discussed on a syntagmatic axle. This will be done in this chapter (1.3.2.).

1.3.1. DEEP CASES, PARTS OF SENTENCE AND
SURFACE CASES IN NOMINATIVE LANGUAGES

On Deep Cases

In primary, complete active sentences the agent or the experiencer becomes the subject and may stand in the nominative: Russ. *Petr čital knigu, Petr videl knigu,* Hung. *Péter olvasott egy könyvet, Péter látott egy könyvet* 'Peter read a book', 'Peter saw a book'. The subject in the theme is typically "determined", usually "definite", therefore, the marking of determination has developed to a lesser degree with regard to its morphological expression as can be observed with the object in various sub-types of nominative languages (see 1.1.2. and 1.2.).

The patient may be expressed by a direct object: Russ. *Petr čital knigu,* Hung. *Péter olvasta a könyvet,* 'Peter read the book'. The derivational history of secondary patient is complex and has not been considered in the theory of deep cases: Russ. *Petr čital o knige,* Hung. *Péter olvasott a könyvről,* 'Peter read about the book'. I shall use the label secondary patient as opposed simple patient. The simple patient has a "central" feature, while the secondary patient has a "non-central" feature. Both may be added to the same verb: Russ. *Petr čital recenziju o knige,* Hung. *Péter olvasott egy recenziót a könyvről,* 'Peter read a review about the book'; Russ. *Petr govoril što-to o knige,* Hung. *Péter mondott valamit a könyvről,* 'Peter told something about the book'. The verb itself contains a feature which requires that the patient be represented in languages possessing a case system by another case than the accusative: Russ. *Petr zanimalsja delom,* Hung. *Péter foglalkozott az üggyel,* 'Peter dealt with the case'.

The addressee may take the role of the direct object instead of the role of surface indirect object, in which instance this takes the accusative characteristic of the surface direct object; Russ. *Petr napomnil Pavlu ob obeščanii* (dat.), Hung. *Péter emlékeztette Pált az igéretre* (acc.), 'Peter reminded Paul of the promise'. Here the expression of the addressee by the accusative is due to the semantic property of the verb. In another instance, it is the speaker who may decide which of the two deep cases he regards as being central; that is, he may or may not attribute a "central" feature to the patient — Hung. *Péter megajándékozta Pált a könyvvel,* 'Peter presented Paul with the book.' and *Péter könyvet ajándékozott Pálnak,* 'Peter presented a book to Paul.' In Serbo-Croatian, the two cases are governed by two different verbs: *Petr je obdario Pavla knigom* (archaic), 'the same as above', *Petr je poklonio Pavlu knigu*, 'the same as above'. Locative may be a central constituent as well; however, the choice between such a locative of a "total" feature and one with no such feature is left to the speaker — Serbo-Croatian: *Radnik je natovario kamion kamenjem*, 'The worker loaded the lorry with stones', and *Radnik je tovario kamenje na kamion*, 'The worker loaded stones on to the lorry'. (The corresponding Russian examples see in 1.2.)

Starting from the "deep cases" we arrive at the direct object of the surface structure, the most important component of the comment, which is derived from a primary patient, or experiencer or locative. When the experiencer and the locative come to the fore, the patient is pushed into the background. This is evoked by the peculiar semantic quality of the verb, and the process may be due to either obligatory or facultative rules. It should be repeated in this context that the semantics of the verb may require a "non-central" object even if no concurrent experiencer or locative is present: Russ. *Peter zanimajetsja lingvistikoj* (instr.), Hung. *Péter foglalkozik nyelvészettel* (instr.), 'Peter studies linguistics', in which case the patient is expressed by a noun in the instrumental.

We have determined the surface object by and large, but have not done the same in connection with the subject. So far we have only said of it that it is the typical expression of the agent and of the experiencer. In the absence of agent or experiencer the role of subject may be taken by the patient and also by the instrumental: Russ. *Petr otkryvajet dver' ključom*. Hung. *Péter kinyitja az ajtót kulccsal*, 'Peter opens the door with a key'; Russ. *Ključ otkryvajet dver'*, Hung. *A kulcs nyitja az ajtót*, 'The key opens the door'; Russ. *Dver' otkryvajetsja* only with a medio-passive verb, Hung. *Az ajtó nyílik* with verb with a medial-suffix 'The door opens'.

This is how the "deep cases" share among themselves the two most important central places in the sentence. If there is no chance for promotion, the addressee will be the indirect object, the locative the adverbial of place, the instrumental the adverbial of instrument.

On Surface Cases

Starting from the "deep cases" or deep relational terms, we arrive, through the analysis of parts of sentence, at the questions of case systems. Case suffixes, pre- and postpositions, as morphological means, express certain grammatical categories. There are two possible modes of expression: a category may express one "meaning", or several at the same time. In the first case, we speak of an agglutinative, in the second of a non-agglutinative representation. Traditionally, this is referred to such morphological categories, as number and case, number and person etc. in morphological typology. The category of case, however, is complex, one must differentiate between grammatical and adverbial "meanings", if I use the traditional terminology, because cases can express both types of relations and deep cases.

The case suffix may denote number and case category, or just the latter, while the preposition and the postposition do not denote case categories. Both the preposition and postposition and the case suffix may express, in principle, one or several syntactic-semantic "meanings" of the given language. These "meanings" manifest universal categories (relations, "cases") in the "context" of the system of categories of individual languages. A case suffix, pre- and postposition which represents one definite semantic-syntactic category, is regarded as agglutinative, while those representing at least two categories are regarded as non-agglutinative. Thus the suffix -*u* of Russian accusative is non-agglutinative not only because it marks accusative and singular simultaneously but also because it expresses at the same time the patient and the locative as well: *Petr videl dom.* 'Peter saw the house', *Petr vošol v dom*, 'Peter entered the house'. In contrast, the suffix -*t* of the accusative is agglutinative in Hungarian, because it expresses only the patient: *Péter látta a házat*, 'Peter saw the house'. The other accusative of Russian, which corresponds to the adverbial of direction, can be parallelled by special case in Hungarian: *Péter bement a házba*, 'Peter entered the house'. But if we continued in this way, it would soon appear that hardly any really agglutinative case suffix could be found even in Hungarian, since the suffix -*t* expresses the surface object in a general sense, that is to say, it may represent, beside the patient, the experiencer and the locative also, provided they become primary argument of the verb with "central" or "total" features, as we have seen above. It seems more appropriate, therefore, to formulate the conditions of agglutination by departing from the deep-structure categories, but thinking, in the final issue, in terms of parts-of-sentence categories of the surface structure. That suffix is agglutinative which is expressive only of one part-of-sentence category of the surface structure (primary object, secondary object or adverbial). In this sense, the suffix -*t* of Hungarian is a nearly agglutinative while the Slavic -*u* case suffix remains a non-agglutinative phenomenon. The preposition *to* of English is not agglutinative either, as it represents secondary, indirect object as well as adverbial modifier of place: *Peter gave the book to Paul*, and *Peter went to the river*. Prepositions going with the Slavic case suffixes, as resultants of a comparatively recent development, have the role of making clear the actual meaning of non-agglutinative, polysemic case suffixes. As against this, the agglutinative case suffixes of Hungarian with a few exceptions— are not fixed to case suffixes but to the absolute stem. It follows from all this that the way to the surface case system as a phenomenon of morphological implications leads via part-of-sentence categories of the surface system. When construing a sentence, one has to shape the surface sentence on the basis of which one is able to bring about the morphological representation of the sentence.

Agglutination is a term used to denote a generally dominating tendency even in agglutinative languages; and we too use the term in this sense. Therefore, it is necessary to ascertain the proper degree of agglutination in every language. Another remark that has to be made here is connected with the historical development of languages: in Proto-Slavic where prepositions were much less frequently used, the non-agglutinative character of the case-endings was not disturbed by prepositions. It was a later development that prepositions (together with case suffixes) came to undertake the function of expressing the locative meanings in the accusative, dative, genitive and ablative (as shown in the examples above).

Nevertheless, it is not only in the differentiation of the objective and the locative "cases" that the agglutinative mode of expression appears; it should also be taken into consideration as a manifestation of the agglutinative character that a set of features of a particular locative case in the non-agglutinative languages finds its parallels not in one, but in several locative cases in the agglutinative languages. For example, the -*u* ending of Russian corresponds to an objectival and two locative case suffixes in Hungarian:

Russ.

*knig***u**

Hung.
könyvet 'the book' (accusative)
Russ.
v knigu
Hung.
könyvbe 'into the book' (illative)
Russ.
na knigu
Hung.
könyvre 'onto the book' (sublative)
In Russian, various prepositions go with the noun—in addition to the *-u* suffix—while in Hungarian *-be* and *-re* are proper case suffixes. In the same way, in Hungarian four other case suffixes correspond to the prepositive and the genitive with the same prepositions *(v, na)*: Russ. *v knige, na knige;* Hung. *a könyvben* (inessive), *a könyvön* (superessive), 'in the book', 'on the book'; *iz knigi, s knigi,* Hung. *a könyvből* (elative), *a könyvről* (delative), 'out of the book', 'from the book'. Even more distinctions than in Hungarian are made among the locative cases in some of the Caucasian languages; for example, in Tabasaran, which L. Hjelmslev classified as belonging to a separate type. Whereas Hungarian has several cases to express locative relations which are represented by identical cases in Russian, always with different prepositions, Tabasaran has case suffixes that correspond to Hungarian postpositions; consequently it possesses more features involved in the expression of cases (Magometov 97—140).

As we have seen above, there is a considerable difference between Russian prepositions and the system of Hungarian postpositions, for the prepositions in Russian are fixed to some case or cases, but Hungarian postpositions—almost without exception—are added to the absolute stem. Russian, as an inflectional language, is characterized by the synonymy of case suffixes, e.g. the accusative is represented by *-u, -a, -o, ф, -y, -i* etc. In Hungarian the accusative is represented by suffix *-t* with morphophonemic variants shaped according to the rules of vowel harmony and other factors. Some cases have no morphophonemic variants. New cases can be readily formed: if a postposition "merges" with a word, a new case will result. Cases of the so-called three-dimensioned languages come about in this manner. Still we cannot say that cases come about by mere chance: they are in harmony with a certain hierarchical order of the locative features. At the same time the cases show a certain degree of numerical variability, depending on whether the possibilities are realized or not.

On the basis of the fairly high number of locative cases supplemented with a series of postpositions, languages like Hungarian are classed among languages which are capable of expressing place relations with a high degree of accuracy. In addition preverbs in Hungarian can represent local relations in more shades of expression than the Slavic system of preverbs can do.

On Deep and Surface Cases

After this survey of the questions of "deep cases", surface constituents of sentence and surface cases I resume the discussion of questions concerning the base-structure features and the surface components characterizable by these.

Agent as a surface subject expressed by the nominative has the following features: [+ active, ± approximation, + central]:
Russ.

> *Mal'čik* (A) *otkryl dver'*.

Hung.

> *A fiú* (A) *kinyitotta az ajtót.*
> 'The boy (A) opened the door.'

Experiencer as a surface subject expressed by the nominative has the following features: [— active, ± approximation, + central]:
Russ.

> *Mal'čik* (E) *vidit dver'*.

Hung.

> *A fiú* (E) *látja az ajtót.*
> 'The boy (E) sees the door.'

In the passive voice the agent or the experiencer has a "non-central" feature and takes the place of a secondary part of sentence: [+ active, ± approximation, — central] in the case of an agent:
Russ.

> *Dver' byla otkryta mal'čikom.* (A)
> 'The door was opened by the boy. (A)'

Passive voice, however, throws up a number of other problems. Just to mention one: it is connected with the loss of the "central" character of the agent, therefore, in the majority of languages with passive con-

6

structions the agent is not indicated: Serbo-Croatian: *Vráta su bila otvorena.* 'The door was opened.'

The patient belongs to the arguments with a "non-active" feature. The patient as a surface direct object expressed by the accusative has the following features: [— active, + approximation, + central]:

Russ.

   Mal'čik otkryl dver'. (P)

Hung.

   A fiú kinyitotta az ajtót. (P)

   'The boy opened the door.' (P)

The "approximation" feature of the patient is problematic if it holds the place of the subject of a sentence in the passive voice: perhaps it is not incorrect to suppose that the patient, assuming the role of the subject, results in a sort of neutralization of the "approximation" feature: [— active, ± approximation, — central] and its features coincide with those of the experiencer.

Russ.

   Dver' (P) *byla otkryta (mal'čikom).*

   'The door (P) was opened (by the boy).'

In Hungarian sentences with a predicate expressed by a medial verb the subject can be a "non-animate" agent:

Hung.

   Az ajtó (A) *kinyílt.* 'The door opened.'

Its features are: [± active, ± approximation, + central]

The deep instrumental has the following features: [+ active, ± approximation, — central] as opposed to the case when it takes the role of the subject and will have the features: [+ active, ± approximation, + central]:

Hung.

   A fiú kulccsal (I) *nyitja az ajtót.*

   'The boy opens the door with a key.'

Hung.

   A kulcs (I) *nyitja az ajtót.*

   'The key opens the door.'

As has been mentioned, in this instance the features of the instrumental agree with those of the agent.

The secondary surface expression of the two "deep cases" result in the same features. Their difference can be revealed by further features.

The set of features I used is not complete from the point of general typology but they show how the difference between various "deep cases" is neutralized in the expression of the surface subject in nominative languages. The neutralization goes even further: the surface representation of the subject is unified in an ideal nominative language.

The patient of base structure may have a "non-central" feature: [— active, + approximation, — central]. Such are the objects which go with verbs of volition requiring an object in the genitive: *Petr želajet sčastja.* 'Peter wishes happiness (lit.)', and the verbs of possession governing the instrumental: *Petr obladajaet prekrasnymi sposobnostjami.* 'Peter possesses excellent abilities.' The patient is a surface indirect object in both cases. The features of the patient in these cases agree with those of the addressee usually expressed by a surface indirect object with features: [— active, + approximation, — central]. The addressee, however, may change its "non-central" to "central" feature; [— active, + approximation, + central] and then its features coincide with the primary features of the patient. This may provide the explanation of the fact that certain verbs govern alternatively the accusative and the dative in representing the patient and the addressee of base structure respectively:
Russ.

    Devuška poblagodarila mal'čika (Ad) *za lentu.* (P)
Hung.

    A lány megköszönte a fiúnak (Ad) *a szalagot.* (P)
    'The girl thanked the boy for the ribbon.'

In Russian the addressee is construed with the accusative, and in Hungarian with the dative; on the other hand, the patient takes the accusative in Hungarian while in Russian it is expressed by *za* plus the accusative. The addressee with a secondary [+ central] feature is represented by the accusative but the expression of a secondary patient varies because the feature [— central] admits various cases.

The deep locative has a "non-active" feature and if an "approximation" feature is also involved, it may take either the accusative or one of the locative cases, dependent on "central" feature being present or absent. A deep locative with a "central" feature implies a "total" feature and such a locative is represented as a surface direct object expressed by the accusative:
1. Hung.

    A munkás a tengelyre (L) *keni az olajat.* (P)
    'The worker smears oil on the axle.'

6*

2. Hung.
  A munkás megkeni a tengelyt (L) *olajjal.* (P)
  'The worker covers the axle with oil.'
3. Hung.
  A munkás letörli a tengelyről (L) *az olajat.* (P)
  'The worker wipes oil from the axle.'
4. Hung.
  A munkás megtörli a tengelyt (L) *az olajtól.* (P)
  'The worker cleans the axle from the oil.'
  These locatives have the following features:
    1. *tengelyre* [— active, + approximation, — central]
    2. *tengelyt* [— active, + approximation, + central]
    3. *tengelyről* [— active, — approximation, — central]
    4. *tengelyt* [— active, — approximation, + central]

In 2. and 4. the change from [— central] to [+ central] is a result of the presence of [+ total] feature. There is no possibility of an alternative use of the accusative and the locative cases if a "limit" feature is involved: Hungarian: *A fiú a háztól* (L) *a parkig* (L) *sétált.* 'The boy walked from the house to the park.'

When dealing with the surface representation of "deep cases", we used only three features. Only one of them: "active" belongs to "deep case" theory. "Central" and "approximation" are terms of surface case-system theories. The former "central" reflects the impact of parts-of-sentence theory because it differentiates the surface subject and the direct object from the other parts of sentence. It can be correlated to the feature "nuclear" of deep grammatical relations as well. This is reasonable because the latter are to be correlated with the parts of sentence in individual languages. The "approximation" feature is essential in the case system because it provides grounds on which to explain why "grammatical" and "adverbial meanings" are expressed by means of the same cases in Slavic. They, however, must be specified when applied in the description of case systems of various types and individual languages (Cf. Deže 1982a).

1.3.2. TYPES OF CASE SYSTEMS REPRESENTED
IN RUSSIAN AND HUNGARIAN: A PARADIGMATIC VIEW

On the Types of Case Systems: Paradigmatic Component
of Syntagmatic Processes

In this point the main problem is the selection of the appropriate form of
the noun in languages that have a case system. The analysis of case
systems belongs to the traditional questions of linguistics; it has been
elaborated first of all in the Indo-European languages, but it has been
dealt with also with regard to other language families. Typologists noticed
the differences in the expression of cases as early as the 19th century
(Misteli 1893, Winkler 1887, 1889). The typology of case systems has been
expanded by L. Hjelmslev (1935, 1937), who set up three types and
examined them on extensive material. We basically accept Hjelmslev's
types, but as regards the description of case systems, we are closer to R.
Jakobson (1936). We consider both the morphological and the syntactic
analysis of case systems indispensable. The former makes it possible for us
to understand and typify the case systems of the surface. The syntactic
approach that was outlined on preceding pages is essential in revealing the
universal invariant behind the types. So in our opinion the results of the
morphological (Hjelmslev 1936, 1937; Jakobson 1936) and the syntactic
trend (Kuryłowich 1960, Isačenko 1954, 123 ff; Fillmore 1968, Anderson
1971) of case system description have to be unified within the framework
of a syntactic approach. I do not believe in a strong version of the localistic
theory, according to which each case is to be derived from the expression
of locality, but I accept a weaker version of it, which attributes an
important role to the local cases in the formation of the non-local ones. In
the following I shall refer to some basic questions of the typology of case
systems and briefly contrast the Russian and Hungarian case systems.

Case systems cannot be typified without complementary, even
intersecting classifications. The three types isolated by Hjelmslev, which
will be represented here by Russian, Hungarian and Tabasaran, are as
important as the differentiation between the ergative and nominative, and
within the latter, between the partitive, semi-partitive and total sub-types.
The latter, however, concerns the grammatical cases and can best be
described with a syntactic approach. This was done in 1.1.2. and here I will
not consider the problems of the ergative and nominative types and the
sub-types of the latter.

From the three types of case systems only two, the Russian and the Hungarian will be described briefly, the third one, represented by Tabasaran, will only be referred to.

From a typological point of view the Russian case system is marked by the fact that the grammatical and lexical or local cases do not separate in it. In Hungarian, on the contrary, they do: the accusative is the case of the direct object, the dative is that of the indirect object, the genitive is that of the "possessor". Some of the local meanings that are expressed by case suffixes and prepositions in Russian, are denoted by a special local case in Hungarian. Let our examples be the Hungarian equivalents of Russian *sumku* (acc.), v *sumk*u (preposition *v* and acc.) and na *sumk*u (preposition *na* and acc.); Hung. *táskát*, *táskába* and *táskára*, which represent three different cases:

[+ appr. + centr.] Russ. acc. *sumk*u, Hung. acc. *táskát*
'bag' (direct object)
[+ appr. + contact, + in] Russ. v *sumk*u, Hung. *táskába*
'into [a] bag'
[+ appr. + contact, + surface] Russ. na *sumk*u, Hung. *táskára*.
'on [a] bag'

'contact' = (physical) contact, [in] is the feature of 'being inside', [surface] the feature of surface.

The Hungarian local cases consistently express the triplicity of directions as well, so it is understandable that in Hungarian there are about twenty cases, while in Russian only six. In Russian the prepositions are associated with the case suffixes; in Hungarian the postpositions usually join the absolute stem, this is typical of postpositions in all languages (Serebrennikov 1974, 303). If they merge into it, new endings come into being. So type 2 represented by Hungarian is open: the postpositions may in principle join the stem. In Tabasaran of type 3, this possibility has been realized, as a result of which the number of cases is about fifty. Hungarian, at the same time, might just as well have much fewer cases, as the emergence of cases is to some extent a morpho-phonological question. Not completely, however, since the process of postpositions turning into suffixes has some semantic regularities as well. In Hungarian, for instance, the cases marked by the features of 'being inside' and 'surface' have come into existence; however, the meanings 'in front of', 'under', 'behind', and 'above' are still expressed by postpositions. In Tabasaran the latter features also correspond to suffixes. 'Being inside' and 'surface', unlike the relations 'under', 'above' etc., constitute two separate cognitive categories.

It should be investigated if the two types of cognitive relations are relevant also for a comparison of type 2 represented by Hungarian and zero-type represented by English. The most common Hungarian case suffixes *-ban* 'in', *-on* 'on', *-hoz* 'to', *-tól* 'from', *-nál* 'at', correspond to English monosyllabic prepositions, whereas Hungarian postpositions are rendered by English non-monosyllabic prepositions (Keresztes 1975). The Hungarian case suffixes mostly express relations of 'being inside', 'surface' and the postpositions mostly denote relations for which these features are irrelevant and which have other relevant features as 'under', 'above', 'behind', 'over' etc.

The existence of a case system is also related to word order types, as was established by Greenberg: "*Universal 41.* If in a language the verb follows both the nominal subject and nominal object as the dominant order, the language almost always has a case system" (Greenberg 1963 (1968), 96). Thus, in a language having SOV word order, there is generally a case system as well, but the relationship of the absence of case system with another word order type has not been possible to point out.

One of Serebrennikov's universals refers to the relationship of the case system and the verbal paradigm: "In languages which have a well-developed case system, the system of tenses is often not highly developed" (Serebrennikov 1974, 300). Further investigations are needed to account for this, as several explanations are possible.

The formal expression of cases is so much a morphological problem that it is not dealt with here (Stankiewicz 1966). One of its essential syntactic implications, however, is emphasized by a universal: "*Universal 38.* Where there is a case system, the only case which ever has only zero allomorphs is the one which includes among its meanings that of the subject of the intransitive verb" (Greenberg 1963 (1968), 95).

Types 1 and 2 of Case Systems in Russian and Hungarian

I propose first to characterize briefly the types of case systems, then to compare the case systems of Russian, Hungarian and Tabasaran. Types 1 and 2 are represented by Russian and by Hungarian, by two nominative languages, and the third by Caucasian Tabasaran, which is an ergative language. In this study I accept Hjelmslev's types, but apply features not quite identical with his. In the analysis of Russian, the conceptions of R.

Jakobson and M. Ivić will be relied on to a considerable extent (Jakobson 1936, Ivić 1953—4 and 1957—8).

In the discussion of the parts of sentence and their expression features "active", "approximation" and "central" were applied. For languages possessing case systems, it will be necessary to select further features concerning cases, prepositions and postpositions. These features will be different for the actants and the circumstants. These two groups of base-structure arguments differ in the sets of features expressed by the case suffixes of the nouns which figure as various parts of the sentence. These features are often called grammatical or adverbial meanings: the former are characteristic of the subject and the object, the latter of the adverbials. While the features "active", "approximation" are universal, the features of the case systems of different types are or can be specific of types or sub-types. When delimiting the different types of case systems, Hjelmslev was led by considerations of what directions are expressible by case suffixes. Accordingly, he established one-, two-, and three-dimensional languages. We call these languages Type 1, Type 2 and Type 3.

In Type 1 the "approximation" feature is common to both actants and circumstants. In the characterization of the latter, of the adverbials, however, it is modified by "contact" and "connecting" features in Russian representing this type. Approximation can be demonstrated in the following way:

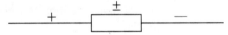

The "approximation" feature has a positive sign when approaching the object, a negative one when away from the object, and plus-minus when at the object. These relations are modified by the "contact" feature, for in the case of a local adverbial, the approximation may result in a contact which ceases in the process of moving away. If the "approximation" feature is irrelevant, then the "connection" or "contact" features may come into play. Later on we shall provide an ample representation of these features; for the while, however, we content ourselves with a few Russian examples:

[+ appr. + contact]: *v sumku* — accusative 'into the bag'
[+ appr. — contact]: *k sumke* — dative 'to the bag'
[— appr. + contact]: *iz sumki* — genitive-ablative 'out of the bag'
[± appr. + contact]: *v sumke* — prepositive-locative 'in the bag'
[± appr. + connection]: *karandašom* — instrumental 'with the pencil'

These three features will do to make differentiation between the cases of Russian, but more are needed by the preposition; thus in the case of the preposition *v* in the above example a feature for the "in" relation is also required. For the preposition *ot* combined with the genitive, a "limit" feature is also to be supposed. Below we use, in addition, the "through" [+ trans.] feature: *šol dorogoj* 'he went on the road', as well as the "societive" feature, to distinguish the adverbial complement of accompaniment; for instance: *igral s mal'čikom* 'he played with the boy'. Then there is the "quality" feature for the state and quality adverbial: *rabotal inženerom* 'he worked as an engineer'; among the latter types, however, we have special syntactic constructions as well, which are denoted by the following feature: *rabotal inženerom*, that is *rabotal i byl inženerom* 'he worked and he was an engineer', *igral s mal'čikom*, that is *on i mal'čik igrali* 'he and the child were playing.'

Case system Type 2 is exemplified by Hungarian in which the case system is based on the feature "approximation".

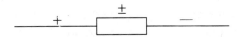

Here, in addition to the "approximation" and "contact" features the "in" and other features are also taken into consideration and diverse local cases come about from the combination of them; e.g.,

[+ appr. + contact, + in] = — BA *táskába* 'into the bag'
[+ appr. + contact, — in] = — RA *táskára* 'on the bag'
[— appr. + contact, + in] = — BÓL *táskából* 'out of the bag'
[— appr. + contact, — in] = — RÓL *táskáról* 'from the surface of the bag'

As opposed to Russian, special cases are used to express the combinations of features which are marked with a preposition and a case suffix in Russian.

Hungarian expresses more cases by means of suffixes than Russian does, but some of these features are denoted by means of postpositions, such as *előtt* 'before', *mögött* 'behind', *fölött* 'above', *alatt* 'beneath', *között* 'between, among', *mellett* 'beside' and *körül* 'around', which are used to determine the external relations of the object more closely. Tabasaran and other Caucasian languages use case suffixes to express them, and consequently the number of cases in them may be some fifty or so.

Next the features will be utilized in order *to compare Russian case system with Hungarian.* Only the outlines of the analysis are given here (for a more detailed description see Deže 1982). Now the Russian case system provides the starting point of the analysis. The fundamental feature of the Russian case system is "approximation". First the nominative case will be examined, then follows the characterization of the accusative and the dative both with "approximation" feature. The latter are distinguished from the genitive by the [+ appr.] feature, the genitive having a [— appr.] feature; finally we will look at the instrumental and the prepositional-locative (briefly: locative) with feature [± appr.].

The nominative case in Russian and in Hungarian, respectively, is characterized by the following features: the "approximation" feature is irrelevant, but the "central" feature is typical, that is [± appr., + centr.] while the meaning of ± irrelevant. For Russian nominative the abbreviation (nom.) will be used, for Hungarian (NOM).

Two of the Russian cases, namely dat. and acc. have an "approximation" feature. They are not expressed with a preposition, but are distinguished from one another by the "central" feature, while those having a preposition are distinguished by the "contact" feature. For instance, acc. [+ appr., + centr.], dat. [+ appr., — centr.], acc. and preposition: [+ appr., + contact], dat. and preposition [+ appr., — contact]. All cases with prepositions are "non-central". The "contact" feature is irrelevant, as a rule, for cases without a preposition, and in this case there is no indication of it below.

In Hungarian case system the approximation and contact features are followed by an "in" feature.

Contrasted with Hungarian, the Russian accusative features are the following:

[+ appr.]	[+ appr.]	[+ appr.]
[+ centr.]	[+ contact]	[+ contact]
	[+ in]	[— in]
		[+ surface]
Russ. acc. (vidit) *sumku*	v *sumku*	na *sumku*
Hung. acc. (látja) *táská*T	*táská*BA	*táská*RA

In Hungarian -BA denotes the illative, -RA marks the sublative. In case of [-in] a further feature is needed; e.g. "surface", but it is not our present concern here. The Hungarian adverbial of purpose may also be classified here; its suffix -ÉRT is the same as that of cause and, therefore, the index number 1 is added: -ÉRT[1]; this, however, is not characterized by the "in" feature; moreover, the "contact" feature is also questionable (in Russian: *za* + acc). In the base structure, the adverbial complement of purpose is a secondary development, expressed by a noun reduced from a sentence: *A könyv*ÉRT *ment el* 'he went for the book', that is *elment, hogy elhozza a könyvet* 'he went to fetch the book.' The Hungarian -VÁ (suffix of the adverbial of result) also belongs to this class; for instance, *róká*VÁ *változott* 'he became a fox', *igazgató*VÁ *nevezték ki* 'he was appointed director'; Russian: *on prevratilsja* v *lisicu; jego naznačili direktor*om. In the Russian equivalents the acc. with preposition *v* may be used, in which case the "approximation" feature is relevant while it is not so in the instrumental case, where it is neutralized. (Old Russian used to have the acc. instead of the instr.) We do not examine the Russian acc. used with a preposition which in Hungarian is expressed not by case suffix but by a postpositional construction. These will be treated below when the system of Hungarian postpositions will be explained.

The features of Russian dat. are simpler:

[+ appr.]	[+ appr.]
[— centr.]	[± contact]
Russian dat. *(daju) Pav*lu	*k sumk*e
Hungarian dat. *(adom) Pál*NAK	*táská*HOZ

In Hungarian -HOZ marks the allative.

The presence of the "approximation" feature characterizes two cases, while its absence only one, that of the genitive with an ablative role, which expresses moving away. The "contact" feature added to this does not have a distinguishing role in Russian.

[— appr.]	[— appr.]	[— appr.]
[— centr.]	[+ contact]	[+ contact]
[+ limit.]	[+ in]	[— in]
		[+ surface]
Russ. gen. *(boitsja) gro*zy	iz *sumk*i	s *sumk*i
Hung. *(fél a) vihar*TÓL	*táská*BÓL	*táská*RÓL

In Hungarian -TÓL markes the ablative, -BÓL is the suffix of the elative and -RÓL is that of the delative.

The "limit" feature is relevant to local relations as well.

[— appr.]
[± contact]
[+ limit]

Russ. ot *sumk*i (*ot* + genitive — ablative)
Hung. *táská*TÓL (TÓL marks the ablative)

In Russian, however, the genitive is used without an ablative role.
When combined with the preposition *do* it also has a "limit" feature. In
Hungarian the case suffix -IG corresponds to the Russian *do:* Hung. *Péter
elkísért engem a színház*IG. Russ. *Petr provodil menja* **do** *teatra* 'Peter
accompanied me to the theatre'; and Hung. *Péter est*IG *dolgozott.* Russ.
Petr rabotal **do** *večera.* 'Peter worked until evening'. The Russian *do* may
correspond also to the Hungarian postposition ELŐTT: **do** *obeda, ebéd*IG
or *ebéd előtt,* 'until lunch or before lunch'. In the first two examples *do* and
-IG have an "approximation" feature while in the last one this is
irrelevant. As an adverbial of time, -IG may denote two limits as well:
Hung. *János öt nap*IG *dolgozott.* 'John worked for five days.' In this
instance, the "limit" feature prevails over the "approximation" feature;
the first is relevant, the second is irrelevant. The "approximation" feature
is relevant, on the other hand, when it is a case of adverbial of cause,
expressed by *iz-za* plus genitive in Russian and by -ÉRT[2] in Hungarian:
Russ. *postradal* **iz-za** *ošibk*i, Hung. *a hibájá*ÉRT *megszenvedett* 'he has
paid for his fault'.

The approximation feature is irrelevant to the Russian loc. and instr.
The locative is exclusively used with prepositions (in Old Russian it might
stand without one). As against the locative, the instrumental may contain
further positive features; namely a "connection" feature when serving as
an adverbial of instrument or of accompaniment, and a "through" [trans]
feature when used as an adverbial of place or quality.

First features of the instrumental are presented (the "deep-case"
categories are also indicated, within brackets):

(i)   [± appr.]
        [— centr.]
        Russ.
        *(dom postrojen) kamen'ščik*om (Agent)
        In Hungarian postposition *által* is required:
        (a ház fel van építve a) kőműves **által**
        'the house has been built by the mason'
        Russ.
        *(zanimajetsja) algebr*oj (Patient)
        Hung.
        *(foglalkozik az) algebrá*VAL
        'he studies algebra'

(ii) [± appr.]   [± appr.]
     [+ connection]   [+ connection]
                           [+ societ.]

Russ.
pisal karandašom (Instrument) *prijechal s mal'čikom*

Hung.
irt ceruzáVAL   *megérkezett a fiúVAL*
'(He) wrote with a pencil.'   '(He) arrived with the boy.'

Russ.
Prijechal vmeste s semjoj.

Hung.
Megérkezett családosTUL.
'He arrived with his family.'

The accompaniment feature [+ societ.] marks a special syntactic structure: namely, the noun to which the suffix -VAL and the synonymous sentence: *Megérkezett ő és megérkezett a fia* (or *családja*) 'He has arrived and also his son (or his family) has arrived', supposing the two actions took place parallel to each other.

The "through" feature is expressed by the instrumental case suffix in Russian:

(iii) [± appr.]
     [+ trans.]

Russ.
šol dorogoj

In Hungarian the suffix -N of the superessive is required: *ment az útON*, 'he went on the road.' The adverbial of quality is distinguished by a certain "quality" feature from the adverbial of place. The former presupposes a special base structure: Hung. *mérnökKÉNT dolgozott; dolgozott és mérnök volt*, 'he worked as an engineer', 'he worked and was an engineer' (at the same time), but this is not obligatory in the case of the suffix -UL of the essive-modal in Hungarian:

(iv) [± appr.]
    [+ trans.]
    [+ qual.]

Russ.
rabotal inženerom

Hung.
dolgozott mérnökKÉNT

Russ.
*služil primer***om**
Hung.
*szolgált példá***UL**, 'it served as an example'.
Although consisting of fairly congruent elements, the instrumental seems to be a heterogeneous category. In Hungarian, the synonymous case-suffix pairs -VAL and -STUL, and -KÉNT and -UL correspond to the Russian adverbials of instrument, accompaniment and quality expressed with the aid of the preposition *s*, or without a preposition. The Russian "noncentral" agent is expressed by the bookish postposition *által* in Hungarian (although agent in the passive voice is rarely used in Hungarian). The Russian "non-central" object may be paralleled by a structure with suffix -VAL, as shown above, but it may correspond to a "central" ACC. as well: Russian: *upravljajet zavod***om***;* Hungarian: *vezeti a gyára***T**, 'He directs the factory.' (Cf. 1.2).

As demonstrated above, the Russian instrumental case corresponds primarily to cases of adverbials of instrument and manner in Hungarian. Corresponding to the locative (the prepositive in Russian grammatical terminology) are the cases expressing locative and temporal in Hungarian. For the "approximation" feature this case is irrelevant, while in respect of the "in" feature there are two locative cases in Hungarian, the inessive: -BAN and the superessive: -N.

	[± appr.]	[± appr.]
	[+ contact]	[+ contact]
	[+ in]	[— in]
		[+ surface]
Russ.	*v sumke*	*na sumke*
Hung.	*táská***BAN**	*táská***N**
	'in the bag'	'on the bag'

The obsolete Hungarian locative case suffix -*T* also belongs here, but the "in" feature seems to be irrelevant in relation to it: *Győröt***T** (Cf. also *Győr***BEN**), *Hódmezővásárhely***T** (Cf. also *Hódmezővásárhely***EN**). The Hung. suffix -NÁL of the adessive can be grouped here too, and in that case it is paralleled by the Russian preposition *pri;* Russ.: **pri** *dome*, Hung.: *ház***NÁL**; 'at the house', since, however, the "limit" feature is also typical of it, it may find its equivalent in the Russ. *u* plus gen. construction, for example, Russian: **u** *Petra*, Hung.: *Péter***NÉL**, 'with Peter'.

The sketchy outlines of the Russian and the Hungarian case systems as given above, deficient as they are, contain more than one element which reveals individual instead of typological characteristic features of Hungarian. Nevertheless, the general tendency can be clearly seen. The Russian case suffixes correspond, as a rule, to a couple of general features: in addition to "approximation", the features of "central", "contact" and "connection" are involved. Of Hungarian, further features are also typical: for example, the "in", the "limit", the "societive" (accompaniment), and the "quality" features, the last-mentioned two being underlain by special structures. In addition, these two features require further detailed analysis in order to make differentiations between the synonymous case endings (-VAL, -STUL, and -KÉNT and -UL). In the foregoing, we have mainly concerned ourselves with the concrete meaning of the suffixes examined, being fully aware of the importance of a more detailed discussion of the abstract meanings which, however, lies outside the scope of this study. Before entering into further analysis, I would like to summarize what has been said so far.

The following table showing the features of Hungarian case suffixes will serve as the basis of our analysis of the case system in the Caucasian Tabasaran language.

Hung.	*Russ.*	*features*
NOM	nom.	[± appr., + centr.]
GEN	gen.	[± appr., — centr.]
ACC	acc.	[+ appr., + centr.]
DAT	dat.	[+ appr., — centr.]
-BA	*v* + acc.	[+ appr., + contact, + in]
-RA	*na* + acc.	[+ appr., + contact, — in, + surface]
-ÉRT[1]	*za* + acc.	[+ appr., + finalis]
-HOZ	*k* + dat.	[+ appr., ± contact]
-BÓL	*iz* + gen.	[— appr., + contact, + in]
-RÓL	*s* + gen.	[— appr., + contact, — in, + surface]
-TÓL	*ot* + gen.	[— appr., ± contact, + limit]
-IG	*do* + gen.	[+ appr., ± contact, + limit]
-ÉRT[2]	*iz-za* + gen.	[— appr., + causalis]
-VAL[1]	instr.	[± appr., + connection]
-VAL[2]	*s* + instr.	[± appr., + connection, + societ.]
-STUL	*vmeste s* + instr.	[± appr., + connection, + societ.]
-KÉNT	instr.	[± appr., + trans, + qual.]
-UL	instr.	[± appr., + trans, + qual.]
-BAN	*v* + loc.	[± appr., ± contact, + in]

Hung.	Russ.	features
-N	*na* + loc.	[± appr., + contact, — in, + surface]
-T	*u/na* + loc.	[± appr., + contact, ± in]
-NÁL	*pri* + loc.	[± appr., — in, + limit]
-VÁ	*v* + acc.	[+ appr., + qual]

The Hungarian GEN differs from the Russian gen., because the Hungarian GEN occurs in the nominal phrase, that is not at the level of sentence. To make differentiation between the suffix pairs -VAL and -STUL on the one hand, and -KÉNT and -UL on the other, involves a further examination that will reveal the differences in their derivation because they assume complex base structures (Cf. above).

Points of completeness cannot be observed in our analysis. What we aim at is no more than to present a typological characterization of the Hungarian case system. Therefore, we have omitted to deal with Hungarian cases which would require more thorough study before contrasting them typologically with the corresponding Russian cases. Such are, for instance the suffix -KOR of the temporal, Russian: *v* plus acc. (where Russian acc. is used to mark point of time instead of the loc.), or the Hungarian distributive suffix of -NKÉNT: of the distributive: *város*o**NKÉNT** 'each town', or -NTA of the distributive-temporal: *nyara***NTAnta** 'each summer', to which the Russian *po* preposition corresponds in combination with the dative of the noun in plural: **po** *let*a**m**, but: *naponta* 'every day' Russ. *každyj den'*, i.e. *každyj* 'each' + the accusative of the noun. Those features which are relevant to lócal adverbials are partly irrelevant to the adverbials of time and manner, that is they are neutralized, therefore acc. may be used to express point of time, and various cases for the distributive meaning. The Hungarian suffix -KÉPP of the formal case (*ajándék***KÉPP** 'as a present') is usually expressed in Russian by means of comparative structure: *kak podarok* (the same), which is also possible in Hungarian: *mint ajándékot*, and is apt to present further problems, showing that their investigation in more detail is a task for the future.

Since only Hungarian case suffixes and their Russian prepositional equivalents have been discussed so far, let us now round off what has been said about the Russian preposition system and characterize briefly also the system of Hungarian postpositions. This time, however, it seems more expedient to approach the question not from the side of case suffixes but from the side of prepositions and postpositions. As has been shown,

Russian prepositions always go hand in hand with cases which make their meanings more precise; for example, *v* marking locative has only an "in" feature by itself, but the direction of the approximation is dependent on the case suffix of the acc. or loc., respectively. Most of the Hungarian postpositions are attached to the noun stem, the unmarked gen. The three form variants of postpositions will impart the features of [— appr.], [± appr.] and [— appr.]: e.g. -BA, -BAN, -RÓL, 'into', 'in', 'from', or ELÉ, ELŐTT, ELŐL, 'before', 'in front of', 'from before'.

The prepositions and postpositions are tabulated below on the basis of their typical features from the point of view of approximation.

		[+ appr.]	[± appr.]	[— appr.]
[+ ante]	*pered*	acc.	instr.	—
	EL-	-É	-ÖTT	-ŐL
[+ post]	*za*	acc.	instr.	*iz(za)* + gen.
	MÖG-	-É	-ÖTT	-ÜL
[+ super]	*nad*	acc.	instr.	—
	FÖL-	-É	-ÖTT	-ÜL
[+ sub]	*pod*	acc.	instr.	*iz(pod)* + gen.
	AL-	-Á	-ATT	-ÓL
[+ inter]	*meždu*	—	*instr., gen.*	—
	KÖZ-	-É	-ÖTT	-ÜL
[+ juxta]	*okolo, rjadom*	—	gen.	—
	MELL-	-É	-ETT	-ŐL
[+ circum]	*vokrug*	—	gen.	—
	KÖR-	-É	-ÜL	—

Except for the last, Hungarian has the triple forms of each postposition. In Russian, the feature (± appr.] is expressed with the help of the corresponding case suffixes of instrumental and genitive, while the [+ appr.] feature is not expressed consistently, and the [— appr.] feature is expressed by the *iz-* element, even though inconsistently. In some of the Slavic dialects (e.g. in the Trans-Carpathian-Ukrainian) the element *iz-* is consistently used in connection with *pered, nad* and *meždu*.

There are Russian prepositions which possess only one variant of the "approximation" feature, which is combined with other features; for instance *čerez* has the meaning; "across a defined surface", that is: [+ trans. + surface, + limes]; *po* + dat.: 'across a non-defined surface', that is [+ trans. + surface, —limit]; *skvoz'* + acc.: 'across an interior part', that is: [+trans. +in]; while *po* tace: 'horizontally to the upper limit' (e.g. *po koleno* 'up to the knee'), etc. All this has been referred to in order to emphasize the complex nature of the Russian system of prepositions, and further to point to missing correspondences in the system of Hungarian postpositions.

We will not enter into the analysis of prepositions of certain adverbials, such as time, manner, cause and purpose: *po, posle* 'after', *krome* 'beside', *radi* (and *iz-za*) 'because of', *dlja* 'for',—the last two being translatable into Hungarian by the -ÉRT[1] and ÉRT[2] cases. This circumstance calls attention to the synonymity of case suffixes and postpositions. It should be noted that some of the Hungarian post-positions are not added to the absolute stem but to the stem + case suffix: -N KIVÜL 'outside', -N BELÜL 'inside', -N KERESZTÜL 'through'.

Type 3 of Case System in Tabasaran

Case system Type 3 is characterized by a further group of features expressed by case suffixes, first of all by the locative suffixes. As has been shown, Hungarian exceeds Russian in that the former is able to express "in" and "limit" place relations with case suffixes. But Tabasaran, in turn, exceeds Hungarian in this respect, for this language, as we shall see later, is able to express further distinctions by means of case suffixes, expressing relations which take the postpositions ALATT, ELŐTT, MÖGÖTT 'beneath', 'before', 'behind' in Hungarian. Because of this the number of case suffixes is considerably increased in Tabasaran. In principle, the postpositions may be attached to the noun as case suffixes in types 2 and 3. Anyway the first steps in this direction have been taken in Hungarian as well, where the postpositions are attached to the absolute stem instead of the case suffix as in the Slavic languages, although there are some exceptions to this rule. Sooner or later the postpositions may merge morphologically with the stem, and then their assimilation will be only a "question of time". Case suffixes of this kind, that is the postpositions welded to the naked stem, show a fair correspondence to the prepositions of English. This fact is well brought out by Hungarian pupils who are easily able to substitute English prepositions for the case suffixes and postpositions of their mother tongue, but have great difficulty in acquiring the sophisticated systems of Russian prepositions and case suffixes.

Now we have arrived at the point where the Tabasaran case system may be subjected to analysis, with special regard to the locative cases. It is typical of Tabasaran that all cases, with the sole exception of the nominative, are formed from the ergative case (the ergative being the marker of the "active" subject). From the ergative are formed the genitive, the dative and all locative cases. From our point of view only the locative cases are of present interest. In Tabasaran these constitute a triple series, the starting point of which can be found in the form of the [± appr.] feature, which gives rise to the formation of all the variants of the [± appr.] and [—appr.] features. In this sense Tabasaran differs from Hungarian where the [± appr.] does not permit of the other two forms derived from it. For instance, -BAN [+ in, ± appr.], -BA [+ in, + appr.], -BÓL [+ in, — appr.]. Departure from the form with a [± appr.] feature is readily permissible in principle, because it is here that the "approximation" feature is irrelevant, while in the other two forms this feature is marked either positively or negatively. In the tabulation below the locative cases of Tabasaran are represented together with the corresponding Hungarian case suffixes and postpositions. The sign / separates the variants from one another.

	Hungarian	Tabasaran
[+ in ± appr.]	-BAN	-(')
[+ surface, ± appr.]	-N	-l / -n
[+ post., ± appr.]	MÖGÖTT	-q
[+ sub., ± appr.]	ALATT	-kə
[+ ante, ± appr.]	ELŐTT	-x ~ / -h
[+ juxta, ± appr.]	MELLETT	-f
[+ inter, ± appr.]	KÖZÖTT	-γ'
[+ surface, + vertical, ± appr.]	-N	-k

Among the Hungarian equivalents of the Tabasaran cases we find both case suffixes and postpositions. The suffixes corresponding to Hungarian ELŐTT may assume a 'beside' meaning as well. Hungarian has no suffix or postposition to refer to vertical surface.

The above forms with a [± appr.] feature serve as a basis for the derivation of sixteen case suffixes through combination with the elements of [+ appr.] or [—appr.] features instead of [± appr.]. These elements correspond to the Hungarian -Á/-É and -OL/ÜL, with features [+ appr.] or [—appr.] respectively, but the Hungarian elements replace the element

7*

-ATT/-ETT/-ÖTT with the feature [± appr.] and are appended to the
roots, for instance:

MÖG + ÖTT   -q   [+ post, ± appr.]
MÖG + É   -q + na   [+ post, + appr.]
MÖG + ÜL   -q + an   [+ post, —appr.]

Thus twenty-four cases develop from the eight, since all three basic
directions have three variants each; consequently the triple-directional
principle prevails just as in Hungarian. In addition, Tabasaran is able to
double the twenty-four cases in the following manner.

Each of the cases may receive a -di element whose meaning in
Hungarian corresponds to ÁT or KERESZTÜL 'through' when combined with a [± appr.] feature, FELÉ 'towards' if with a [+ appr.] and
FELŐL 'from the direction of' if with a [—appr.] feature. The role of -di
can be exactly paralleled with the Hungarian postpositions ÁT,
KERESZTÜL 'through', which, however, are attachable to one particular case suffix (-N) only, for example, a mezőN ÁT 'through the field',
while the Tabasaran -di is attachable to every case suffix. In this way the
twenty-four cases in Tabasaran will be doubled, and forty eight cases will
be obtained. To these is added the case with -di element combined with
dative—locative (in Hungarian this construction would equal házNAK
FELÉ 'towards the house').

This is enough perhaps to illustrate how the locative cases of
Tabasaran differ from Hungarian: in the former language, suffixes are
used to express place relations which are designated by postpositions in
Hungarian; furthermore, in addition to triple division of locative relations
according to the "approximation" feature, there has developed also a
division by the "through" [trans] feature. In Slavic languages "through" is
a component of the instrumental case, but in Hungarian, as well as in
Tabasaran, this feature combined with approximation brings about a
further division of case suffixes. The "trans" feature, like triple approximation, has developed into a system, while in Hungarian only the -N
ÁT/KERESZTÜL construction corresponds to it. Hungarian did not
follow this trend of development any further; it coupled the -N case with
various new locative postpositions, thus producing forms with suffix -N
and postposition, e.g. -N BELÜL 'inside of' -N KÍVÜL 'outside of' -N
ALUL 'under' -N FELÜL 'over' which have a [± appr.] feature, with
possible extension with other features, e.g. -N KÍVÜLRŐL 'from
outside'.

We will not discuss here how abstract case meanings are expressed in Tabasaran; let it suffice to mention only that cause relation is of course indicated by the locative case with [—appr.] feature (cf. the Hungarian elative: *irigység*BŐL 'out of envy'), for adverbials of instrument and accompaniment it uses the ergative or some of the variants of the locative with a "through" feature (cf. the Russian instr. which designates local adverbial with a "through" feature, as well as modifier of instrument and accompaniment).

Tabasaran also has postpositions combined with possessive cases; their semantic construction agrees with that of Hungarian inasmuch as triple approximation is typical of them in place relations. They express relations which are not indicated by cases (Magometov 324 seq.).

Part 2

Word Order Types, Topic and Comment
in Hungarian and Russian

2.1. On the General Typology of Topic and Comment

This part of the book contains my paper on diathesis and the chapters of my book on syntactic typology published in Hungarian in 1972. Their revision before the publication of their English version as Part 2 of this book was a very hard task. The development in the general theory of topic and comment in the typology of word order was great and the theories proposed are heterogeneous, often contradictory. Even a brief summary of them cannot be given because it would require my comments. They need explanation for some statements of various theories I can accept, others I cannot. It must suffice to call the attention of the reader to some publications.

There are various approaches to communicative organization, usually formulated as a theory of topic and comment and presented in *Papers on Functional Sentence Perspective* (ed. by F. Daneš, Praha 1974) and *Topic and Comment, Contextual Boundness and Focus* (ed. by Ö. Dahl, Hamburg 1974), to mention only two publications. The development of topic-comment theory was summarized in P. Sgall, E. Hajičova, E. Benešova in *Topic, Focus and Generative Semantics* (Kroneberg 1973) up to the mid-seventies.

The theory of diathesis is formulated in various ways. I accepted here the one elaborated by the Leningrad typologists and presented in the volumes: *Typology of Passive Constructions, Diatheses and Voices* (in Russian: Tipologija 1974), *Problems of the Theory of Grammatical Voice* (in Russian: Problemy teorii grammatičeskogo zaloga. ed. by V. S. Khrakovskij, Leningrad 1978) and *Satzstruktur und Genus verbi* (ed. by R. Lötsch and R. Růžička, Berlin 1976). The last two volumes also present more or less different views on diathesis.

The typology of word order and the questions of topic and comment, subject and object are treated in *Word Order and Word Order Change* (ed. by Charles N. Li, Austin 1976) and in *Grammatical Relations* (ed. by P.

Cole and J. M. Sadock, New York 1977), in an American theoretical context. In Fr. Antinucci's book *Fondamenti di una teoria tipologica del linguaggio* (Bologna 1977) the problems of communicative organization and those of word order play an important role. Word order is approached from theoretical, typological and contrastive viewpoints in *Reports on Text Linguistics: Approaches to Word Order* (ed. by N. E. Enkvist and V. Kohonen, Åbo 1976).

Our presentation of diathesis will be based on the Leningrad approach. The types of diathesis have not been formulated clearly, there is no passive in Hungarian, and neither the Russian nor English diathesis has been described in the Leningrad theory, the questions of diathesis, therefore, are discussed very briefly.

I will pay more attention to the types of word order and characterize Hungarian word order in detail with special regard to its function in topic-comment relations. The discussion is empirical but is related to our general approach to grammar which takes the theory of deep cases and that of grammatical relations into consideration.

The rules of word order belong to a larger set of ordering rules including those of extended noun phrase and the rules ordering the elements in an analytic or a synthetic word. This larger set of ordering rules will also be outlined briefly in 2.1.

2.1.1. COMMUNICATIVE ORGANIZATION: TYPOLOGY
OF DIATHESIS AND WORD ORDER TYPES

Diathesis in the Framework of Syntactic Typology

In approaching this problem from the viewpoint of base structure, I left out of account both the semantic description of individual predicates and arguments and the question of how semantic units are made up of various components. Only the various types of predicate and their arguments were considered even though they are realized differently in the lexemes of individual languages. Such an assumption seems to be permissible and it is accepted by adherents of various conceptions. The base structure also provides 'auxiliary' information on aspect and tense in the predicate, on the number and identification of the arguments, etc. The description of predicates and of 'auxiliary' information may be fixed by means of features. In addition, the very same level furnishes information on the communicative organization of the sentence: on diathesis and word order used for the expression of topic-comment or theme and rheme relations. (These two pairs of terms denote the same relations in our terminology.)

Operations of diathesis may be defined as a peculiar cycle of rules in communicative organization, preceding the arrangement of actants and circumstants in surface structure. Variants of diathesis serve as starting points for the typology of word order, of which, only the typology of permutations of full nominative sentences in basic diathesis is more or less elaborated (Greenberg 1963, Cholodovič 1966, Firbas 1964, Dezső— Szépe 1974, *Word order* 1975). At the same time, diatheses serve as a starting point for the typology of sentence stressing, determining sentence stress and places for pause. Rules concerning word order and sentence stressing are means of topic and comment and constitute the next cycle of rules in communicative organization. The typology of topic and comment has not as yet been fully elaborated, nevertheless there are available reliable data on languages of various types (on Hungarian: Dezső 1980, on Russian: Adamec 1966).

In the volume on the typology of diatheses produced by the Leningrad group, initial and derived diatheses with one, two or three actants are distinguished, and their universal patterns (Tipologija 1974, 15—16), diverse operations (Tipologija 1974, 54—72), and global and partial constraints (Tipologija 1974, 22) are determined. Their realization, however, may depend on factors of the typology of aspect and tense. Two types, relevant for the typology of diatheses, can be observed as regards the formation of the predicate: languages possessing fully developed paradigmatic means for expressing the passive and languages expressing the passive lexically or by means of word formation. English, for example, disposes of a well-developed paradigm of passive forms, which are widely used, in contrast to Hungarian, which employs suffixes, e.g. *merít* 'immerse': *merül* 'submerge', 'be immersed', although it also exhibits a tendency for paradigm formation. If passive voice is expressed grammatically, attention must also be paid to synthetic and analytic means of expression on the one hand e.g. Russ. *statja pisalas'* 'the article was being written' and *statja (byla, budet) napisana*, 'the article is (was, will be) written', Hung. *a cikk meg van (volt, lesz) írva* 'the article is (was, will be) written', and on the other hand, as the various ways of expressing the passive may be bound up with the aspect of the verb (e.g. in Russian and in Hungarian), the typology of aspect and tense must also be taken into account. At this juncture, problems relating to morphological typology (paradigms of the verb and their formal means of expression) also come into play. In the history of many languages, the morphological passive is a secondary development, for it comes into being in individual branches or languages of various language families, so that the process of transition from synthetism to analytism may also be reflected in the formation of the passive.

The formation of actants raises a whole series of questions relating to grammatical typology, which affect the typology of diathesis as well. In typology there is a considerable amount of knowledge amassed on number, identification or determination and on means of expressing them like grammatical number, numerals, pronouns, articles etc. (Greenberg 1966, 1972, Majtinskaja 1969, Ingram 1971, Moravcsik 1969, Bese—Dezső—Gulya 1970, Hetzron 1970, etc.). The very issue of the primary actant or subject and the secondary actant or object raises fundamental questions in syntactic typology and, as a result, the typology of diathesis becomes a central problem. I shall resume the discussion of this problem after a survey of points of intersection in various sub-systems of grammatical typology. In the work of the Leningrad group referred to above, some problems concerning ergative and nominative structures are also taken into consideration in connection with the formation of actants (Tipologija 1974, 23, 34—36). It stands to reason that no detailed analysis of these problems could have been set as the task of the book, all the more so that such an analysis exceeds the bounds of grammatical typology proper and poses the question of a certain attitude to contensive types (Klimov 1973) and of typological constructions where phonological, morphological and syntactic characteristics merge into one type (Skalička 1973). Comparatively little attention has been paid to the partitive type of expressing the subject and object (Tipologija 1974, 21—23), which is connected with the typology of aspect and definiteness in Estonian and in other languages. Active, ergative, nominative and within the latter partitive and total constructions are expressed by inflections, which, in the process of 'selection' (R. Jakobson's term), can be chosen from three types of case system, possessing their own morphological questions (Hjelmslev 1935, 1937, Jakobson 1936, Ferguson 1971). One of the actual but complex tasks is to establish contacts at the intersection of the syntactic and paradigmatic axes and to connect the syntactic and morphological typology of paradigms.

If the deep subject and object are universal categories, the surface categories 'subject' and 'object' must be classed among such categories of individual languages as differ in their realization from language to language, for the peculiar morphological ways of expressing them must also be taken into consideration in their definition. In Hungarian grammar, for example, only a noun in the nominative can be regarded as a subject, and a noun in the accusative as object, while there is no indirect object. This can be accounted for not simply by the peculiarity of the attitude adopted by Hungarian grammarians, as this treatment is also supported by the existence of a special type of nominal paradigm, the second by Hjelmslev, which differentiates more strictly between 'grammatical' cases and adverbial ones than is usual in the analysis of languages of the first type (e.g. Russian), where the accusative is the case for the direct object and direction with contact, etc. *šapku* 'cap' (acc.), *v šapku* 'in cap', *na šapku* 'on cap'. Therefore, behind the peculiarities of grammars of individual languages there exists a considerable portion of the general and the particular, which demands that these problems be included among questions of parts of sentence to be dealt with in typology (Meščaninov 1963). The morphological formation of parts of sentence is completed by rules of concord, whose typology is already in the process of elaboration (Moravcsik 1971).

If in base structure one predicate is subordinated to the other, in surface structure the result is subordinate clauses, non-finite constructions and attributive noun phrases. Besides, the synonymy of these constructions must also be taken into account. Mainly subordinate clauses have been subjected to typological analyses (Korš 1877, Seiler 1960, The Chicago witch-hunt 1972, Schwartz 1971, 1972), although there exist studies of noun phrases as well (for bibliography: Dezső 1983).

Typologists have investigated almost exclusively declarative sentences. Of other types only the problems of interrogative sentences have been studied (Moravcsik 1971b, Ultan 1969).

When examining the typology of the sub-systems of syntax, I do not endeavour to present a complete picture even of questions closely bound up with diathesis. Nor do I intend to demonstrate how particular typologies are related to one another. Nowadays syntactical typology is a conglomeration of particular typologies, whose meaningful connections are well enough observed by specialists; nevertheless, these connections do not as yet form a compact system. Also, partial theories exist for the interpretation of the phenomena of sub-systems (e.g. theories of aspect, ergativity and case systems), but they do not constitute parts of a uniform syntactic theory. General grammatical theories are not as yet able to grasp the laws of typology and to incorporate partial theories. The question of complex or contentive types is not yet clear in either empirical or theoretical respects, although the appropriate answer to this question would have very great explanatory power. At present, typology is in this unenviable state, and, thus, the elaboration of the category of diathesis, one of the central problems of typology within the framework of a conception corresponding to modern interpretations of syntax and brought into proper correlation with other conceptions would certainly mean a significant step forward.

Now I touch on the basic question, the definition of diathesis, which I shall go into in greater detail below. In my view, it is necessary to distinguish diathesis and passive voice. The term 'diathesis' must be preserved for the system of correlations between deep and surface structures, irrespective of the fact whether or not they are marked on the verb and to retain the term 'passive' for those diatheses as are marked on the verb with the help of the passive paradigm. That these two terms must be kept apart is advisable not only from the terminological point of view, but also from that of the following considerations specifying my standpoint.

If one distinguishes between invariant base structure and the "surface" structures of individual languages, consequently, it is indispensable to separate the typological set of rules of diatheses from active and passive voices of individual languages. In the latter, form is given priority. If, however, it is also accepted that the rules of diathesis represent one of the first cycles of communicative organization, correlations between arguments in base structure and sentence constituents in surface structure come to the fore and the way the verb is expressed becomes secondary in importance. Much as I recognize the importance of the morphological expression of the passive, I regard as fundamental the correlation between base and surface structure components. But if such a viewpoint is adopted, diathesis has to be considered in the system of rules of communicative organization and be connected with other cycles of these rules. The latter also includes the typological rules of word order and sentence stressing (i.e. the establishment of the place of sentence stress as well as the determination of places for pause), serving for the topic-comment relations in a sentence. The typological questions of word order have so far been elaborated only for full sentences with subject and object in the active voice, whereas passive or impersonal sentences have not been studied in detail. This illustrates the normal advance in linguistics as a discipline, the progress from primary phenomena to secondary ones. In addition, it is the forms that are first described, to be followed by an analysis of their function, and that is why the typology of topic and comment as a field of research began only in the very recent past.

What kind of correctives does the typology of diatheses introduce into word order typology? If one starts from the fact that diatheses constitute a cycle of rules preceding those of topic and comment realized with the help of word order and sentence stressing, several conclusions follow. 1. Each diathesis has its 'paradigm' of variants according to changes in word order as well as in stress patterns of sentences with given communicative functions. (On paradigms in syntax see Jakobson 1972.) 2. As a result of their study, universals as well as rules of types and individual languages must emerge as clearly established, accompanied with their interpretation within the framework of communicative organization as a part of general syntactic theory. 3. In addition, the variants of individual diatheses must be correlated from the viewpoint of their function, and their functional laws must be revealed, which will lead to elaborating the general typology of functions in the given type, in which the system of these functions and the means for their expression are determined.

On the Typology of Diathesis

The correlation of deep and surface structures as 'objects' is considered by the Leningrad group whose approach will be analyzed. One of them is a 'situation' which is semantic in character, the other is a sentence being of a syntactic nature. (In my view, the first object is a semantic-syntactic universal invariant, the second belongs to the syntax of individual languages, I shall, however, use the terms of the Leningrad group.) The semantic predicate of the first possesses semantic 'variables', obligatory participants and attributes (as kinds of argument). In his earlier paper (Khrakovsky 1973, 5—45), Khrakovsky regards only participants as relevant for diatheses, while attributes are also included in his later paper (Khrakovsky 1975), for they can also participate in passive transformations, e.g. *The bed has been slept in by John* (Tipologija 1974, 7; 1975, 35—36). The other 'object' is constituted by the syntactic predicate possessing syntactic variables: actants and circumstants (Tipologija 1974,

10—11, 1975, 37—38). The subject and object are termed as actants, whereas the label 'circumstant' refers to adverbials. It should be noted, however, that the question of the relationship between the typological categories 'actant' and 'circumstant' on the one hand and such categories of individual languages as 'subject', 'object' and 'adverbial' on the other is considerably more complex than is presented in Khrakovsky's papers. Naturally, I am aware of the fact that the analysis of this problem was not his aim, as it would also have required a study of parts of speech in various languages and in various grammars (Členy predloženija 1972).

The questions of diathesis are determined in the book as follows: "Let us call the equivalents of parts of sentence to the participants of a situation diathesis. Then, the equivalence of parts of sentence with the participants of the situation to be fixed in the initial construction can be called initial diathesis. In the process of transition from the initial construction to the derived one, the initial diathesis undergoes a change. The essence of the change consists in the participants no longer being denoted by the same parts of sentence as in the initial construction. Moreover, these participants may not be designated on the lexical level at all. The diathesis to be fixed in the derived construction will be covered by the term 'voice'" (Tipologija 1974, 13). It is clear from the quotation what is meant by the term 'diathesis', hitherto unknown in linguistics, and how the author has modified the range of application of the term 'voice'. In my view, the meaning of the term 'voice' ought not to be expanded, it should rather be retained in its traditional sense for the designation of those diatheses in which the change in the initial form of the predicate takes place. Further on, the task of research becomes narrower: "not all derived constructions of voice will be described, only those where the equivalence subject-participant X, which usually represents the deep subject, is upset" (Tipologija 1974, 13). Such limitation is wholly justified, otherwise the aim of the analysis could not be attained. Such a definition of diathesis operates with the traditional categories of parts of sentence which are well-known from the descriptions of individual languages, but whose typological status is unclear because of their close relationship with the properties of various languages as well as tradition (for example these categories in Russian and Hungarian). That is why Khrakovsky, in his second paper, was right in operating only with the terms 'actant' and 'circumstant' and giving them syntactic weight, on the basis of which the parts of speech of individual languages can be properly described, e.g. the syntactic weight of the direct object is greater than that of the indirect one if both types of object are manifested (Khrakovsky 1975, 39). The concretization of semantic terms is also problematic: further on in the analysis they appear as 'agent', 'patient', 'addressee', etc. They are universal categories and a considerable consensus of opinion can be observed in their interpretation, although divergent views concerning details can also be found. The author was right in applying them in the analysis of concrete structures, but not including them in his definitions.

In their research much attention was devoted to various questions of the formation of diatheses, namely to the formal means serving for marking verbs and nouns in derived diatheses, to the correlation of active and passive voice, to ergative constructions as well as to syntactical valency. Nevertheless, the correlations of diatheses remained unclear because of a lack of proper understanding and presentation of the calculus. It was developed in Khrakovsky's second paper, where the approach to diatheses is also made more precise. The calculus method is well-known, for it is also used in the typology of word order, as e.g. in the simple example: of two semantic variables (A, B), the following chains are derived on the syntactic level: AB, BA, and in the absence of one variable or both, the absence being marked by the symbol X, the resulting chains are: AX, BX, XX, where the variables are the 'arguments' of the predicate. A shift in diathesis indicates a change in weight: Russ. AB; *Metrostrojevcy* (A = 1) *postroili metro* (B = 2) 'The builders (A = 1) built the underground (B = 2)'; *Ja* (A = 1) *vspomnil jego slova* (B = 2) 'I (A = 1) remembered his words (B = 2)'; BA: *Metro* (B = 1) *postrojeno metrostrojevcami* (A = 2) 'The underground (B = 1) has been built by the builders (A = 2)', and *Jego slova* (B = 1) *vspomnilis' mne* (A = 2) 'His words (B = 1) occurred to me (A = 2)' (Khrakovsky 1975, 39 ff). Such an abstract calculus is then filled with abundant data from concrete languages, without which it is uninteresting, but it would be a mistake to underestimate its generalizing role. As the illustrative examples demonstrate, the rich material presented in the book is placed in the framework of calculuses, which must naturally be further developed and made more precise.

Not even an outline presentation of diathesis typology can be undertaken here. Only a few examples will be presented from one of Khrakovsky's papers, which appeared in English and expounded the core of the conception (Khrakovsky 1973).

A structure consisting of an agent, a predicate and a patient reveals the following possibilities of diathesis (Khrakovsky 1973, 63):

8

(0)
Molnija (Sb) razbila (Pr) stenu (C_1).
'Lightning destroyed the wall.'
(1)
Stenu (C_1) razbilo (Pr).
'The wall was destroyed.'
(2)
Stenu (C_1) razbilo (Pr) molniej (C).
'The wall was destroyed by lightning.'
(3)
Stena (Sb) razbita (Pr).
'The wall is (has been) destroyed.'
(4)
Stena (Sb) razbita (Pr) molniej (C).
'The wall is (has been) destroyed by lightning.'
In (1) and (2) the verb is active but used impersonally, the object (C_1) is in
the accusative, and in (1) the agent is missing while in (2) it is in the
instrumental (C_1). The verbs of (3) and (4) are passive, the object appears
as the subject, while the agent is missing in (3) and it is in the instrumental
in (4). Perhaps what has been presented gives a notion of the framework
serving as the basis of typological research, in which not only the diathesis
variants but also the formal means have to be taken into account. Instead
of entering into typological details, let us examine the Russian equivalents
of a structure containing three actants: agent, object-patient, addressee
represented by subject (Sb), direct object (C_1), indirect object (C_2). Only
three of the six possibilities can be realized in Russian (Khrakovsky 1973,
63):

(0)
Otec (Sb) podaril (Pr) bratu (C_2) knigu (C_1).
'Father gave brother a book.'
(1)
Bratu (C_2) podarili (Pr) knigu (C_1).
'Brother was given a book.'
(3)
Kniga (Sb) byla podarena (Pr) bratu (C_2).
'The book was given to brother.'
(4)
Kniga (Sb) byla podarena (Pr) bratu (C_2) otcom (C).
'The book was given to brother by father.'

The following ones are not realized: (2) Pr $+ C_1$ (Ob) $+ C_2$ (Adr) $+ C$ (Ag); (5) Sb (Adr) $+$ Pr $+ C_1$ (Ob); and (6) Sb (Adr) $+$ Pr $+ C_1$ (Ob) $+ C$ (Ag). In English, on the other hand, with the exception of (1) and (2) all the variants can be found (C is an agent represented as a secondary constituent):

(0)

He (Sb) gave (Pr) me (C_2) a book (C_1).

(3)

A book (Sb) was given (Pr) to me (C_2).

(4)

A book (Sb) was given (Pr) by him (C) to me (C_2).

(5)

I (Sb) was given (Pr) a book (C_1).

(6)

I (Sb) was given (Pr) a book (C_1) by him (C).

As is shown also by the examples, the typological framework is suitable also for the purposes of contrastive analysis.

Khrakovsky (1973, 63—4) also formulated an essential universal statement: "Passive constructions with an agent are only found where there are passive constructions without an agent. On the other hand, passive constructions with an agent are not at all obligatory for passive constructions without an agent. This phenomenon, which is apparently universal, allows us to presume that passive constructions with an agent are genetically secondary and have been generated from passive constructions without an agent." So far this has only been suspected, among other things on the basis of languages like Russian, Serbo-Croatian and Hungarian, which express passive diathesis in different ways: in Hungarian there is no passive voice but passive diathesis can be expressed without the agent; in Serbo-Croatian there are passive verb forms but the agent usually is not expressed; and in Russian a passive voice exists and the agent is also expressed. This must also be the way in which the passive voice has come into being: in Hungarian it exists only as a diathesis, while in the two Slavonic languages it has already become fixed in verb forms as well. (It has to be mentioned that these are diachronically secondary phenomena in all three languages.)

Before turning to the analysis of word order typology in the field of topic and comment I shall also venture to presume a universal: if a language has fixed word order, it must possess a marked form of diathesis, which is most likely to be the passive verb form.

8*

The Rules of Theme and Rheme: Word Order Typology

Diathesis has stated certain variants and arranged them in neutral or primary word order. The next cycle of the rules of communicative organization starts from this point; the different variants of diathesis can be regarded as the basic variants of word order types. The task of word order typology is to establish types and universals on the basis of the possible permutations. It is closely connected with accentuation typology, which examines the types of sentence-stressing with regard to the word order types.

The results of word order and accentuation typology are interpreted by a theme–rheme theory, which so far has generally been set forth within separate languages and on the basis of their data of word order and accentuation. As the theme–rheme theory necessarily has to account also for primary word order, it is expedient to formulate it so that it may serve as a basis not only for the typology of word order and accentuation but also for the typology of diathesis. This will lead to a theory of communicative organization. It has to be linked with the theory of actualization. The two of them should be integrated into a theory of a wider scope, which is connected with the theory of case and through this with the problems of morphology.

Having posited the theory of topic and comment including the typology of word order and accentuation into a broader framework I shall outline only a small segment of the whole: the word order types of sentences made up of an object, predicate and subject, together with the data of accentuation typology and within the framework of a topic-comment theory. I cannot undertake to present the works and views on word-order typology (Greenberg 1963; Cholodovič 1966; Lehmann 1972a, 1972b; Ross 1967; Schwartz 1972), or to be confronted with the theme–rheme theories (Halliday 1967, 1968; Dahl 1969; Daneš 1957; Firbas 1964; Adamec 1966; Sgall 1967). In the typology of word order I shall supplement Greenberg's study of universals by an analysis of the types. As regards topic-comment theory, the many-sided if not homogeneous approach of the Prague linguists is closer to mine and the views adopted here have also been influenced by Hungarian linguistic tradition going back to the 1880's.

Up to the present, word order research has analyzed active sentences unmarked from the point of view of diathesis. It is very important in the examination of word order and accentuation to distinguish the primary word order unmarked in respect of topic and comment from the other marked variants. If passive sentences marked from the point of view of diathesis are analyzed, and if diathesis constitutes a part of a theory of communicative organization, passive sentences may be marked not only in respect of diathesis but also in respect of topic and comment: (1) *Devuška napisala pis'mo.* 'The girl has written a letter'. (2) *Pis'mo napisana devuškoj.* 'A letter has been written by the girl'. where in the second sentence the communicative perspective has changed: instead of the agent the object is the topic but both sentences are unmarked from the point of view of topic and comment and are opposed to marked variants: (3) *Pis'mo napisala devuška* 'It is the girl who has written the letter' and (4) *Devuškoj napisano pis'mo* 'It is the letter that has been written by the girl'.

For the moment I am interested in sentences that are unmarked in respect of diathesis, e.g. *Peter wrote a letter.* They display the principle of activity; the 'active' argument becomes the topic, or, if the topic consists of more than one element, the kernel, the 'central' part of the topic: the subject in nominative languages *(Peter).* The non-active argument tends to become a part of the comment and obtains the feature 'approximation' and in case it has the feature 'central' as well, it is called object *(a letter)* and constitutes the kernel of the comment. A constituent having the feature 'approximation' but not being 'central' is an indirect object: *(Peter wrote a letter) to his mother,* or an adverbial of direction: *Peter went to the forest.* As in the latter sentence the non-central adverbial of direction constitutes the kernel of the comment. The marking of the different kinds of subjects and objects is important because it will serve as a basis for the analysis of the case system as well, in which the differentiation of central and non-central, i.e. peripheral cases is of significance.

That is how one arrives at the surface subject (S) and object (O) categories of the active sentence, which, together with the verbal predicate (V) constitute the traditional terms of word order typology. The sentence of active primary word order did not undergo any change, it is unmarked with respect to communicative organization, i.e. from the point of view of the text, situation and speaker. The subject is the topic, the object is the comment: *Peter wrote a letter.* The topic is equivalent to the starting part of the message, while the comment to its informing part. The latter is the marked category. The main pause of the sentence takes place between the topic and comment; still the dividing line between them is not always clear, which is a manifestation of the wave-like nature of language (Pike

1967, 468). Sentence stress, however, always emphasizes the kernel of the comment, while the kernel of the topic may obtain a secondary stress.

Stress may mean slight prominence (focus), e.g. in case of primary word order and primary accentuation; emphasis, when a certain presumed context is completed by the information of the comment; and contrast, when what is asserted is contrary to the previous text. In some languages of free word order, e.g. in Hungarian, the application of emphasis and contrast brings about a change of word order, the stressed element being posited before the verb:

SVO:

Péter # levelet ír.

'Peter is writing (a) letter.'

SOV:

(*Mit ír Péter?*

'What is Peter writing?')

Péter # levelet ír.

'Peter is writing (a) letter.'

OVS:

(*Péter leckét ír.*

'Peter is writing (a) homework.')

Levelet *ír # Péter.*

'It is (a) letter that Peter is writing.'

In primary word order the subject constituting the topic precedes the object constituting the comment in most languages. This is main type **A**, the sub-types of which are determined by the position of the verb:

(1) SOV   (2) SVO   (3) VSO

SOV:

Hung. *Péter levelet ír.*

SVO:

E. *Peter is writing a letter.*

Russ. *Petr pišet pis'mo.*

The pause comes after S, and the stress is on O, though if O is known and V contains more important information, V can also be stressed in languages of the SVO type: *Peter is writing the letter.*

Type 3 will not be demonstrated and main type **B** will only be referred to. In main type **B**, to which, among others, Malagasy belongs, O precedes S: VOS.

If O has already been mentioned in what immediately precedes, it obtains the feature 'anaphora' and appears before S, giving rise to the following permutations:

(1) OSV   (2) OVS

The verb invariably appears at the end or middle of the sentence, the S is usually stressed:

OSV:

Hung. *Levelet* **Péter** *ír.*

OVS:

Russ. *Pis'mo pišet* **Petr.**

This order of O and S corresponds to a variant of passive diathesis: *Pis'mo pišetsja Petrom;* but in it the sentence stress is usually on S, so S cannot be omitted, not to speak of the morphological differences. However, this active word order bears a certain relation to the variant of passive diathesis, therefore, in Hungarian, which has no passive voice, it can be used for the translation of English passive constructions.

In types 1 and 2 the third word order variant is rare, it occurs in far fewer languages than the first variant or the first and second together. VSO is more frequent in type 2 than in type 1. The sentence begins with the verb and continues with S in both types:

(1) VSO   (2) VSO

(1) VSO:

Hung. *Ír Péter levelet.*

(2) VSO:

Russ. *Pišet Petr pis'mo.*

In Hungarian and Russian V is emphasized, but in Swahili, which also belongs to type 2, S is stressed. The remaining variants of languages having free word order will not be presented; in the case of Hungarian and Russian they would be equivalent to the three missing permutations. It is, however, important to mention that the rules of accentuation are not identical in Hungarian, which belongs to type 1 and in Russian which belongs to type 2: in Hungarian sentence stress is usually on the element before the verb, while in Russian it is on the element after the verb:

SOV: *Péter* **levelet** *ír.*

SVO: *Petr pišet* **pis'mo.**

It is not part of my task here to analyze sentences of four and more members; I only refer to the fact that each type has its place of extension, which is denoted by O O O:

(1) S O O O V   (2) S V O O O   (3) V S O O O

(1) is extended between S and V, while (2) and (3) after S and V:

(1) SMOV:

Hung. *Péter a szobában levelet ír.*

(2) SVOM:

Russ. *Petr pišet pis'mo v komnate.*

'Peter is writing a letter in the room.'

In the case of four member sentences mixed types also occur:

(1) and (2) SOVM:

Péter levelet ír a szobában.

In this the order of O corresponds to type 1, the order of M (of adverbial modifier) to type 2. The word order type of Hungarian in fact seems to tend from type 1 towards type 2, and that is manifested among other things also in the double primary word order. The primary word order of the sentences analyzed up to now was SOV. In them, however, O always appeared without an article and the verb was imperfective. In the case of O with an article, especially if the verb is perfective, the primary word order is SVO.

SVO:

Péter megírta a levelet.

Diachronic word order typology has not been elaborated upon yet, but it is known that the Proto-Indo-European language was of the SOV type, and present-day Indo-European languages have either preserved this or become type SVO or VSO. The Uralic proto-language belonged to the SOV type as well, and the present-day languages represent either type SOV or SVO, while Hungarian is in a transitory state. The change of type may have another direction, too, and may result in languages with a double word order. The reason for the change is uncertain: in all probability complex reasons have to be taken into account, though the role of one factor may have been more significant than that of others. For instance, the change of the type of aspect and the formation of a new system of determination must have played an important role in Hungarian and perhaps in other languages, too.

Even these simple illustrative examples have demonstrated that word order and accentuation typology together with theme–rheme theory can be used for contrastive analysis. If this is what one is aiming at, one has to describe the individual properties of the two languages in detail; one cannot content oneself with a number of general statements. The topic-comment analysis has to be put in the centre: variants of the same function have to be compared with regard to usage. Typology can also be used in predictions: with the knowledge of synchronic and diachronic typology one can predict the optimal strategy if the target language and the base language are of different types (Dezső—Nemser 1973, 18 ff.). This is not merely a theoretical question. In Hungarian textbooks for Serbo-Croatian students the author has to apply a definite strategy in teaching Hungarian word order because he cannot teach two word order types at the same time. This question is not so complicated in the case of languages with fixed word order, but if languages of free word order are to be contrasted, one has to follow a definite strategy, in the settling of which typology may be helpful.

On the Order of Attributes and Actualizing Elements

A noun may have an element for determination (article and pronoun) and its number may be determined by a numeral but it may also have several attributes which belong to different parts of speech (adjective, noun, derived adjective). Attributes may also be expressed by constructions (participial constructions, subordinate clauses). There are some laws concerning the position of actualizing elements and attributes, which have been partly established by typology. The order of the element of determination (Dt), a numeral (Num) and a qualifying attribute (A) is the following: 1. if they precede a noun, only: DtNumAN, (2) if they follow it: NDtNumA or NANumDt. If the qualifying attribute figures before the noun, all its kinds precede the noun, but if it figures after it, some of its kinds may precede it nevertheless, e.g. in French (Greenberg 1963, 68). The attributive clause may precede the noun if the qualifying attribute also precedes it or if the noun may receive a postposition or if both apply (Greenberg 1963, 71).

H. Seiler dealt with the internal order of actualizing elements and attributes (Seiler 1980). His statements made on German material correspond to what I have found when examining the word order of the Hungarian noun phrase (Dezső 1983). In Seiler's view actualizing elements are the indicators of specification, while attributes are those of characterization. These constitute the two poles of determination in a broad sense, whose means of expression have been dealt with. There is a certain gradation expressed in word order: the range of function of a determining element increases as it is shifted further from the noun: the potential of a determiner for singling out the object referred to increases proportionally with its positional distance from the head noun. Thus, the potential of specifying elements is greater than that of characterizing ones, with further grades within the latter (mass noun, colour, evaluating attribute), as is shown by the following example. This question, considering its full content, is naturally much more complicated in individual languages as is suggested by the example below (Dezső 1983), nevertheless the data of German and Hungarian demonstrate well the two processes of determination in general, and one type of the position of actualizing and qualifying attributes in particular. On the basis of Greenberg's universals mentioned above it can be assumed that the order of elements preceding a noun remains the same or is re-arranged in a mirror image way if they are shifted behind it, provided the gradation assumed by Seiler is of universal validity and determines the internal order of actualizing elements and mainly that of qualifying attributes. The phenomenon under investigation is illustrated by a German and a Hungarian example having identical meaning:

Ger.

Alle diese meine erwähnten zehn schönen roten hölzernen Kugeln, die ich dir jetzt gebe.

Hung.

Mindezek az én említett tíz szép piros fa golyóim, amelyeket én neked most adok. (lit.)

In the string of determination the borderline between specification and characterization is to be found at the numeral, as transformation into a subordinate clause is no longer possible to the left of the numeral or is feasible only through certain changes in the case of a numeral or pronoun in both languages. The Hungarian equivalent of the German adjective *hölzern* formed from a noun is a noun in attributive function *(fa)*, while the genitive of the Hungarian personal pronoun corresponds to the German possessive pronoun. This seems to prove that differences in part of speech status do not affect the stages of determination or the position of determining elements. The semantics of the given participle is peculiar as it refers to the occurrence in a text. Participial constructions with a different meaning would also figure at this place or they would take the place of the numeral in Hungarian. Non-extended participles, with an adjectival function and more of a characterizing nature may, however, be shifted nearer to the noun—depending on their meaning.

On the Complex Linear Types

Greenberg established certain interconnections between the word order types of the sentence, the word order of the noun phrase (including the possessive attribute as well), and the order of words of an analytic character (noun and preposition or postposition) as well of the morphemes of synthetic words. These will not be presented here in the order of Greenberg's universals in question. Since two series of universals reveal themselves, they will be presented separately, as the manifestations of two complex types.

The complex type (A) can be characterized as follows. (1) ,,*Universal 4*. With overwhelmingly greater than chance frequency languages with normal SOV order are postpositional" (Greenberg 1963 (1968), 79) and (2) in languages with postpositions the genitive almost always precedes the governing noun (Greenberg 1963 (1968), 79), although (3): if the genitive follows the noun in languages with SOV order, the adjective does the same (Greenberg 1963 (1968), 79). The following can be stated about analytic verb forms, or more exactly about full verbs and inflected auxiliary verbs: (4) "In languages with dominant order SOV, an inflected auxiliary always follows the main verb." (Greenberg 1963 (1968), 85.) The relationship between synthetic and analytic words is the following (5): "*Universal 27*. If a language is exclusively suffixing, it is postpositional" (Greenberg 1963 (1968), 93). In this complex type, it can be stated about the order of morphemes in a synthetic word that "*Universal 28*. If both the derivation and inflection follow the root . . . the derivation is always between the root and the inflection." (Greenberg 1963 (1968), 93.) It is, incidentally, universally valid that "*Universal 29*. If a language has inflection, it always has derivation" (Greenberg 1963 (1968), 93). Inflection falls into two parts in the case of agglutinative means of expression: the number affix and the case suffixes. The universal rule about the order of the latter is that "the expression of number almost always comes between the noun base and the expression of case" (Greenberg 1963 (1968), 95), therefore, the order in this type is: (7) Base + Number + Case.

Let us briefly sum up the relations of this complex linear type:
(1) if SOV then N + Post,
(2) if N + Post then N_{gen} + N,
(3) if SOV and NN_{gen} then NA,
(4) if SOV then V + Aux,
(5) if Root + Suf then N + Post,

(6) Root + Deriv + Infl,

(7) Base + Num + Case.

The linear complex type (B) can be characterized by rules opposite to those above. It can be stated about the relationship between the word order of the sentence, that of the noun phrase and the analytic word that (1) *"Universal 3.* Languages with dominant VSO order are always prepositional" (Greenberg 1963 (1968), 78) and (2) *"Universal 2.* In languages with prepositions, the genitive almost always follows the governing noun" (Greenberg 1963 (1968), 78), (3) *"Universal 17.* With overwhelmingly more than chance frequency, languages with dominant order VSO have the adjectives after the noun" (Greenberg 1963 (1968), 85). The relationship between the synthetic and the analytic word is the following: (5) *"Universal 27.* If a language... is exclusively prefixing, it is prepositional" (Greenberg 1963 (1968), 93). In this complex type, it can be stated about the order of morphemes in the synthetic word: (6) *"Universal 28.* If both the derivation and inflection... precede the root, the derivation is always between the root and the inflection" (Cf. Greenberg 1963 (1968), 93). Incidentally, it is universally valid that: *"Universal 29.* If a language has inflection, it always has derivation" (Greenberg 1963 (1968), 93). In the case of an agglutinative means of expression, the inflection falls into two parts: the number affix and the case ending. The order of the latter presents the following picture in this type: (7) Case + Number + Base.

Let us sum up in brief the interrelations of this complex linear type:

(1) if VSO then Prep + N,

(2) if Prep + N then N + N_{gen},

(3) if VSO then N + A,

(4) if VSO then Aux + V;

(5) if Prep + Root then Prep + N,

(6) Infl + Deriv + Root,

(7) Case + Number + Base.

Interrelations are not always obligatorily valid and do not form an uninterrupted series, nevertheless two linear types can very clearly be revealed. These have been known by typology for some time and characterized by means of the principles *regens post rectum* or 'dominant after dominated' and *regens ante rectum* or 'dominant before dominated'. On the basis of the above universals the relationship of the SVO word order type with other rules of linearization is problematic. Historical examination shows that languages with a SVO word order may either have originally been of this type or the SVO type may be the result of a secondary development, both being represented among the languages examined by Greenberg. Languages originally of the SVO type conform to linearization on the basis of the second principle, that of *regens ante rectum*, while languages whose SVO word order is the result of a secondary development, may more or less have preserved the rules of the principle *regens post rectum* of linearization (for instance the Indo-European languages having a SVO word order).

The two types of linearization may be related with other type properties as well: e.g. the principle *regens post rectum* with the use of non-finite constructions in many languages. These issues, however, will not be tackled here.

Some of the relationships between the above two types will be illustrated on the basis of respective languages. Type (A) will be represented by Hungarian, whereas type (B) by Swahili. The rules of linearization have also been extended by stress rules, which are presumably typologically valid for word groups: In type (A) (1) it is the first word that is stressed, while in (B) (1) it is the second. The stress patterns of a word in the two languages correspond to those of word groups: in (A) (2) the stress falls on the beginning of the word, while in (B) (2) it falls on the word end. The typological implications of this must, however, be clarified.

(A) (1) in the word groups the dominant word is preceded by the dominatum, and the accent of the sentence or tone group falls on the latter; with Hungarian examples:

O + V:

levelet *írt*
'[he/she] has written [a] letter'

A + N:

hosszú *levél*
'long letter'

N_g + N:

Péter *levele*
'Peter's letter'

(A) (2) in the word the main morpheme of an analytic word or the stem morpheme of a synthetic word precede the subsidiary morpheme or affix morpheme; the stress falls on the former:

N + Post:
a **levél** *alatt*
'under the letter'
V + Aux:
írni fog
[he] 'will write'
N + Suf:
a **levél***ben*
'in the letter'

The Hungarian language must have been characterized only by this type of linearization until the word order VO appeared: *irta (a levelet)*. Consequently, Hungarian is not of a pure type now.

Hungarian is basically a language of the agglutinative type and expresses number and case endings by means of separate morphemes. These can easily be differentiated from affixes. Their position correspond to the above type (A):

Root + Deriv + Infl (Case):
ír — ó — hoz 'to a writer'
Base + Num + Case:
iró — k — hoz 'to writers'.

Type **B** consists of rules opposite to the previous ones. The examples are from Swahili:

(B) (1) in the word groups the dominant word is followed by the dominatum and the accent of the sentence or tone group falls on the latter:

V + *O:*
anaandika **barua**
'[He] is writing a letter'
Aux + *V:*
nilikuwa **nikiandika**
'[I] was writing'
N + *A:*
barua **refu**
'long letter'
N + *Ng:*
barua ya **Peter**
'Peter's letter'

(B) (2) in the words the main morpheme of an analytic word or the stem morpheme of a synthetic word are preceded by the subsidiary morpheme or suffix morpheme; the stress falls on the former:

Prep *N:*
katika **barua**
'in [the/a] letter'
Pref — *V:*
*nime***andika**
'I have written'
Swahili does not represent type **B** clearly either, but the deviations will not be discussed here.

Referring to the data of present-day Hungarian, we have already pointed out that the mixed type has come into being through a development from type **A** towards type **B**. In Swahili, in my opinion there seems to be a new tendency in the opposite direction (on Swahili typology see Skalička 1944).

Such a complex type is comparatively easy to explain by general rules, since only linearization is concerned. Though the structures are different, they are related to each other in a particular way: the attributive noun phrase can be derived from two propositions, one of which is subordinated to the other. This way a specific derived structure comes into being. The postpositions and prepositions were originally independent words in the sentence (e.g. adverbs), or parts of possessive constructions, and lost their independence afterwards. This also applies to case endings to a certain extent: Hung. *-ben* evolved from a noun denoting possession into a postposition, then into a case ending. The Swahili *ni-* element is a shortened form of the pronoun *nini* etc., even though the etymology is not always so clear or the development so understandable. So the correspondence of the linearization rules of different structures is due to various derivational relations. The differences between the rules of word groups and words are easy to understand: they represent different types of structures, the former belonging to syntax, the latter to morphology. The only common feature they share is that the stress falls on the word carrying the more important information, i.e. in type **A** on the first, in type **B** on the second element.

The complex types pose even more complicated riddles for typologists (see Skalička 1974 and 3.3.), but their research is exciting since it throws light on the relations of the types of the partial systems of language. Concerning practice, knowledge of clear types and dominant types comprises rules for different languages and within the given range of problems it draws attention to neglected fields, such as the accentuation of tone groups.

2.1.2. ON THE TYPOLOGY OF WORD ORDER

Word order types

Our analysis of the typology of word order is based on the data of hundreds of languages. Their examination is beyond the scope of this part
of the book. I shall present only some conclusions of their analysis.

Word order typology classifies sentences containing subject, verbal
predicate and object into two main types. In Main Type A the basic word
order is so constructed that S is placed before the pause separating topic
from comment and O after the pause: S # O; Main Type B shows the
picture in reverse: O # S (relatively few languages belong to this type).
Main Type A is divided into three subtypes according to the place of the
verb:

1. S # OV. Hung:

Péter # levelet ír 'Peter writes a letter.'

2. S # VO. Russ.:

Petr # pišet pis' mo. 'Same.'

3. VS # O. Arabic:

Yaktubu # 'Alī al-ḥiṭāba. 'Same.'

Main Type B is represented by one type only which can be
exemplified from the Malagasy, language of Madagascar:

4. VI # S. Malagasy:

Manorartra taratasy # Rakoto. 'Rakoto writes a letter.'

The Hungarian example, which is relevant anyway, needs to be
further analyzed below, because of the more complicated nature of the
Hungarian word order system. The former examples show the rule of
sentence stress as well: sentence stress is placed on the element preceding
the verb in Type 1; on the element following the verb in Type 2; on the
element standing by itself in Type 3; and on the element after the verb in
Type 4. Nevertheless, Types 3 and 4 should be examined in more detail.

Here only the basic word order has been demonstrated in non-
contextual relation. Other possible variants will be shown in Types 1 and 2
only (for Types 3 and 4 see Dezső and Szépe 1974). Within Types 1 and 2 in
sub-type (a) of languages with an absolutely fixed word order there occurs
only one variant; in sub-type (b) of languages with a semi-fixed word
order a further possible variant can be contextually used when the object
has occurred in the preliminaries. In sub-type (c) of languages with a semi-
free word order, still another variant occurs, in addition to the two

mentioned, where the sentence is headed by the verb. Free word order tolerates all six variants, this sub-type (d), however, will not be considered here. (In the following example the number refers to the Type, the letter to sub-types.)

1 (a) S # OV   (b) S # OV   (c) S # OV
                    O # SV   O # SV
                                    VS # O

Three Hungarian examples will illustrate the three variants:

S # OV.
Péter # levelet írt
'Peter wrote a letter.'
O # SV.
*Levelet # **Péter** írt.*
'It is Peter who wrote a letter.'
VS # O.
Írt *Péter # levelet.*
'Wrote Peter a letter.'
('There has been a letter written by Peter.')

Type 2 has the following possibilities of forming sub-types:

2 (a) S # VO   (b) S # VO   (c) S # VO
                    O # VS   O # VS
                                    VS # O

Sub-type (a) is represented by English which is of fixed word order; sub-type (b) by German, which is of semi-fixed; sub-type (c) by Rumanian, which is of semi-free; while Russian is of free word order. The next three examples are Russian:

S # VO.
Petr # pisal pis' mo.
O # VS.
*Pis' mo # pisal **Petr**.*
VS # O.
Pisal *Petr # pis' mo.*

Type 1 lays primary stress on the element before the verb. Type 2 that after the verb. This is only a general rule of sentence stress. The speaker may transfer, within certain limits, the accent to another element, if so required by his communicative purpose. (We shall enter into a more detailed analysis of this question in Chapter 2.2.) In the variant headed by a verb, the verb is accented, but this rule is not valid for every language of Type 2; for instance, S receives stress in Swahili.

9

The above statements refer to affirmative sentences in the indicative mood. Interrogative sentences are characterized by peculiar accentuation rule, apportioning stress to a nominal element, or to an interrogative pronoun, but very often to the verb. If interrogation is directed onto S, O or V, then S, O or V respectively will come to the front in languages of Type 1 and in some of the languages of Type 2; for example, English and German. In the latter the interrogative pattern is identical with that of declarative sentences except VSO order admitted only in interrogative sentences: *Schrieb Peter den Brief?* In English the interrogative sentence with an interrogative pronoun has a specific device, the auxiliary verb *do* and admits three variants of word order:

Who *wrote the letter?*

What *did Peter write?*

Did *Peter write the letter?*

The auxiliary verb *do* is used in interrogative sentences in a word order OVS (actually OAuxSV) which would be impossible in a declarative sentence: **The letter did write Peter*, or **The letter write Peter* except infrequent occurences of OVS under special conditions. Similar is the case when the interrogation concerns the verb: **Did** *Peter write a letter?* Finite auxiliary verbs in English take the place of the main verb in Type 2 and English has a special rule which places the main verb after the subject irrespective of whether a question refers to the object or the verb. Accordingly, the following three variants occur in English:

2 SVO

    OVS (= OAuxSV)

    VSO (= AuxSVO)

Variant SVO, OVS, VSO are typical for SVO languages with more freedom of word order.

Interrogation and reference to an element in the antecedent are not expressible simultaneously in the languages of Type 2 with limited freedom because it would require order SOV or OSV characteristic of Type 1. Therefore, the Hungarian word order SOV. *Péter mit ír?* 'Peter what writes?' (lit.) or OSV: *Levelet ki ír?* 'The letter who writes?' (lit.) has no corresponding variants in languages belonging to Type 2, since their fixed word order would not admit SOV or OSV even in an interrogative sentence.

Sentences with interrogative pronouns have their peculiarities in Type 1 because they tend to be posited at the beginning of the sentence. Hungarian has to use a word order characteristic of Type 2 when the interrogation concerns the subject: *Ki írt levelet?;* and a sentence **Ki levelet írt?* would be impossible, although such is the word order in the affirmative (SOV). The word order OVS, characteristic of Type 2 languages, is used in Hungarian if the interrogation affects the object: *Mit írt Péter?* instead of OVS: **Mit Péter írt?* Hungarian can do all this, being a language with a free word order and able to utilize all six variants. Certainly, the anomalies mentioned indicate the peculiar nature of problems associated with interrogative sentences with an interrogative pronoun. These anomalies may be avoided in Hungarian if the interrogation is directed to a noun in sentence patterns like the following:

SVO. *Péter* **levelet** *írt?*
OSV. *Levelet* **Péter** *írt?*
VSO. **Írt** *Péter levelet?*

In sentences expressing direct command or order the accent is usually placed on the verb, in which case the subject is omitted this being the second person:

VO. Hung.:
Írj *levelet!*
English:
Write *a letter!*

This results in a sentence pattern of a universally valid word order. We will not detail here the cases of indirect orders addressed to a third person. Questions of negative sentence patterns, as well as those of subordinate clauses must be ignored, too, since to touch them superficially would be worse than plain omission.

Keeping, therefore, within the sphere of simple affirmative sentences, we would like to examine implicational universals, which are valid only if certain conditions are fulfilled. These are characterized by simple logical implications ('if...then'). In order to approach them, let us survey the possible word order variants of the diverse types, supplementing at the same time the scheme presented above:

Main Type A

Type 1.

(a) SOV	(b) SOV	(c) SOV	(d) SOV
	OSV	OSV	OSV
		VSO	VSO
			and SVO
			OVS
			VOS

Type 2.

(a) SVO	(b) SVO	(c) SVO	(d) SVO
	OVS	OVS	OVS
		VSO	VSO
			and SOV
			OSV
			VOS

Type 3.

(b) VSO

SVO or VOS

Main Type B

Type 4.

(a) VOS

Examples have been given for the basic variants and there is no need to illustrate further possibilities of permutation, since they can be realized by a simple inversion of the word order. In Arabic, belonging to Type 3, there are VSO and SVO variants, while VSO and VOS are characteristic of Murle. Variants given in the first place are always the basic word order, while those following them are used in certain definite contexts only. On the basis of the word order system, implicational universals can be established; from these it can be inferred if certain word order patterns exist in a language in case another kind of word order pattern is already known of the same language (Greenberg 1963). Obviously, the implicational universals are useful in such instances when only very short texts are available of a language whose word order system is of some interest for research. All this, however, is no concern of ours, except for one thing: it is a typical feature of the implicational universals that from a given contextual order of sequence conclusion can be made as to the type of the basic word order pattern; for instance:

if there exists   then there exists

(i) OSV   SOV

(ii) OVS   SVO

Investigation of child language has shown that after a short period of uncertainty, the basic word order pattern develops first before all other patterns. Historical changes of the types of languages, on the other hand, provide evidence of the fact that first the basic variant comes into prominence. Let us exemplify the latter statement by Hungarian sentence patterns. Finno-Ugric had SOV as basic word order; that is, it belonged to Type 1. This word order pattern survives in sentences with an object with zero article: *Péter levelet írt.* 'Peter letter wrote (lit.).' If the object takes an article the basic word order will be changed into SVO: *Péter írta a levelet* 'Peter wrote the letter', *Péter írt egy levelet* 'Peter wrote a letter.' Contextual variants, however, may come up in the form of OSV: *A levelet* **Péter** *írja.*, as well as in the form of OVS: *A* **levelet** *írja Péter.*, depending on the emphasis. Some languages are characterized by the co-occurrence of SVO and OSV word order, being mixed types, which means that by the time their word-order system reached the stage of consolidation, their basic word-order patterns had already been transformed, but their contextual ones had not (e.g. in Dongo in Africa).

All this amounts to saying that the basic word order develops first and changes first. It follows, therefore, that when it comes to teaching foreign languages, the basic word order patterns have to be practised first. This suggestion may seem trivial with reference to languages which possess but one type of basic word order, but may not seem so self-evident in the case of some other languages where the basic word order changes with the changing pattern of sentence structure, displaying characteristics of several word order types, as in the Hungarian examples quoted above. Here we have to consider the fact that the basic word order is used also when the subject has been mentioned in a previous sentence of the same context. Consequently, over and above the basic word order and the concomitant accent and intonation—the latter is often neglected—the pupil has to learn how and when to use them.

The same applies to the contextual word order, the importance of which is evident in the case of pupils in whose mother tongues this kind of word order is either absent or little used (for instance, in English). Similar obstacles have to be overcome in the instruction of pupils whose mother tongues belong to Type 3 with basic word-order patterns VSO, since this pattern finds its equivalents in Types 1 and 2 in variants where the verb is placed at the beginning of the sentence and has emphatic stress. In languages of Type 3 SVO is the contextually fixed order which is the basic order in Type 2. This is also a circumstance that is apt to make things worse.

Lesser difficulties are encountered when different patterns of basic and contextual word order are considered in languages without a fixed word order belonging to Types 1 and 2. Nevertheless, the system of word-order rules must be thoroughly clarified in such instances as well, for neglect of this duty will give rise to numerous sources of error, as experience has shown: similar though not quite identical word order rules are a constant source of blunder for Hungarians speaking Russian and vice versa. It is only by a careful revaluation that the application of these rules can be acquired.

Summing up what has been said so far, a universal principle is valid for the development of word order systems, the change of their types, and their acquisition: basic word order takes precedence over the contextual. It develops first, it changes first, and it is to be acquired first. A peculiar reflection of this principle can be observed in linguistic history: if the word order of a language becomes fixed and fossilized, its basic word order (SOV, SVO) will subsist (such has been the case with English). If there be another possible variant, it is the variant with the anaphoric object in sentence initial position (OSV, OVS, the latter being exemplified by German); much less frequently still another variant offers itself (VSO) in which the sentence is headed by the verb.

These last statements of ours hold true only for languages of Types 1 and 2. In respect of Type 3 there are two possible variants given: VSO, SVO or VSO, VOS. The secondary variant VOS corresponds to the basic variant VSO, but SVO requires special examination.

In the foregoing, sentences of three parts—one being the object—have been analyzed. Six variants may be obtained by permutation of the three elements, therefore, they are easy to survey. On the other hand with the four-element sentences the number of permutations is twenty-four. Next we propose to examine sentences consisting of subject, verbal predicate, object and adverbial modifier of place (M) with an approximation feature; for example, *Péter széket hozott a szobába.* 'Peter brought a chair into the room.' Six of the twenty-four variants start with the subject: S . . . ; six with the object: O . . . ; six with the adverbial: M . . . ; and six with the verb: V . . . . In languages of Types 1 and 2, the basic variants have to be looked for among those beginning with the subject (S), and the contextual ones among those beginning with O and M; V always heads variants in which the verb has a contextually anaphoric function. All this is in full harmony with the statements made in connection with the three-membered sentences.

A certain trend of complementation can be served in the b a s i c w o r d o r d e r of certain language types: the complements tend to be situated in a systematic order, proceeding either to the left (in Type 1) or to the right (in Types 2, 3 and 4) from the verb. In all the types the obligatory constituents (object, adverbial) stand next to the verb, while the non-obligatory ones (for instance, free modifiers) somewhat farther off:

(1) SMOV   (3) VSOM
(2) SVOM   (4) VOMS

There is a highly complicated typological regulatory system at work to determine, depending on the semantic features of the verb and other features of the constituents, the order of sequence in which the sentence constituents have to be arranged. Nevertheless we try to present the question in the simplest possible form: six with initial O . . . and six with initial M . . . . The dividing line between unmixed Types 1 and 2 may be drawn on the basis of the three-membered variant. Let us recall:

Type 1 OSV and Type 2 OVS

that is S precedes V (—SV) in Type 1, and follows it in Type 2 (—VS): consequently, six variants of SV sequence belong to Type 1, while the other six variants, with a reverse order VS, are characteristic of Type 2:

Type 1	*Type 2*
OSMV	OVMS
OMSV	OMVS
OSVM	OVSM
MSOV	MVOS
MOSV	MOVS
MSVO	MVSO

Our illustrative material will be selected from Types 1 and 2. Earlier, when characterizing Type 1, we referred to Hungarian and examined three-member sentences of that language, although it is not a pure representative of Type 1. When it comes to analyzing four-member sentences, we have to face the fact that Hungarian is a mixed-type tongue bearing traits of Types 1 and 2. Therefore, we have to adduce an example from Mongol (by courtesy of Lajos Bese) in illustration of Type 1.

For a characteristically Type 1 language like Mongol only some of the variants of the first column will be correct, while in languages belonging to Type 2 only some of the second column. Let us analyze our Mongol example from this point of view. The sentence, borrowed from this unmixed Type 1 language, reads like this:

SMOV.

Damdin gert talx *avč irev.*

'Damdin into the house bread brought.' (lit.)

Type 2 can be characterized by a German example:

SVOM.

Peter brachte einen Stuhl ins Zimmer.

In mixed-type Hungarian the unarticled object is followed by the modifier, provided the object precedes the verb:

SOVM.

Péter székett hozott a szobába.

'Peter chair brought into the room.' (lit.)

If the object takes an article, it is placed after the verb, and the modifier before the verb:

SMVO.

Péter a szobába hozta a széket.

'Peter into the room brought the chair (lit.).'

The following two variants, one representing unmixed Type 1, the other unmixed Type 2, are not of basic word order:

(1) SMOV.

*Péter a szobába **széket** hozott.*

(2) SVOM.

Péter *hozta a széket a szobába.*

On the other hand, if the verb takes a preverb, the word order SVOM of Type 2 is preferable:

(1) SVOM.

Péter behozta a széket a szobába.

although SOVM is not precluded either:

Péter a széket behozta a szobába.

but in this case it is supposed that the object *a széket* has already come up in the text. Thus, the verb has a determining function in Hungarian word order. If its aspectuality is perfective the basic word order is SVOM, in which case it is impossible to use an unarticled object: **Péter széket behozott a szobába.* If the verb is of an imperfective aspect, the placing of the object depends on whether it has or has not an article: unarticled object stands before the verb; articled after the verb: *Péter széket hozott a szobába. Péter a szobába hozta a széket.*, and the modifier is positioned after or before the verb, respectively. Thus, in the case of verbs of an imperfective aspect mixed word order is preferable.

In the above examples of Type 1 and mixed word order the element preceding the verb is stressed, that is its accentuation is characteristic of Type 1:

*Péter **széket** hozott a szobába.*

(Cf. *Péter **levelet** ír.*) In word order SVOM of Type 2. the stress is put on either the verb with prefix or the element following the verb:

Péter behozta *a széket a szobába.*
Péter behozott egy széket *a szobába.*
as well as:
Péter megírta *a levelet.*
Péter megírt egy levelet.

Placing a mild stress is dependent on whether the object does or does not take an indefinite article; if the case is the former, that is the object has the function of introducing a new communication element, emphasis is lent to the object, otherwise it is lent to the verb.

We obtain an emphatic variant instead of the basic word order, if the object and the modifier are interchanged:

Péter a szobába *hozott széket.*
Péter a széket *hozta a szobába.*

Many similar instances might be given of the possible variants beginning with S, but the general picture would remain the same.

As to the contextual variants beginning with the object or a modifier, we may distinguish twelve.
In Mongolian contextual variants the order of sequence of the subject and the verb is SV:

MSOV.
Gert damdin **talx** *avč irev.*
OMSV.
Talx gert **Damdin** *avč irev.*
The element preceding the verb receives stress.

Type 2 will be exemplified by a Swahili basic sentence which reads:
Juma amezijaza ndoo maji. 'Juma poured water into the buckets.'
MVOS.
Ndoo amezijaza maji Juma.
OVMS.
Maji amezijaza ndoo Juma.
In both sentences the order is VS. German similarly belongs to Type 2. Its contextual variants are different but, in the case of inverse word order VS obtains:

MVSO.
Ins Zimmer brachte Peter den Stuhl.
OVSM.
Den Stuhl brachte Peter ins Zimmer.
OVMS.
*Den Stuhl brachte ins Zimmer Peter.

MVOS.
*Ins Zimmer brachte den Stuhl Peter.
All twelve possible variants are acceptable in Hungarian. We omit to analyze them in detail, because twice twelve possibilities of permutation are given, in respect of sentences with objects with and without an article. Further problems are involved with sentences construed with an unarticled object. All variants, which receive a marked stress in preverbal position. Sentences construed with a perfective verb in the basic variant consistently represent Type 2, while the contextual variant of the same sentence shows a hardly discernible difference, from the point of view of communication:
OVSM.
A széket behozta Péter a szobába.
OSVM.
A széket Péter behozta a szobába.
This seems to show that in the contextual variant Type 2 is not so firmly established as it is in the basic variant. But the difference is more explicit in sentences of three elements:
OVS.
A széket **behozta** Péter.
OSV.
A széket Péter **behozta**.
where OSV is somewhat more neutral than OVS.

Elliptical sentences receive comparatively little attention in word-order typology whereas some languages often use constructions without a subject, and others deprive the unemphatic object of its fixed place in the word order pattern. Only languages of Types 1 and 2, and the transitions between the two, will be examined here from this point of view. In a decisively mechanical approach, the complete variants will be reduced to become elliptical, and even so only typologically characterizable results will be considered.

First sentences of three elements will be reduced so that the subject is eliminated. In these instances the subject is denoted with lower-case character (s).

Type 1	Type 2
OVs	sVO
OsV	OVs

In the basic variant the difference in the order of the two types will prevail: (1) OV, (2) VO, for example, (1) Hung. **Levelet** *írt* 'Letter wrote' (lit.), (2)

Russ. *Pisal* **pis'mo**. 'Wrote letter', but it will disappear in the contextual variant: OV: Hung. **Levelet** *írt*, Russ. *Pis'mo* **pisal**.

If the object is omitted or becomes unaccented, the following picture will be seen:

Type 1	Type 2
SoV	SVo
oSV	oVS

In the basic variant there is no difference between the two types: (1) *Péter* **írt**., (2) *Petr* **pisal**., while in the contextual variant there is a difference (1) **Péter** *írt*., (2) *Pisal* **Petr**.

It has to be noted that within Type 1 the difference between the basic and the contextual word order will be eliminated both when the subject is missing: *Levelet írt*, and when the object is omitted: *Péter írt*. Nevertheless, there is a difference in the accentuation: if the subject is omitted in the basic variant, the stress is placed like this: *Levelet írt*, while in the contextual variant: **Levelet** *írt;* and also when the object is missing: *Péter írt*, **Péter** *írt*. As has been mentioned, Hungarian linguistic data are not wholly relevant here, and it would be more reasonable to use data of an unmixed Type 1 language instead, if they were not more difficult to interprete.

The variants of four-member sentences beginning with S show the following structure after S is eliminated:

Type 1	Type 2	Mixed Types 1 and 2
sMOV	sVOM	sOVM
sOMV	sVMO	sMVO

For example, (1) *A szobába széket hozott.* 'In the room chair brought' (lit). (MOV), (2) *Prines stul v komnatu.* 'Brought chair in the room'. (lit.) (VOM), mixed: *Széket hozott a szobába.* (OVM). The difference between Types 1 and 2 remains, and also the mixed type shows a difference. In the case of variants beginning with O and M, respectively, we have the following picture:

Type 1	Type 2	the result of the two
OsMV	OVMs	OMV
OMsV	OMVs	OVM
OsVM	OVsM	MOV
MsOV	MVOs	MVO
MOsV	MOVs	
MsVO	MVsO	

For instance: *Stul prines v komnatu* 'Chair brought in the room' (lit). (OVM). Thus, the differènce between the two types of word order disappears but the difference of accent remains.

When the object is omitted, the word order of four-member sentences starting with S shows the following picture:

Type 1	Type 2	Mixed Types 1 and 2
SMoV	SVoM	SoVM
SoMV	SVMo	SMVo

For example: (1) **Péter a szobába hozott*. (SMV), (2) **Petr prines v komnatu*. (SVM).

The difference between Types 1 and 2 will obtain, while the mixed type will agree with Type 1 and Type 2, respectively.

Variants beginning with O and M show the following picture:

Type 1	result	Type 2	result
oSMV		oVMS	
oMSV	SMV	oMVS	VMS
oSVM	SVM	oVSM	MVS
MSoV	MSV	MVoS	VSM
MoSV		MoVS	
MSVo		MVSo	

For instance: (1) **Péter a szobába hozott*. (SMV), (2) **V komnatu prines Petr*. (MVS).

As has been shown, the differençe between the elliptical variants of Types 1 and 2 is not eliminated. This is understandable since the collocation of S and V is decisive, and, therefore, these two elements will preserve their original positions. The variants of Type 1 beginning with S and O show partial agreement (SMV).

We should like to emphasize once more that the analyses given above have been carried out with a general typological end in view, and that the examples adduced have to be regarded as illustrative material only. It cannot be considered our task here to examine in what cases our sentences are correct, whether in Hungarian or in Russian.

Correlations and Changes of Word Order Types

Let us briefly sum up the most important facts before we examine the universal implications and the problems of diachrony. It can be supposed that the topic-comment rules demonstrated above have a general applicability: within the given conditions the agent, the experiencer and the instrumental will always qualify as the typological subject and the topic in the word order Main Type A, occupying the place before the pause in the sentence, according to the primary topic-comment rules. It is in this way that the three types of basic word order patterns are construed within the first main type of word order (Cf. the examples given before):

Type 1   Type 2   Type 3
S # OV   S # VO   VS # O

The topic will maintain its place even when it receives the "anaphoric" feature. When, however, the anaphoric element is the object (O), it takes the place at the head of the sentence, that is the position of the topic, in word order Types 1 and 2, provided a possibility of two variants is given (Cf. the examples above):

Type 1   Type 2
O # SV   O # VS

Type 3 (VSO) comprises two secondary variants: SVO and VOS. In the latter, O is put in the first part of the sentence, as in the contextual variants of Types 1 and 2, which is not the case in connection with SVO. Apparently, the order O # S is only a frequantal in the secondary variants of Main Type A.

The basic order and the only variant of Main Type B is VO # S; for instance, Malagasy: *Manoratra taratasy # Rakoto* 'Writes letter # Rakoto' (lit). The differentiation between Main Types A and B has been made on the grounds that in Main Type A the topically featured S precedes O in the basic word order, the former being separated by a pause from the latter: S # O, while Main Type B shows the picture in reverse: O # S. Presumably the two are connected by the mere fact that S with a topic feature is not primarily stressed, and O may have, and often has, the stress. Presumably in the case of variants of reverse word order S may have, and often has, emphasis; at least such inference can be made from the examples as follows (Dezső and Szépe 1974): *Examples:*

Type 1: O # S*V*; *Type 2:* O # V*S*; *Type 3:* *S* # VO;
Hung.
(1) *Levelet* # **Péter** *írta.* 'Letter # Peter wrote' (lit.).
Russ.
(2) *Pis'mo* # *pisal* **Petr.** 'Letter # wrote Peter' (lit.).
Arabic
(3) **Ali** # *yaktubu al-ḥiṭāba.* 'Ali # writes the letter'.

Thus, Types 1 and 2 bear in relation to each other a higher degree of agreement than in relation to Type 3. let alone Type 4, as regards the realization of topic-comment function.

It is a known fact that Types 1 and 2 are wide spread, Type 3 occurs fairly frequently, but Type 4, that is Main Type B, can be observed only in certain areas. In this connection the question arises whether Type 3, and chiefly Type 4, are not secondary developments, of which more particulars will be given below.

The various types are characterized by peculiar rules of accentuation as appears from the examples analyzed above: in Type 1 the element standing before the verb should be stressed, in Type 2 the element after the verb, and the same applies to Type 4, while in Type 3 sentence stress is placed on the element standing on its own. The element heading the sentence is stressed both in Type 1 (**Ír** *Péter* # *levelet.*) and in Type 2 (**Píšet** *Petr* # *pis'mo.*), although the latter needs to be further investigated. Here, however, we encounter special problems, connected with Types 1 and 2, in which three variants are possible (and in the case of completely free word order, all six variants are possible). That is to say the variants are capable of fusing into one another and developing, through restructuring and restricting word order, into Types 3 and 4. Therefore, we have to deal with a new factor here which should be considered in panchronic typology.

When it comes to analyzing sentences which are more complicated constructions or different in structure the typological system will be modified, augmented and diversified. The division into four types will be retained; nevertheless, we have to take into account possible mixed types. Without going into the problem in detail, we would like to point out that the trend of complementation is as follows: if the verb takes, in addition to S and O, a further complement (second object or adverbial modifier), then the new nominal element occupies, in the unmixed types, the next vacant place in the basic word order:

(1) S # -OV; (2) S # VO-; (3) VS # O-; (4) VO- # S.

As by analysis of extended simple sentences the question would become complicated, only the mixed type will be mentioned here, exemplified by the following Hungarian sentence: *Az anya* # *kenyeret vágott* + *a fiának* 'Mother # (some) bread cut to her son' in which the object stands, in conformity with the rules of Type 1, before the verb, while the indirect object in the Dative, after the verb, according to the rule of Type 2.

Let us, therefore, abide by the SVO structures and try to compare Greenberg's universals with ours.

"*Universal 1:* In declarative sentences with nominal subject, the dominant order is almost always one in which the subject precedes the object." (Greenberg 1963 (1968), 77).

This universal is not fully valid, because it refers to Main Type A only; Type 4 mentioned above was unknown to Greenberg who regarded it as an uncertain exception.

"*Universal 6:* All languages with dominant VSO order have SVO as an alternative or as the only alternative basic order." (Greenberg 1963 (1968), 79).

This universal does not seem to be unexceptional either, for there exist languages which have got the VSO and VOS word-order patterns, this sub-type of Type 3, however, requires further investigation.

"*Universal 7:* If in a language with dominant SOV order, there is no alternative basic order, or only OSV as the alternative, then all adverbial modifiers of the verb likewise precede the verb. (This is the "rigid" sub-type of III.") (Greenberg 1963 (1968), 80).

Our universals will be similar to *Universals 6 and 7* established by Greenberg inasmuch as they also follow from type rules. In order to make this statement clear, let us tabulate here the possible types and sub-types on the basis of the data we actually have at hand. (In this survey (a) is used to denote a sub-type with one variant, (b) and (c) sub-types with half-bound two and three variants, respectively, and (d) the free sub-type with six variants.)

Main Type A

Type 1.

(a) SOV	(b) SOV	(c) SOV	(d) SOV
	OSV	OSV	OSV
		VSO	VSO
			SVO
			OVS
			VOS

Type 2.

(a) SVO	(b) SVO	(c) SVO	(d) SVO
	OVS	OVS	OVS
		VSO	VSO
			SOV
			OSV
			VOS

Type 3.

(b) VSO	or	VSO	
SVO		VOS	

Main Type B

Type 4.

(a) VSO

In respect of these data, certain implications, called implicational universals, are derived from the type system:

If a language has	then it also has
I. OSV	OSV
II. OVS	SVO

The topic-comment grounds for these two universals are constituted by the fact that SVO and SOV are always given as bases if the contextual arrangements OSV and OVS are detectable in Types 1 and 2; since no OVS and OSV are possible in Types 3 and 4, their universal character is not restricted. Exceptions to this rule may come up when the language does not represent a pure tye: its basic order has undergone certain changes, but its contextual word order has been preserved, and its free word order has been reduced to two variants belonging to two different types: to SVO and OSV.

III. VSO	SOV	or	SVO
non-dominant	OSV		OVS

Also this universal is based on topic-comment rules: a non-dominant word order opening with a verb as an anaphoric element is only possible if there exists a basic order (SVO or SOV) and a variant with an anaphoric object (OVS or OSV).

IV. VOS	VSO	or	SOV
non-dominant			SVO
			OSV
			OVS
			VSO

The exceptional position of VOS is documented by this universal: it can be observed as a secondary variant in Type 3, but is met with in Types 1 and 2 only in cases when all the other variants are also available.

V. OSV, OVS	SOV, SVO, VSO, VOS
VI. SOV, SVO	OSV, OVS, VSO, VOS

These two universals have their bases in the characteristic features of Type 1 and 2; to wit, the basic and the contextual variants of these two types may come up only in free word order patterns, otherwise they mutually preclude each other. Types 3 and 4 do not contradict this rule, therefore, it is universal.

These universals can be easily deduced from the system of types and have a heuristic significance as well: with the help of these universals the word order types of a given language can be inferred even from fragmentary texts of the same language. Furthermore, they may be instrumental in making historical reconstructions, for which they provide historical grounds (identity is also expressed by numbers):

if this exists now —	then this existed before
(*I) SOV	SOV — OSV
(*II) SVO	SVO — OVS
(*III) (a) SOV, OSV	SOV, OSV — VSO
(b) SVO, OVS	SVO, OVS — VSO.

Of course, these implications are valid only if the freedom of word order in a given language is restricted. Such processes have been met with in languages belonging to Types 1 and 2. Universals (*II) and (*III) (b) can be exemplified by word order patterns of English, German, Rumanian, in which the universals mentioned have come about as a result of the consolidation of fixed word order patterns.

If any of the four word order types can change into any of the others, then we have to consider twelve possibilities, even if we suppose only one change takes place:

$$
(1)\ SOV
\begin{cases}
(i) \to SVO \\
(ii) \to VSO \\
(iii) \to VOS
\end{cases}
$$

$$
(2)\ SVO
\begin{cases}
(i) \to SOV \\
(ii) \to VSO \\
(iii) \to VOS
\end{cases}
$$

$$
(3)\ VSO
\begin{cases}
(i) \to SOV \\
(ii) \to SVO \\
(iii) \to VOS
\end{cases}
$$

$$
(4)\ VOS
\begin{cases}
(i) \to SOV \\
(ii) \to SVO \\
(iii) \to VSO
\end{cases}
$$

SOV etc. represents not one or another variant but the whole of the type in our schematic survey. One can suppose, however, a type changing twice, that is the combination of rules (1)—(4) with the partial rules of (i)—(iii) can be imagined, for instance SOV→SVO→VSO, which results in a combination of (1) (i) with (2) (ii). The twelve possibilities, or their combinations, can be considered hypothetical possibilities only. As has been mentioned, there are relatively few (4) VOS type languages, and there is but little probability of, let us say, a change of (4) (i) and (4) (ii) having occurred in the past, although the possibility of such a change is not precluded for the future. We do not know the past history of a considerable number of languages, and, therefore, we are not able to state whether or not changes affecting their types of word order patterns have taken place in them, although it can be surmised, and is also justifiably supposed in general, that even if the various languages of a given language family represent different types, the proto-language of these tongues must have been characterized by a unique word order. Thus late Indo-European must have been, in all likelihood, of a free SOV word order and the SVO type European languages have developed as an outcome of a change of the type. The same may be stated in connection with the Celtic languages, which have actually VSO as basic word order, but it is not yet settled whether this VSO type has developed from some primitive Indo-European SOV word order or from another word order type of SVO going back to type SOV, that is through the process of a double change: SOV→SVO→VSO, which would agree with the result of a combination of (1) (i) with (2) (ii) in the scheme above. Finno-Ugric or Uralic may also have had SOV word order type; the recent SVO in Balto-Finnish languages is secondary, and in Hungarian at its initial stage of development. In the Indonesian and the Oceanic languages the SVO type may have been the preliminary of the VSO or VOS types, although it can also be imagined that the latter has come about from one of the subtypes of VSO (VSO, VOS).

Let us now go into the question of change. A precondition of change of type is that the initial type should have had the variants that are characteristic of the type developed from it. For instance, a change of (1)→(2) presupposes the existence of the variants SOV, OSV (VSO) characteristic of Type 1, as well as the variants SVO, OVS characteristic of Type 2. The change set in progressively, SVO came slowly to undertake the role of basic word order from SOV, while the contextual word order went over from OSV to OVS. In consequence of the change in function a change of frequency of occurrence has also taken place: instead of SOV, SVO became the most frequent variant. The process is well discernible in Old and Middle English, in the data of the Anglo-Saxon Chronicle and Ormulum. The process of type-change made a marked headway in the basic word order of the Anglo-Saxon Chronicle, this having been represented in SOV with a frequency of 35 per cent and in SVO with 30 per cent, while the number for OSV in the contextual variant was 11 per cent, indicating a much higher frequency than that of OVS, which was 3 per cent (Shannon 13). As against this, in the Ormulum the SVO variant greatly exceeds SOV (69 against 14 per cent), and the contextual word order is rather rare; the word order shows an advanced stage of consolidation, but OVS has gained the upper hand (4 per cent) and the frequency of OSV is less (1 per cent) (Dalmatier 1969 54). Some, if not the majority, of European languages between 800 and 1500 were characterized by a high frequency ratio of the VSO variant (18 per cent in the Anglo-Saxon Chronicle, *loc. cit.*), which may well have given rise to either VSO or SVO types of word order; the former was the case in the Celtic languages; in English SVO was not pushed into the background.

This single example may offer an insight into the process of SOV→SVO and SVO→VSO change of type, and perhaps also SOV→SVO→VSO change, although no details can be given here and no other type-shift can be analyzed in this study.

As has been mentioned, the change of word order goes hand in hand with the process of grammatical reorganization, and as a result, different variants will express the basic and the contextual functions, a fact that can be well demonstrated by statistical methods. Certain structural-functional correlations are replaced by others, and in the transitional period even the shift is expressible in statistical terms, which means that the transition from one structure into another can be captured through statistical regularities.

It is difficult to determine the causes that give rise to a change in word order. They probably vary in importance. There are several languages for which a double word order type is characteristic, and in which the aspectuality feature of the verb determines which word order is to be followed (e.g. SVO or VSO in Koalib, SVO or SOV in Moru). Maybe, the change of the aspect type is decisive from the point of view of word order change. Some of the Indo-European languages (Slavic, English, etc.) provide instances of change of aspect, but the aspectuality of ancient Greek can not have been unlike that of ancient Indo-European, yet it was characterized by SVO word order. It is more plausible that change of aspect reflects only one side of a certain change in the syntactic structure, which gave rise to the change of the word order type. To tell the truth, it is highly questionable if the change of the word order can be attributed to the change in certain parts of the syntactic structure, and if so which part has a substantial role in the change.

As has been expounded in Part 1, aspectuality is closely interrelated with "determination" so decisive in the communication process. In some languages its features are expressed by means of definite pronouns and definite articles, in others by accusative suffixes (cf. the accusative and the absolute cases of the Altaic languages) or by an opposition of the accusative and partitive cases (in Finnish), or by objective conjugation (Hungarian), or by verbal infix (the Bantu languages), and so on. For example, in Hungarian the sentence: *A fiú megírta a levelet* 'The boy has written the letter' has a perfective verb and an object with definite article, and it has SVO order; at the same time, SOV basic order is used with verbs which do not take a preverb with a perfective function *(meg-)*; and with an object without article: *A fiú levelet írt* 'The boy wrote (a) letter', and the former sentence with SOV order: *A fiú levelet megírta* would be impossible. As the function of the word order mainly concerns the realization of the communication, and as aspect and definiteness have a similar function (even though in another relation), it may be supposed that the change in the word order is primarily responsive to the changes in the system of actualizing rules (aspectuality, definiteness), but all these are correlated with the whole structure of the sentence. For the time being we cannot account for changes in word order; perhaps a multiplicity of causes are involved, and, therefore, only some of the essential components can be pointed out.

As mentioned above, morphological changes can hardly result in changes of word order type, but within a type morphological change may induce the consolidation of word order (e.g. in Middle English) thereby bringing about a new subtype. Thus word order, in the absence of certain morphological means, assumes a distinctive function in respect of the parts of sentence.

Correlation and Changes of Sentence Stress in
Types 1 and 2

The most important word order variants are usually described in the studies of individual languages and typology could formulate their regularities. Very little is known about the principles of sentence stress. What I am going to say should be regarded only as tentative and temporary statements based on the data of Uralic, Altaic and some Indo-European languages.

The usual place of sentence stress and hence that of comment is the position immediately preceding the verb in Type 1. If this position is occupied by an element that cannot be moved from this place (e.g. an indirect object in absolute case in Turcic languages), an element further before the verb can be stressed. If X denotes a stressed element, Y an unstressed one, then:

(i) XV   (ii) XYV

demonstrate the variants of the preverbal stressing principle. In languages having no elements with fixed preverbal position (e.g. in Hungarian) only variant (i) is possible, i.e. a stressed element must immediately precede the verb. In languages with both variants, a stressed element may be separated from the verb under special conditions.

In rigid SOV languages, no element can follow the verb. If a postverbal position is admitted, the element following the verb is either unstressed or has an emphatic or contrastive stress denoted by X:

(iii) VY   (iv) VX

In SVO languages, the usual place of the focused element is after the verb either in an immediately postverbal position of after an unstressed element:

(i) VX   (ii) VYX

In a preverbal position the stress expresses emphasis or contrast in SVO languages with free word order:

(iii) XV

Thus, the principles of stressing the comment are the opposite in SOV and SVO languages. The rules of individual languages are more complicated because they are often of mixed type. If in SOV languages an element does not stand close to the verb, as a result of the semantic cohesion principle, but is stressed, it moves to an immediately preverbial position, if it can do so, and instead of $SAO^{id}O^dV$ one finds:

$SAO^dO^{id}V$ or $SO^{id}O^dAV$ or $AO^{id}O^dSV$ etc., where O^{id}, A, S are stressed. (Of course, the position of unstressed nominal elements may vary.) If the immediately preverbal position is occupied, the stressed element stands before the verb and tends to the closest possible position; e.g. $SO^{id}AO^dV$ or $AO^{id}SO^dV$ etc.

The verb may be stressed in any position, but if it is in sentence initial position, it has an obligatory emphasis or contrast.

If a language changes its type of word order from SOV to SVO, it has to change the principles of sentence stress as well. The restricted sub-types of both types have no common variant:

(1) SOV   (2) SVO
    OSV   OVS

and no change of type is possible. The existence of a common variant VSO is of no relevance. A change of type is possible in cases of free word order, when the basic order and the stressing principles of the two types differ but the untypical variants are also used:

(1) SVO   (2) SOV
    OVS   OSV

The untypical variants of SOV languages have one or (in cases of 4 elements) several elements in postverbal position. They may be either unstressed or contrasted but they cannot have simple focus.

An SOV language must change its stressing principles to those of SVO:

SOV: (i) XV   (ii) XYV   (iii) VX or VY
to SVO: (i) YX   (ii) VYX   (iii) XV

The postverbal position must also be a focused one instead of unstressed or in addition to a contrasted position of SOV type. The preverbal position cannot be used in cases of focus, but it will preserve its emphatic or contrastive status (that was not specially mentioned earlier).

The main principle of preverbal stressing changes to a postverbal one. Thus one arrives at the principles of Russian. Proto-Indo-European and Proto-Slavic were SOV languages, Modern Russian belongs to SVO languages with free word order. It has preserved the stress on the sentence initial verbs: *V*SO instead of V*S*O with a stressed S in such an originally SVO language, like Swahili.

2.2. Typological Characterization
   of Hungarian Word Order

I think it will be useful to present to the reader the system of the word order
and sentence accentuation of a language with free word order. Hungarian
has been chosen because it demonstrates the relationship between
sentence structure, aspectuality, determination, on the one hand, and
word order and sentence accentuation, on the other. The system of topic
and comment in Hungarian will be simplified even if it seems to be
sophisticated enough to the reader (for a detailed analysis see Dezső 1980).
I could not simplify it more than I did, but I tried to use a very limited
number of lexical items. The chapter on the word order of sentences with
an object can easily be followed, if you remember the lexemes: *fiú* (nom.)
'boy', *levelet* (acc.) 'letter', *újságot* (acc.) 'newspaper', *olvas* and *el + olvas*
'read' (imperfective *vs.* perfective), *visz* 'take', *el + visz* 'away take'
(imperfective *vs* perfective), *visz + el* (imperfective or continuous), *a/az*
'the', *egy* 'a', 'one', *nem* 'no'.

First sentences with an object (2.2. 1.), then particulars of sentences
with an adverbial (2.2. 2.) and those with an object and an adverbial (2.2.
3.) will be surveyed, and the chapter will close with an analysis of the
sentences containing a pronoun (2.2. 3.).

2.2.1. SENTENCES WITH AN OBJECT

In this subchapter we shall deal first with questions of sentences construed with verbs which do not take a preverb and in the next with sentences in which the verb does take a preverb; in both cases affirmative
sentences will be treated first, negative ones second.

By way of introduction we have to mention the features used in the
analysis. The noun element of the topic containing a given information
may either be such as has been mentioned in the preliminaries, in which
case it has an "anaphora" feature [+ anaph.] or such as has not been

mentioned previously, but implied in the situation and, therefore, felt as given in the text, when it is called topic feature [+ topic]. Topic and anaphora features are not usually marked in the examples but are still considered in the course of analysis; this mainly obtains for the latter. The phrase in which the new communication is called comment and it may include a slightly emphatic element which receives a "focus" feature [+ foc.], or an emphatic element [+ emph.], or a strongly stressed element expressing contrast [+ contr.]. The examples given below might be read with different stresses, but we endeavour to make the sentence stress unambiguous by using emphatic features and pause symbols. Accentuation as given in the following examples has been considered typical by our informants. (As to the letter types used, s p a c i n g is used for slight stress, bold face for emphasis and strong stress, # pause, and + short pause.)

Of the sentences construed with verbs without a preverb those will be examined whose subject takes a definite article and whose object has a definite, an indefinite or a zero article. Analysis will be carried out according to the following order of variants: SVO, SOV, OSV, OVS, VSO and VOS.

SVO.

A fiú # o l v a s s a [+ foc.] *a levelet.*
'The boy reads the letter.'
A fiú # *olvas egy* l e v e l e t [+ foc.).
'The boy reads a letter.'
A fiú* # **olvas [+ emph.] *levelet.*
'The boy reads letter.'

The difference of a slight accent between the two first sentences is due to the use of the article: a new element is introduced by the indefinite article, therefore, it receives a mild accent. The third sentence does not make sense; *A fiú* # **olvas** *újságot* would be correct, since *újság* 'newspaper' rather denotes species, which can be contrasted with nouns like *könyv* 'book', *folyóirat* 'journal'.

SOV.

A fiú # **a levelet** [+ emph.] *olvassa.*
'It is the letter that the boy is reading.'
A fiú # *egy* **levelet** [+ emph.] *olvas.*
A fiú # l e v e l e t [+ foc.] *olvas.*

In the first sentence the object preceding the verb has probably been mentioned, therefore, it is emphatic and may express contrast as well. The second sentence which is construed with an object taking the indefinite article *egy* 'a' seems problematic: it would be correct only if *egy* were used in the connotation of *az egyik* 'one of the' indeterminate pronoun: *A fiú az egyik levelet olvassa.* 'The boy reads one of the letters.', in which case it would refer to an unidentified object of a known set. The third sentence is the basic variant of the sentence with an object taking zero article.

OSV.

A levelet ≠ *a* **fiú** [+ emph.] *olvassa.*
'It is the boy that reads the letter.'
*Egy levelet ≠ *a* **fiú** *olvas.*
Levelet ≠ *a* **fiú** [+ contr.] *olvas.*

The first sentence has an anaphoric object, its subject is emphatic. The subject of the third sentence expresses contrast by means of the object: the O article indicates that the *levél* 'letter' refers to species which may be compared to, say, 'newspaper', and that there is no problem in of identifying the specimen. The sentence begun with the article *egy* is impossible, because an object imparting new meaningful content cannot stand at the head of the sentence.

OSV.

A **levelet** [+ contr.] *olvassa* + *a fiú.*
*Egy **levelet** [+ contr.] *olvas* + *a fiú.*
Levelet [+ contr.] *olvas* + *a fiú.*

In our opinion, the object standing at the head of the sentence is stressed only in case of particular, strong emphasis (contrast). The second sentence construed with the indefinite article *egy* is not correct: zero article should be used instead, for the object *levél* with a marked emphasis refers to the specific category.

VSO.

Olvassa [+ emph.] *a fiú* ≠ *a levelet.*
Olvas [+ emph.] *a fiú* ≠ *egy levelet.*
***Olvas** [+ emph.] *a fiú* ≠ *levelet.*

The verb has to be placed at the head of the sentence if the action is important for the speaker. This is usually required by the preliminary text. In such cases the verb denotes, as a rule, action in progress. Since the noun *levél* is not used as a specific term, the last sentence is not correct, although the sentence with *újságot* 'newpaper': *Olvas a fiú újságot.* is correct. In contrast to the two former sentences, no concrete action is involved in this last-adduced example.

Essentially the same may be stated in connection with the VOS variants to follow. The difference between VSO and VOS is that the former word order has the subject before the pause while the latter has the object, and the object and subject, respectively, after the pause. That is to say, the difference is caused by the placing of the secondary sentence stress.

VOS.

Olvassa [+ emph.] *a levelet* # *a fiú.*

Olvas [+ emph.] *egy levelet* # *a fiú.*

***Olvas** [+ emph.] *levelet* # *a fiú.*

It can be summarily established that sentences with articled object have SVO as basic word order; SOV and OSV as well as VSO and VOS are emphatic, while OVS is mainly used to express contrast. Otherwise, contrast expressed by proper accentuation can be imagined in the other variants as well. Simple contrast is indicated by the primarily emphatic element:

SVO.

A fiú # **olvassa** *a levelet.*

'The boy is reading (and not writing) the letter.'

SOV.

A fiú # *a* **levelet** *olvassa.*

'The boy is reading the letter (and not the newspaper).'

OSV. *A levelet* # *a* **fiú** *olvassa.*

'The letter is being read by the boy (and not by the girl).

VSO.

Olvassa *a fiú* # *a levelet.*

'The letter is being read (and not written) by the boy.

VOS.

Olvassa *a levelet* # *a fiú.*

We omit to deal here with questions of double contrast. Nor will we enter into discussion of sentences construed with indefinite- or zero-articled object; let it suffice to mention here that no contrast can be formed in the SVO variant in the presence of the indefinite article *egy:*

SVO.

A fiú # **olvas** *egy* **levelet.**

'The boy is reading a letter (and not a newspaper).'

but correct usage prefers the word order SOV instead:

SOV.

A fiú # *egy* **levelet** *olvas.*

It should be noted, however, that the variant with zero article is usually preferred to the variant with the indefinite article *egy:*
SOV.
A fiú # **levelet** *olvas.*
The indefinite article is used only in cases where the speaker feels it important to direct attention to the circumstance that not the species in general but a specimen is being referred to by the object.

A further and more delicate problem arises when the subject of the sentence takes the indefinite article. If the unaccented subject takes the initial position in the sentence as the topic of the sentence, then it is usually supposed to be known. In such cases the article *egy* is interpreted as *az egyik* 'one of the', that is as an unidentified element of a known set:
SVO.
Egy fiú # olvassa [+ foc.] *a levelet.*
'One of the boys is reading the letter.'
Egy fiú # *olvas egy* levelet [+ foc.].
**Egy fiú* # olvas *levelet.*
In contrast, when the object also takes the indefinite article, the same interpretation is not relevant:
SOV.
Egy fiú* # *a* **levelet [+ emph.] *olvassa.*
Egy fiú* # *egy* **levelet [+ emph.] *olvas.*
Egy fiú* # **levelet [+ foc.] *olvas.*
To use the pronoun *az egyik* would make all three sentences correct: *Az egyik fiú a levelet olvassa,* and so on.
OSV.
A levelet # *egy* **fiú** [+ emph.] *olvassa.*
Egy levelet* # *egy* **fiú *olvas.*
Levelet # *egy* **fiú** [+ emph.] *olvas.*
In these examples the subject taking the indefinite article *egy* is placed in the second half of the sentence and it may denote a completely unknown subject as well. The collocation of the article *egy* with the object is not felt to be very satisfactory in these instances either; zero article would certainly be preferable.
OSV.
A **levelet** [+ contr.] *olvassa + egy fiú.*
Egy* **levelet *olvas egy fiú.*
Levelet [+ contr.] *olvas + egy fiú.*

This variant needs no further explanation. Variants which start with the verb may be classed into two groups:

VSO.

Olvassa [+ emph.] *egy fiú* ⧺ *a levelet.*

Olvas [+ emph.] *egy fiú* ⧺ *egy levelet.*

***Olvas** [+ emph.] *egy fiú* ⧺ *levelet.*

VOS.

Olvassa [+ emph.] *a levelet* ⧺ *egy fiú.*

Olvas [+ emph.] *egy levelet* ⧺ *egy fiú.*

***Olvas** [+ emph.] *levelet* ⧺ *egy fiú.*

The verb is emphatic in both variants. The correlation of an emphatic verb with zero articled object has been expounded above. In neither of the variants is it obligatory to interpret the word *egy* as a pronoun, although *az egyik* is possible here as well as in other cases.

The subject taking the indefinite article *egy* may occur in three positions: at the head of the sentence: SVO. *Egy fiú* ⧺ olvassa *a levelet.*, where *az egyik* is to be understood, and especially in SOV *az egyik* would do better: *(Az) egy(ik) fiú* ⧺ *a* **levelet** *olvassa.*, since an unidentified element of a known set is involved. The subject with the indefinite article is located in the second half of the sentence in the variant starting with an object: OSV. *A levelet* ⧺ *egy* **fiú** *olvassa.* OVS. *A* **levelet** *olvassa* + *egy fiú.* The subject may be undetermined in both sentences, although in the OVS variant rather *az egyik* is understood. In the variants beginning with a verb we have the basic word order VSO where the subject with an indefinite article stands in the first part, and VOS where the same stands in the second part of the sentence, but since the verb is emphatic it seems that a completely unknown subject may be possible in both cases.

In the range of negative sentences only sentences construed with a subject with definite and zero articles, will be examined, since the use of the indefinite article would not give a correct meaning:

SVO.

**A fiú nem olvas egy levelet.*

SOV.

**A fiú egy levelet nem olvas.*

OSV.

**Egy levelet a fiú nem olvas.*

OVS.

**Egy levelet nem olvas a fiú.*

VSO.
*Nem olvas a fiú egy levelet.
VOS.
*Nem olvas egy levelet a fiú.
Negated action can refer to an identified object: *A fiú nem olvassa a levelet.*, 'The boy does not read the letter' or else the action does not require a precise identification of the object: *A fiú levelet nem olvas.*, 'The boy does not read letter(s).' This latter example also indicates that it would make better sense to use a specific noun, for instance *újságot* 'newspaper(s)': *A fiú újságot nem olvas.* In this sentence the negative particle *nem* is coupled with the verb. Since this particle always has an emphatic function, it is essential to consider whether the verb or some noun receives primary emphasis in the affirmative counterpart of the negative sentence. If in the affirmative form the primary stress falls on the verb, in the negative form the same verb will receive both the negative and the primary emphasis. If, however, it is some noun that takes the primary emphasis, the particle *nem* will represent a counterpole to it, as shown in the examples to follow. First those three variants are adduced where the verb receives the primary emphasis:

SVO.
A fiú # **nem** *olvassa az újságot.*
A fiú # **nem** *olvas újságot.*
VSO.
Nem *olvassa a fiú* # *az újságot.*
Nem *olvas a fiú* # *újságot.*
VOS.
Nem *olvassa az újságot* # *a fiú.*
Nem *olvas újságot* # *a fiú.*
These do not differ at all from the corresponding affirmative sentences. If the primary emphasis fell on some noun, then either the negated verb would receive emphasis or the noun would form a contrast. Let me take the former case:

SOV.
A fiú + *az újságot* + **nem** *olvassa.*
A fiú + *újságot* + **nem** *olvas.*
OVS.
Az újságot + **nem** *olvassa* + *a fiú.*
Újságot + **nem** *olvas* + *a fiú.*

OSV.

Az újságot + *a fiú* + **nem** *olvassa.*

Újságot + *a fiú* + **nem** *olvas.*

Strong emphasis may be placed on the noun, but less frequently:

SOV.

A fiú ⧺ *az* **újságot** *nem olvassa.*

OVS.

Az **újságot** *nem olvassa* ⧺ *a fiú.*

OSV.

Az újságot ⧺ *a* **fiú** *nem olvassa.*

I shall not enumerate the variants with a zero article. In the case of a negated noun only that word order variant is correct in which both the primary emphasis and negation affects the same word. In such instances the noun phrase is accented:

SOV.

A fiú ⧺ **nem** *az újságot olvassa.*

A fiú ⧺ **nem** *újságot olvas.*

OVS.

Nem *az újságot olvassa* ⧺ *a fiú.*

Nem *újságot olvas* ⧺ *a fiú.*

OSV.

Az újságot ⧺ **nem** *a fiú olvassa.*

Újságot ⧺ **nem** *a fiú olvas.*

By accentuating the SVO variant, the subject receives special emphasis:

SVO.

Nem *a fiú olvassa* ⧺ *az újságot.*

Nem *a fiú olvas* ⧺ *újságot.*

The following examples make no sense, because in them the emphasis is laid on a negated noun located far from the verb, although the negative particle ought to have a strong emphasis:

VSO.

*Olvassa a fiú nem az újságot.

OSV.

*Nem az újságot a fiú olvassa.

Of elliptical sentences only those will be examined here in which the subject is omitted since it is known either from the situation or from the context. By combining the verb and the object, we may bring about two groups consisting of three sentences each:

VO.

Olvassa [+ foc.] *az újságot.*

Olvas egy újságot [+ foc.].

Olvas [+ emph.] *újságot.*

In principle, VO can result from both the SVO and the VOS variants, but it should be derived from SVO if the emphasis relations are taken into consideration. The three sentence patterns in the OV variant are the following:

OV.

Az **újságot** [+ emph.] *olvassa.*

*Egy **újságot** [+ emph.] *olvas.*

Újságot [+ foc.] *olvas.*

The variant OV may result from SOV as well as OVS and OSV variants, although the emphasis relations permit the derivation of the first variant from OVS, the second from SOV exclusively.

In negative sentences the emphasis is placed on the negated verb, as in the full variant:

VO.

Nem *olvassa az újságot.*

Nem *olvas újságot.*

OV.

Az újságot **nem** *olvassa.*

Újságot **nem** *olvas.*

In case the object is negated, the word order OV is obligatory:

OV.

Nem *az újságot olvassa.*

Nem *újságot olvas.*

In the analysis of verbs taking a preverb only typical phenomena will be surveyed. To start with, sentences construed with a zero article are incorrect; that is to say, they are only correct in certain special contexts, whether a perfective or a lexical meaning is expressed by the preverb.

SVO.

**A fiú elolvas újságot.*

**A fiú elvisz újságot.*

But sentences construed with an object with the indefinite article *egy* are correct:

SVO.

A fiú # elolvas *egy újságot.*

'The boy # (will) read a newspaper.'

But if the emphasis is not strong, it is received by the verb in the SVO variant. Similar is the case with sentences containing an object taking the definite article. I choose to analyze this latter type of construction, this being more suitable to demonstrate the characteristics of sentences construed with verbs with preverb, and also because every variant can be deduced from it.

SVO.
A fiú # elolvassa [+ foc.] *az újságot.*
SOV.
A fiú + *az újságot* + **elolvassa** [+ emph.].
OVS.
Az újságot + **elolvassa** [+ emph.] *a fiú.*
OSV.
Az újságot + *a fiú* + **elolvassa** [+ emph.].
VSO.
Elolvassa [+ emph.] *a fiú* # *az újságot.*
VOS.
Elolvassa [+ emph.] *az újságot* # *a fiú.*

Emphasis has been placed on the verb in each variant and we find the focus in the SVO basic variant, while emphasis in the rest. Pause relation of sentences without preverbs does not change, provided the verbs are emphatic in them (SVO, VSO, VOS): in the remaining three examples a short pause is perceptible before and after the verb, respectively, and the same is the case with locative preverbs replacing the purely perfective:

SVO.
A fiú # elviszi *az újságot.*
'The boy # away-takes the newspaper' (lit.)
SOV.
A fiú # *az újságot* + **elviszi.**

We get the primary emphasis relations only when the preverb is placed after the verb. In such cases the emphasis is laid on the same part of the sentence as in sentences without a preverb:

SOV.
A fiú # *az* **újságot** [+ emph.] *olvassa el.*
OSV.
Az újságot # *a* **fiú** [+ emph.] *olvassa el.*
OVS.
Az **újságot** [+ contr.] *olvassa el* + *a fiú.*

Nevertheless, it is not quite obvious whether there is such a great difference between the emphasis in SOV and OSV and that in OVS which would give us reason enough to call the former simple and the latter strong emphasis. In the SVO variant it is the subject and not the verb that takes the emphasis:

SVO.
A **fiú** [+ emph.] *olvassa el* # *az újságot.*

The two variants starting with the verb are impossible since there is no need for the postposition of the preverb in these instances. To wit, there is no noun to be stressed before the verb:

VSO.
*Olvassa el a fiú az újságot.
VOS.
*Olvassa el az újságot a fiú.

It should be noted, that both sentences would be correct if the verb were to express command (in the imperative mood). If the verb has also an approximation feature, the sentence pattern in question is acceptable, but not with a perfective aspectuality only with a progressive aspectuality:

VSO.
Viszi *el* [+ emph.] *a fiú* # *az újságot.*
VOS.
Viszi *el* [+ emph.] *az újságot* # *a fiú.*

Also the SVO variant can be accentuated so that the verb receives a mild emphasis. In such cases the verb will obtain a progressive aspectuality:

SVO.
A fiú # v i s z i e l *az újságot.*

In the rest of the variants where primary emphasis is laid on the noun, such an accentuation would be problematical, for instance, SVO: **A fiú* + *az újságot* + v i s z i *el.*

In sentences where the v e r b is n e g a t i v e, the particle *nem* will receive the emphasis and the preverb will be retrojected:

SVO.
A fiú # **nem** *olvassa el az újságot.*
SOV.
A fiú + *az újságot* + **nem** *olvassa el.*
OSV.
Az újságot + *a fiú* + **nem** *olvassa el.*
OVS.
Az újságot + **nem** *olvassa el a fiú.*

11

VSO.

Nem *olvassa el a fiú* # *az újságot.*

VOS.

Nem *olvassa el az újságot* # *a fiú.*

As to accentuation, these sentences are essentially identical with those construed with verbs without a preverb. Negative particles are possible also in sentences where the verb takes a prepositive preverb, in a particular context, for instance:

SVO.

A fiú nem **elolvassa** *az újságot.*

'The boy does not peruse the newspaper (but he puts it on the fire).',
when the verb is markedly emphatic and needs to be complemented.

When we negate the noun the sentence is only correct if we negate the primarily accentuated part.

SOV.

A fiú # **nem** *az újságot olvassa el.*

OVS.

Nem *az újságot olvassa el* # *a fiú.*

SVO.

Nem *a fiú olvassa el* # *az újságot.*

OSV.

Az újságot # **nem** *a fiú olvassa el.*

In the SVO variant the subject instead of the verb receives the emphasis.

2.2.2. SENTENCES WITH AN ADVERBIAL

The analysis of sentences with an object given in the previous chapter makes it possible for us to save time in the examination of sentences with an adverbial: we omit to deal with sentences containing a subject with the indefinite article *egy;* also, adverbials taking an indefinite article will be discussed in brief; further, negative and elliptical sentences will also be disregarded here. We propose to start investigating sentences with verbs not coupled with preverbs, and then go on with sentences with a preverb.

In order to characterize sentences with an adverbial I have thought it best to single out a verb which is frequently used in common speech and is apt to be complemented with all kinds of adverbial modifiers (**M**); such a verb is *megy* '(he) goes', which can be complemented as follows:

adjective with a suffix of modifier of manner:
A fiú gyorsan megy.
'The boy walks fast.'
noun as modifier of manner:
A fiú vonattal megy.
'The boy travels by train.'
noun as modifier of direction:
A fiú az erdőbe megy.
'The boy goes to the woods.'
noun as modifier of place:
A fiú a réten megy.
'The boy walks in the meadow.'
noun as modifier of purpose:
A fiú fáért megy.
'The boy goes to fetch wood.'

A suffixed adjective standing for modifier of manner cannot be actualized (that is, it cannot go with an article or a pronoun): *A fiú gyorsan megy.*, while a noun with the same syntactic role can be actualized: *A fiú vonattal megy. A fiú ezzel a vonattal megy.*, 'The boy travels by this train.' *A fiú valamelyik vonattal megy.* 'The boy travels by one of the trains.', and to quote an example of articled noun as modifier of manner: *A fiú a vonattal megy.* 'The boy travels by the train.', which is not impossible though the preceding example with the demonstrative pronoun is more idiomatic. *A fiú egy vonattal megy.* is correct in my opinion only if *egy* is used with the meaning *az egyik* 'one of'. The possibilities of permutation with nouns taking zero article and a demonstrative pronoun will be specially analyzed below, but first the variants of the sentence *A fiú gyorsan megy.* will be examined.

SMV.
A fiú # gyorsan [+ foc.] *megy.*
SVM.
A fiú [+ contr.] *megy* # *gyorsan.*
MSV.
Gyorsan # *a* **fiú** [+ contr.] *megy.*
MVS.
Gyorsan [+ emph.] *megy* # *a fiú.*
VSM.
(*)**Megy** [+ emph.] *a fiú* # *gyorsan.*

11*

VMS.
(*)**Megy** [+ emph.] *gyorsan* ⧧ *a fiú.*
The sign (*) denotes a sentence correct under specific conditions.

SMV is basic variant, while the rest are either emphatic or contrastive, although it is not always easy to differentiate between the two. It depends on the context whether the variant characterized here as emphatic will not turn out to be contrastive and *vice versa;* what is accepted here as contrastive may well be emphatic when the sentences require so. Nevertheless it seems to us as if the modifier and the verb are more ready to receive emphasis.

SMV.
A fiú ⧧ vonattal [+ foc.] *megy.*
SVM.
A **fiú** [+ contr.] *megy* ⧧ *vonattal.*
MSV.
Vonattal ⧧ *a* **fiú** [+ contr.] *megy.*
MVS.
Vonattal [+ emph.] *megy* ⧧ *a fiú.*
VSM.
(*)**Megy** [+ emph.] *a fiú* ⧧ *vonattal.*
VMS.
(*)**Megy** [+ emph.] *vonattal* ⧧ *a fiú.*
The emphasis relations of the different variants of this sample sentence are identical with those of the previous set of examples, that is there is no difference in this sense between the adjective with a modifier suffix and an articled noun with a modifier suffix.

SMV.
A fiú ⧧ ezzel *a vonattal* [+ foc.] *megy.*
SVM.
A **fiú** [+ contr.] *megy* ⧧ *ezzel a vonattal.*
(*)*A fiú* ⧧ **megy** [+ emph.] *ezzel a vonattal.*
MSV.
Ezzel a vonattal ⧧ *a* **fiú** [+ contr.] *megy.*
MVS.
Ezzel *a vonattal* [+ emph.] *megy* ⧧ *a fiú.*
VSM.
(*)**Megy** [+ emph.] *a fiú* ⧧ *ezzel a vonattal.*
VMS.
(*)**Megy** [+ emph.] *ezzel a vonattal* ⧧ *a fiú.*

The use of modifiers collocated with a demonstrative pronoun does not involve any particular change. Only the second variant of SVM, which emphasized the verb, may be regarded as a deviation, indicating the influence of word order Type 2.

Of the modifiers of direction, those construed with the definite article offer themselves for a detailed analysis.

SMV.
A fiú # az erdőbe [+ foc.] *megy.*
SVM.
A fiú # megy [+ foc.] *az erdőbe.*
MSV.
Az erdőbe # **a fiú** [+ contr.] *megy.*
MVS.
Az erdőbe [+ emph.] *megy* # *a fiú.*
VSM.
Megy [+ emph.] *a fiú* # *az erdőbe.*
VMS.
Megy [+ emph.] *az erdőbe* # *a fiú.*

As against the former examples, it is an essential difference that SVM here, just as in sentences with an object, is a focal variant. The focus is on the verb denoting a concrete progressive action. However, in the SVM variant S may have contrastive stress: *A* **fiú** *megy az erdőbe.* The emphasis in VSM is weak, nearing a mild stress.

Of the modifiers of place, those taking an article will be examined from the point of view of word order.

SMV.
A fiú # az úton [+ foc.] *megy.*
SVM.
A fiú # megy [+ foc.] *az úton.*
MSV.
Az úton # *a* **fiú** [+ contr.] *megy.*
MVS.
Az **úton** [+ emph.] *megy* # *a fiú.*
VSM.
Megy [+ emph.] *a fiú* # *az úton.*
VMS.
Megy [+ emph.] *az úton* # *a fiú.*

SVM here again receives a mild emphasis, and the stressed verb denotes a concrete action in progress, however, S may have contrastive stress, too: *A*

fiú megy # *az úton*. The stress given to VSM is weak also here, and the verb in it indicates progressive action.

In sentences denoting direction or place, even in their SMV variants, those with zero article are less frequent than in the group of sentences containing a modifier of manner (in the examples: *ment* 'walked'):

A fiú # érdőbe *megy (ment)*.

(*)*A fiú* # járdán *megy (ment)*.

'The boy is walking on the pavement.'

The modifier of place is less suited to denote a specific notion than are the modifiers of manner. For this the modifier of direction is more suitable, and, therefore, we may take the following sentence as a perfectly correct example: *A fiú iskolába megy*. 'The boy goes to school.' In the SVM variants the subject will receive emphasis:

A fiú *megy (ment) erdőbe*.

(*)*A fiú megy (ment) járdán*.

But in the case of the modifier *iskolába* stress may be laid on the verb as well:

A fiú # megy (ment) *iskolába*.

While it would have been more appropriate to place the verb in the past tense *(ment)* in the SMV variant, in which the purpose of the action is emphasized *(A fiú* iskolába *ment)*, in the SVM word order it is more usual to keep the present tense *(A fiú megy iskolába.)*, provided the verb is stressed and the progressive form is involved. There is nothing peculiar in the rest of the variants, as concerns emphasis:

MSV.

Erdőbe # *a* **fiú** *ment*.

MVS.

Erdőbe *ment* # *a fiú*.

VSM.

Megy *a fiú* # *erdőbe*.

VMS.

(*)**Megy** *erdőbe* # *a fiú*.

Very few sound sentences can be construed with the adverbial modifier of place (other than direction), (*)*Réten a fiú ment.*, *Réten ment a fiú.* (*) *Megy a fiú réten is.*, (*) *Megy réten is a fiú.* It is not only the kind of modifier that is to blame for this, in part the lexemes are also responsible, for sentences like *Gyárban dolgozik a fiú.* 'The boy is working in a factory.' *Gyárban a fiú dolgozik.*, 'It is the boy that works in the factory.' are unobjectionable although not all variants of them are so: (*)*Dolgozik a fiú* *gyárban is.*, (*)*Dolgozik gyárban is a fiú*. It should be noted that adverbial modifiers of place more often occur with an article than without one, and that the use of zero article is considerably determined by the lexical properties of the verb and the modifier proper.

The modifier of purpose may take both the definite and the zero article:

SMV.
A fiú # a fáért [+ foc.] *megy.*
A fiú # fáért [+ foc.] *megy.*
SVM.
A fiú # megy [+ foc.] *a fáért.*
A fiú # megy [+ foc.] *fáért.*
MSV.
A fáért # **a fiú** [+ contr.] *megy.*
Fáért # **a fiú** [+ contr.] *megy.*
MVS.
A **fáért** [+ emph.] *megy* # *a fiú.*
Fáért [+ emph.] *megy* # *a fiú.*
VSM.
Megy [+ emph.] *a fiú* # *a fáért.*
Megy [+ emph.] *a fiú* # *fáért.*
VMS.
Megy [+ emph.] *a fáért* # *a fiú.*
Megy [+ emph.] *fáért* # *a fiú.*

Emphasis relations in sentences with a modifier of direction or with a modifier of purpose are identical, which can be partly explained by the semantic affinity of the two kinds of modifiers: both are expressive of controlled action, and the direction, at least in part, indicates purpose, and purpose—at least in the given example—indicates, to some extent, also direction.

In the above analysis of sentences with an object I adduced examples in which the verb takes a preverb. From data of corresponding sentences with an object it can be made clear that there is an essential difference between sentences construed with modifiers taking a definite and modifiers taking a zero article: namely, a prepositive preverb cannot be used in collocation with a zero-articled object:

**A fiú elolvas újságot.*
**A fiú elvisz újságot.*,

while the construction is correct if the object takes an article:

A fiú elolvassa az újságot.

It is questionable, however, whether the same statement applies to sentences with a modifier as well. In examining our set of examples we shall not go through the various kinds of adverbials but treat the material comprehensively. First sentences with the definite article will be introduced.

SVM.

A fiú # elmegy *a vonattal.*

A fiú # elmegy *az erdőbe.*

A fiú # elmegy *a fáért.*

A fiú # átmegy *a mezőn.*

SMV.

A fiú + *a vonattal* + elmegy.

A fiú + *az erdőbe* + elmegy.

A fiú + *a fáért* + elmegy.

A fiú + *a mezőn* + átmegy.

SVM being the basic variant, the verb receives a mild accent. The peculiarity of SMV lies in the noun with the modifier suffix having possibly an anaphora feature (it has been mentioned or understood in the previous sentences), consequently it precedes the verb though it is not placed at the sentence head which is the position maintained for the subject probably also mentioned before. In the variant starting with adverbial complements the latter have been mentioned or understood from the context.

MVS.

A vonattal # **elmegy** *a fiú.*

Az erdőbe # **elmegy** *a fiú.*

A fáért # **elmegy** *a fiú.*

A mezőn # **átmegy** *a fiú.*

MSV.

A vonattal + *a fiú* + **elmegy.**

Az erdőbe + *a fiú* + **elmegy.**

A fáért + *a fiú* + **elmegy.**

A mezőn + *a fiú* + **átmegy.**

Emphasis is always laid on the verb, and the difference between the two variants concerns the placing of the subject and the verb (as the difference in the previous group concerned the collocation of the modifier and the verb). The variants SMV and MSV agree inasmuch as they both have the verb at the end, but disagree as regards the distribution of the subject and the modifier.

Of the variants opening with the verb, only VSM will be considered here.

VSM.

Elmegy *a fiú* # *a vonattal.*

Elmegy *a fiú* #ᵗ *az erdőbe.*

Elmegy *a fiú* # *a fáért.*

Átmegy *a fiú* # *a mezőn.*

Here again the verb is emphatic, but it is not preceded by another part of sentence.

Since these constructions with the definite article show a full agreement with the objective constructions, there is no need for a more detailed collation of them.

Sentences with zero article will also be discussed in the order of variants. First those starting with the subject will be analyzed. Sentences construed with an adjective plus modifier suffix will be included in the examination because these bear a close resemblance of those without an article:

SVM.

(*)*A fiú* # elmegy *erdőbe.*

A fiú # elmegy *fáért.*

A fiú # elmegy *vonattal.*

A fiú # elmegy *gyorsan.*

(*)*A fiú* # átmegy *mezőn.*

Construed with another modifier of direction, the first sentence is acceptable: *A fiú elmegy iskolába;* the last sentence would be correct if complemented with a different lexeme: *A fiú átmegy hídon (is).,* 'The boy crosses the bridge (also).'

SMV.

A fiú + *erdőbe (iskolába)* + elmegy.

A fiú + *fáért* + elmegy.

A fiú + *vonattal* + elmegy.

A fiú + *gyorsan* + elmegy.

(*)*A fiú* + *mezőn* + átmegy.

The first of these two variants (SVM) appears to be the basic one, while the second presupposes still some other restricting information, for example: *A fiú fáért elmegy, de mást nem hoz.,* 'The boy goes to fetch wood, but he will not fetch anything else.' In this respect it agrees with the objective construction: *A fiú leveleket elvisz, de egyebet nem tesz.*, 'The boy carries letters but he does not do anything else.' In the case of adjectives taking a modifier suffix there is no need for complementary information: *A fiú gyorsan elmegy.*

Essentially the same can be said in connection with the two variants starting with adverbials, although these rather presuppose a contrast:

MSV.

Erdőbe (iskolába) + *a fiú* + **elmegy.**

Fáért + *a fiú* + **elmegy.**

Vonattal + *a fiú* + **elmegy.**

*Gyorsan + *a fiú* + **elmegy.**

Mezőn + *a fiú* + **átmegy.**

MVS.

Erdőbe (iskolába) ⧺ **elmegy** *a fiú.*

Fáért ⧺ **elmegy** *a fiú.*

Vonattal ⧺ **elmegy** *a fiú.*

Gyorsan ⧺ elmegy *a fiú.*

Mezőn ⧺ **átmegy** *a fiú.*

The sentence construed with adjective plus modifier suffix in the MSV group is dubious unless it is complemented with other words while its MVS counterpart is not of a contrastive character. Variants opening with the verb are correct without exception, therefore, only the variant VSM will be introduced:

VSM.

Elmegy *a fiú* ⧺ *erdőbe (iskolába).*

Elmegy *a fiú* ⧺ *fáért.*

Elmegy *a fiú* ⧺ *vonattal.*

Elmegy *a fiú* ⧺ *gyorsan.*

(*)**Átmegy** *a fiú* ⧺ *mezőn.*

The correctness of the last sentence is dubious, but construed with a different lexeme the same construction pattern would be more acceptable: *Átmegy a fiú hídon (is).*, 'The boy crosses the bridge (as well).' The sentence construed with the adverbial modifier of place offers least possibility of a zero articled modifier collocated with a perfective verb. In sentences expressing direction, purpose and manner we find it easier to determine all these without actualizing and concretizing the modifier, but concretizing the verb by means of a preverb.

By retrojecting the preverb, the noun preceding the verb is made emphatic. In the case of sentences construed with the definite article the result will be the same as in sentences with an object: correct sentences will be obtained in which the emphasis is received by the noun preceding the verb:

SVM.

A fiú # *az* **erdőbe** *megy el.*

A fiú # *a* **fáért** *megy el.*

A fiú # *a* **vonattal** *megy el.*

A fiú # *a* **réten** *megy át.*

In the group of the next three variants only the first example is interesting from our point of view, because S has a strong stress.

SMV.

A **fiú** *megy el* # *az erdőbe.*

MVS.

Az **erdőbe** *megy el* # *a fiú.*

MSV.

Az erdőbe # *a* **fiú** *megy el.*

The variant starting with a verb whose preverb is retrojected makes sense in case the preverb denotes a concrete place relation:

VSM.

Megy el *a fiú* # *az erdőbe.*

Megy el *a fiú* # *a fáért.*

Megy el *a fiú* # *a vonattal.*

Megy át *a fiú* # *a réten.*

Notably, the preverb *el* has a locative meaning in these sentences, although it does not considerably modify the semantic content of the verb. Therefore, in variants where direction or purpose is emphasized, the use of the preverb *el* seems to be unnecessary (SVM, MVS).

To sum up: verbs with preverbs are of perfective aspectuality if they have the preverb placed before the verb. Verbs without a preverb and verbs with a prepositive perfectivizing preverb, or less consistently, verbs with a postpositive lexical preverb, and with the same preverb in preposition, form aspectual pairs: the first are imperfective, the second perfective. Sentences containing a verb with a prepositive preverb and an object or an adverbial have peculiar rules of word order: the verb with prepositive preverb is usually focused, not all permutations are correct etc. In addition, the article selection of the complement of the verb is restricted. One of the typological consequences of this is that SVO or SVM (M = modifier) are the basic variants of word order and SOV or SMV as well as OSV and MSV are special variants with a two-member theme (S and O or M). Unfortunately, we have no detailed description of the languages possessing similar phenomena and we can not draw any typological conclusions from the comparison of various languages sharing the same properties, and our observations remain as a contribution to future investigations.

2.2.3. SENTENCES WITH AN OBJECT
AND AN ADVERBIAL

Sentences with an object and an adverbial modifier have already been discussed above (2.1.), although we omitted there to enter into details of the Hungarian data. To make good the omission, I propose here to survey the class of sentences consisting of a verb with an object and an adverbial of place or instrument. Since these sentence contructions consist of four members, the number of possible permutations is twenty-four. However, the scope of this study permits discussion of only two sentences:

A fiú olvassa a könyvet a szobában.
'The boy is reading the book in the room.'
A fiú ceruzával írja a levelet.
'The boy writes the letter with a pencil.'

The first example contains an object with a definite article and an adverbial of place with a definite article. Sentences with an object have the basic word order SVO: *A fiú olvassa a könyvet.*, while those with an adverbial complement have two basic word orders, between which a difference of focus can be observed: *A fiú olvas a szobában. A fiú a szobában olvas.* Let us start analyzing the six variants with the subject at the head of the sentence.

SVOM.
A fiú ‡ olvassa [+ foc.] *a könyvet* + a *szobában.*
SVMO.
A fiú ‡ olvassa [+ foc.] *a szobában* + a *könyvet.*

These two variants are typical of languages belonging to Type 2 inasmuch as the verb is followed by two complements; of the two, SVOM is more usual, this being the basic word order. In the next two variants the verb is wedged in between the two complements:

SOVM.
A fiú ‡ *a* **könyvet** [+ emph.] *olvassa* + a *szobában.*
SMVO.
A fiú ‡ a szobában [+ foc.] *olvassa* + a *könyvet.*

The complement preceding the verb is stressed in both sentences. This kind of word order belongs to the mixed type, because the complement preceding the verb characterizes Type 1 while the complement following the verb characterizes Type 2.

The following two variants represent Type 1: the two complements are situated between the subject and the verb:

SMOV.

A fiú + *a szobában* # *a* **könyvet** [+ emph.] *olvassa.*

SOMV.

A fiú + *a könyvet* # *a* **szobában** [+ emph.] *olvassa.*

The complement preceding the verb is emphatical, while the one following the subject has presumably been mentioned in the preceding context.

There exist twelve such variants which have a complement in the initial position. Such complements' have been mentioned in the preceding text. Languages of Type 2 are characterized by a VS constellation. First I propose to examine constructions starting with an object, then those with an adverbial complement in the initial position:

OVSM.

A **könyvet** [+ emph.] *olvassa* # *a fiú a szobában.*

OVMS.

A **könyvet** [+ emph.] *olvassa* # *a szobában a fiú.*

OMVS.

A könyvet # *a* **szobában** [+ emph.] *olvassa* + *a fiú.*

MVSO.

A **szobában** [+ emph.] *olvassa* # *a fiú a könyvet.*

MVOS.

A **szobában** [+ emph.] *olvassa* # *a könyvet a fiú.*

MOVS.

A szobában # *a* **könyvet** [+ emph.] *olvassa* + *a fiú.*

From the variants symmetrically arranged the identical features are readily discernible. Here it is even more difficult to qualify the degree of emphasis than in other cases: possibly, some of the sentence patterns can be used to express contrast only. The emphatic element may stand at the head of the sentence (in four variants), but it may occupy the second place as well (OMVS, MOVS).

Of the twice three variants characteristic of language Type 1, first of all those beginning with the object will be introduced:

OSVM.

A könyvet # *a* **fiú** [+ emph.] *olvassa* + *a szobában.*

OSMV.

A könyvet + *a fiú* # *a szobában* [+ emph.] *olvassa.*

OMSV.

A könyvet + *a szobában* # *a fiú* [+ emph.] *olvassa.*

Examples beginning with the adverbial modifier:

MSVO.

A szobában # *a fiú* [+ emph.] *olvassa* + *a könyvet.*

MSOV.

A szobában + *a fiú* # *a könyvet* [+ emph.] *olvassa.*

MOSV.

A szobában + *a könyvet* # *a fiú* [+ emph.] *olvassa.*

In two variants the emphasis is placed on the second element, and in four variants on the third. The words preceding the emphatic element have presumably occurred in the preceding context.

In two of the variants opening with the verb, the subject precedes both the object and the adverbial modifier:

VSOM.

Olvassa [+ emph.] *a fiú* # *a könyvet a szobában.*

VSMO.

Olvassa [+ emph.] *a fiú* # *a szobában a könyvet.*

In two of the remaining four variants it is the object and in another two the adverbial complement that follows the verb which is emphatic in every case:

VOSM.

Olvassa [+ emph.] *a könyvet* # *a fiú a szobában.*

VOMS.

Olvassa [+ emph.] *a könyvet* # *a szobában a fiú.*

VMOS.

Olvassa [+ emph.] *a szobában* # *a könyvet a fiú.*

VMSO.

Olvassa [+ emph.] *a szobában* # *a fiú a könyvet.*

The basic order of the sentence analyzed above is SVOM: *A fiú* olvassa *a könyvet a szobában,* where the object comes after the verb and the modifier comes last. This agrees with the basic word order of languages of Type 2, for example English: *Peter is reading the book in the room.* In the variants SOVM, SMOV, and SOMV the noun preceding the verb receives emphasis. In the SMVO variant: *A fiú* a szobában *olvassa a könyvet.*, there is a mild stress placed on the modifier, which follows also from the circumstance that the modifier would receive a focus even if it were not collocated with an object: *A fiú* a szobában *olvas.* SVMO is a less frequent, peculiar order of words: *A fiú* olvassa *a szobában a könyvet.*

The next example: *A fiú ceruzával írja a levelet.* 'The boy writes the letter with a pencil.' will not be analyzed in all its possible variants. Only those variants will be examined in which the subject holds the initial position. The emphatic and contextual variants starting with the object, the adverbial modifier or the verb will be neglected. Even of the variants beginning with the subject only the basic one is interesting from our point of view; here the adverbial of instrument precedes the verb, which again is followed by the object:

SMOV.

A fiú # a ceruzával *írja* + *a levelet.*

It is less customary to place the instrumental after the object, and still less customary to place it after the verb:

SVOM.

A fiú # írja *a levelet* + *a ceruzával.*

SVMO.

A fiú # írja *a ceruzával* + *a levelet.*

If the instrumental takes no article, as is usually the case, the word order remains unchanged:

SMVO.

A fiú # ceruzával *írja* + *a levelet.*

The word order would remain similarly unchanged, if the adverbial modifier of instrument were replaced by a modifier of manner:

SMVO.

A fiú # szépen *írja* + *a levelet.*

'The boy writes the letter beautifully.'

A fiú # örömmel *írja* + *a levelet.*

'The boy writes the letter gladly.'

But what happens if the object does not take an article and so occupies the position before the verb?

SOV.

A fiú # levelet *ír.*

Let us survey the six possible variants resulting from such a change. First of all, the mixed types are interesting:

SMVO.

A fiú # ceruzával *ír* + *levelet.*

SOVM.

A fiú # levelet *ír* + *ceruzával.*

Of the two, SMVO appears to be more natural: in the SMVO variant the modifier receives a lesser emphasis than does the object in SOVM.

In word-order variants typical of languages of Type 1 the noun preceding the verb is emphatic:

SMOV.

A fiú + ceruzával # **levelet** *ír.*

SOMV.

A fiú + levelet # **ceruzával** *ír.*

In fact, a slight contrast can also be felt. Let us also mention two variants characteristic of Type 2:

SVOM.

A **fiú** *ír* # *levelet ceruzával.*

SVMO.

A **fiú** *ír* # *ceruzával levelet.*

In these variants the subject *a fiú* is emphatic. Interestingly enough, the basic word order turned out to be *A fiú ceruzával ír levelet.*, which is a mixed type, whereas if the two complements were to be applied separately, the Type 1 word order would be necessary: *A fiú levelet ír., A fiú ceruzával ír.;* we see here the instrumental gaining the upper hand in the struggle for the position before the verb, relegating the object to the place after the verb. This is the more surprising since we should find it natural if the two complements stayed between the subject and the verb, resulting in the basic word order SOMV, or SMOV: *A fiú levelet ceruzával ír., A fiú ceruzával levelet ír.;* but these sentences, expressing a peculiar contrastive meaning, cannot be regarded as representing basic order.

2.2.4. ON THE WORD ORDER OF SENTENCES CONTAINING A PRONOUN

In Chapter 2.1 we presented a brief survey of word order typology and some aspects of the typology of sentence accentuation (stress, pause). Now we propose to proceed with an examination of questions relating to determination and aspectuality, since these may influence the word order, as appeared from the data on Hungarian word order. Hungarian as well as a number of other languages possess double word order, whose application is dependent on aspectuality and determination. But we focus our investigation on Hungarian, because in this language determination can be expressed by well developed linguistic means which provide ample grounds for comparative analysis of the Slavic languages in particular. In turn, the latter have more developed means for expressing aspectuality. Determination can be expressed by particular means: such are definite pronouns, articles, both determining the noun, but pronouns may stand as substitutes for nouns, adjectival or numerical attributes (for details see 1.1.2.).

Here we confine ourselves to analyzing demonstrative, interrogative and general pronouns and the more important features of articles, and use mainly Hungarian examples, although our statements will be compared with the results of general typology.

In the analysis of the definite pronouns and articles we have to pay special heed to the categories as element of a set, whole and part. The central category here is "definite", which is universally expressed by the demonstrative pronoun, the other means of morphological expression being not universal. The "definite" identifies the individual, if it is in the singular; in the plural, it identifies a set:

A fiú **azt a** *könyvet olvassa.*
'The boy reads that book.'
A fiú **azokat a** *könyveket olvassa.*
'The boy reads those books.'

It is more usual to find a noun before the verb with the demonstrative pronoun rather than without it referring to a situation as expressed in the above examples, because deixis is often combined with emphasis, and the latter requires the position before the verb, although it may stand after the verb as well, in which case, however, the definite article lacking stress is more usual:

A fiú **olvassa** *azt a könyvet.*
A fiú **olvassa** *a könyvet.*
'The boy reads the book.'

Thus, the deictic demonstrative pronoun may take both the stressed position (preceding the verb) and the non-stressed position, the stress falling on the pronoun in the former case (the article cannot receive accent). If a pronoun is used, reference may be made, in addition to the situation, also to the context, but when an article is used, the differentiation is not essential. A peculiar anaphoric pronoun has developed from the demonstrative pronoun in many languages, for instance in Swahili; in Hungarian the two kinds of demonstrative pronouns do not differ morphologically, but the anaphoric variety is unstressed and it is customarily placed at the head of the sentence:

Azt a könyvet a **fiú** *olvassa.*

12

In most cases the object that takes such a demonstrative pronoun is not stressed, although it may receive a stress if so required by the speaker's intention.

Azt a *könyvet olvassa a fiú.*

In such instances, however, a selective contrasting takes place: selection is made among several books, just as in the case of emphatic pointing: one element of a set is pointed out.

A further problem may arise with the use of verbs with a preverb: after a focused, emphatic or contrastive object, the preverb separates from the verb:

A fiú **azt a** *könyvet olvasta el.*

Azt a *könyvet olvasta el a fiú.*

To sum up: both the definite article and the demonstrative pronoun express identification, and in the case of a demonstrative pronoun, reference to the thing implied in the situation (deixis) or to what has been mentioned in the context formerly (anaphora) has an important role.

Notice, however that sometimes the demonstrative pronoun replacing a noun does not have an identifying but an anaphoric function, that is it refers to the preliminary but does not specify the individual thing:

János **bort** *ivott. Péter is* **azt** *iszik.*

'John drank wine. So does Peter.'

'Peter too that drinks.' (lit.)

János **tanító** *volt. Péter is* **az** *lesz.*

'John was a teacher. Peter will be one, too.'

The demonstrative pronoun identifies any noun phrase in the situation or the context, while the personal pronoun identifies the speaker and his partner only in the situation, differentiating one from the other (*én, te* 'I, you') and both from a third person who stands apart from the communication situation, that is, has a negative relation to it, being neither a speaker nor a partner (*ő,* 'he'). It is not by mere accident that in many languages the 3rd person pronoun has its origin in a demonstrative pronoun (such is the case in Russian). The close affinity of the two kinds of pronouns is well brought out by the circumstance that the deictic demonstrative pronoun may be classified according to whether it points to something near the speaker or the speaking partner or to something that is far off. For example, Serbo-Croatian: *ja — ovaj* 'I' — this'; *ti — taj* 'you' — 'that one here'; *on — onaj* 'he — 'that one there'. Of course, such varieties may come about only in case of triple division; such division is not feasible in Hungarian where a dual opposition of *ez — az* 'this' —

'that' prevails. In Slavic, the 3rd personal pronoun is often used anaphorically, and this causes much difficulty for Hungarian pupils:

Russ.:

Petr čital knigu, ja jeje tože čital, ona byla interesnoj.

'Peter read the book, so did I, it was interesting.'

Hung.:

Péter olvasta a könyvet, én is olvastam, igen érdekes volt.

This simple example shows the difference in usage of the two languages: the first anaphoric personal pronoun of Russian is replaced by a personal suffix of objective conjugation in Hungarian, and the second has zero representation.

Structurally, t h e p o s s e s s i v e p r o n o u n may be explained from the personal pronoun, because it stands for a pronominal possessor and its possession at the same time. In Hungarian its origin is detectable in its morphology: *én-é-m* 'I-that-my' (lit.), 'that of me' results in *enyém* 'mine', e.g. *Péter olvasta az enyémet* 'Peter r e a d mine', *Péter* az e n y é m e t *olvasta* 'Peter m i n e read' (lit.). The word order rules of the sentences with an object expressed by a possessive pronoun are similar to those with an object with a demonstrative pronoun. The Russian *moj* 'my, mine' does not yield to further parsing; on the other hand, the 3rd person possessive pronoun is the genitive of the personal pronoun (Russian: *jego*, Hungarian: *ö-v-é* 'he-that-his' (lit.), 'that of he', 'his').

From the point of view of sentence order, the personal pronoun is interesting also because in some languages its use is obligatory (for instance in English and German), while in others (Hungarian and some Slavic) the unemphatic pronominal subject is often omitted when it can be inferred from the personal suffix of the verb. The objective conjugation of Hungarian makes it possible to omit the unemphatic pronominal object as well, and in some Slavic languages the unemphatic personal pronominal complement in the accusative and dative may be expressed by enclitic pronouns placed after an emphatic word, while in others the 'full' pronoun occupies an unemphatic position. In the following Slavic sentences an unemphatic personal pronoun is required by the Russian, and an enclitic pronoun by the Serbo-Croatian usage.

Hung.

Ismerem. '(I) know (him).'

Russ.

Ja jego *znaju.*

'I him know' (lit.).

12*

Sr.-Cr.:
Znam ga.
'(I) know him (encl.)'.
These sentences also show that the pronominal subject is more frequently used in Russian than in either Hungarian or Serbo-Croatian. Pronominal subject is obligatory in Hungarian in case of emphasis or contrast:
Ki ismeri Jánost? Én **ismerem.**
'Who knows John?' 'I know him.'
Én **ismerem** *Jánost. Te* **nem,** or **Én** *ismerem Jánost.* **Nem** *te.*
'I know John, you do not.'
On the other hand, the pronoun should not be used when two verbs next to each other are of the same person:
Hung.:
Te *elmégy haza, (*te) lefekszel.*
'You go home, (*you) go to bed.',
even languages susceptible of pronominal use (like Russian) will omit the pronoun in such constructions. Not even in case of a change of person is the pronoun necessary:
Hung.
Ismered Jánost? Ismerem.
'Do you know John? Yes, I do.', rather than:
Ismered Jánost? Én ismerem.,
unless the speaker wishes to emphasize the pronoun.

By way of comparison with nominal object we mentioned that the object taking a demonstrative pronoun pursuant to the rule of nouns with a definite article usually came after the verb, although not infrequently it preceded the verb when in an emphatic position. The same is true of the personal pronominal object, but it should be mentioned that the stress is often laid on the verb even when it is preceded by an object:
Hung.:
A fiú őt **ismerte.**
'The boy **knew** *him.*'
A fiú **őt** *ismerte.*
'The boy knew **him.**'
In the second example it is supposed that *őt* has an anaphoric function. The pronoun that comes after the verb can be more readily omitted, provided there is no doubt whom the discarded pronoun represents:
A fiú **ismerte** *(őt).*
'The boy knew him.'

Not for a moment do we entertain the idea that by presenting the above analysis we have solved the problems connected with word order and sentence stress in Hungarian sentences which include a "definite" pronoun. Our aim was to give indication of the difficulties a pupil with a foreign mother tongue is likely to face when learning Hungarian. We had no room to discuss in detail the reverse situation, although a comparison of Hungarian with a foreign language from the point of view of a Hungarian pupil learning a foreign language would be equally important for an adequate understanding of the question.

Of the personal and demonstrative pronouns with a "definite" feature it may be stated that they are universal and historically primary. Furthermore, the possessive pronoun is etymologically associated with the personal pronoun (Cf. Majtinskaja 1969, 284—8).

To sum up: the use of pronouns requires the introduction of further rules. They were demonstrated on Hungarian examples. The deictic demonstrative pronouns prefer a stressed position: in Hungarian this is before the verb, but secondarily they may be placed after the verb and not be stressed. The anaphoric demonstrative pronouns are placed primarily in sentence initial position without stress, but secondarily they may be followed by the verb and be stressed. The personal pronouns are often in zero form, i.e. omitted; in case of emphasis or contrast they are in a stressed position, before the verb. They may be used without stress, but this is specific and not obligatory.

Hungarian applies the objective conjugation when the object is expressed by a demonstrative, a possessive or a personal pronoun, except where 1st and 2nd person pronouns are involved, for instance: *A fiú lát engem.*, and *A fiú lát téged.* 'The boy sees me., The boy sees you.' Objective conjugation, however, is used in Hungarian in connection with certain kinds of interrogative, indefinite, negative and general pronouns (such as pronouns with *-ik* particle: *melyik, valamelyik, semelyik* etc.), which are generally regarded as "indefinite" pronouns, and which are expressive of a specific identification. A better understanding of this usage makes it indispensable to survey briefly the general problems connected with them.

As regards the class of "indefinite" pronouns the interrogative pronoun is diachronically primary and indefinite. Negative pronouns, as well as certain kinds of general pronouns, derive from the interrogative pronoun in a considerable number of languages, like the Hungarian *ki, valaki, senki, bárki,* 'who, somebody, nobody, anybody', although indefinite and general pronouns may come about in another way as well (Cf. Majtinskaja 1969, 285—6). The specific feature of interrogative pronoun is "question", that of the negative is "negation", and of the general "totum" ("everything"). The interrogative pronoun is emphatic, and as such it claims a word order in which it may receive due stress, for example:

Ki *látta a fiút* ? *A fiút* **ki** *látta?*
'Who saw the boy?'
Melyik *könyvet olvasta János?* *János* **melyik** *könyvet olvasta?*
'Which one of the books did John read?'
No other word order is possible for them:
Ki a fiút látta (meg)?
Melyik könyvet János olvasta?
In contrast, the indefinite pronoun is unaccented but the noun it is collocated with may be stressed.

A fiú **olvasott** *valamit.*
'The boy read something.'
A fiú **olvasott** *valami könyvet.*
'The boy read some book.'
A fiú **olvasta** *valamelyik könyvet.*
'The boy read one of the books.'
The object preceding the verb is emphatic, though the pronoun in the same collocation is not:

A fiú valami **könyvet** *olvasott.*
'The boy read some book.'
A fiú valamelyik **könyvet** *olvasta.*
'The boy read one of the books.'
This is very specific in Hungarian, because the pronouns, adjectives and numerals preceding the noun head are stressed. The substantival pronoun placed in an emphatic position cannot be stressed:

A fiú valamit **olvasott.**
'The boy was reading something.'
Applied as a noun or a determiner, *valami* 'some(thing)' is non-definite, while *valamelyik* 'some(one)' signifies an unidentified element of a definite set, and therefore it has a selectively identifying function. The same can be said of the other pronouns ending in *-ik* (for instance, *melyik* 'which one'). The indefinite article corresponds to both kinds of indefinite pronouns: it may designate either an unknown individual or a member of a set given in a situation, and the difference between the two comes to be neutralized just

as the difference between deictic and anaphoric pronouns is neutralized when these pronouns are replaced with a definite article.

A fiú olvasott egy **könyvet.**
'The boy read a book.'
*Egy könyvet a fiú olvasott.
'The boy read one of the books.'

The element to be selected from a set is better known than the unknown individual. Another question is how many elements a set consists of. The Russian *kotoryj* 'which one' permits of selecting between two things; the Hungarian *melyik* 'which one' allows a choice among an unspecified number of elements of a given set (Majtinskaja 1969, 277). A further question of typological investigation is connected with a situation where an element put up for selection from a set known to both parties may be known to one of the parties, for example: *Elhoztam neked egy könyvet.*, where the speaker knows the book and is able to identify it. This is not enough in the case of definiteness, where both parties have to know the thing: *Elhoztam neked a könyvet.* 'I have brought the book for you.' Nevertheless, the forms of objective conjugation may be used in connection with an identified set without the elements specified.

The use of general and negative pronouns requires specific principles and rules in sentences consisting of a verbal predicate and of a preverb. The examination of general pronouns with "totum" feature and that of negative pronouns with "nil" feature must be extended to other parts of speech with the same feature. The transitory features between "totum" and "nil" are also relevant to word order.

From sentences with preverbs we will examine those which contain a constituent with a "totum" feature. But what we are primarily interested in are not sentences with an object and an adverbial but sentences with only one of them, whether object or adverbial, for sentences with both an object and an adverbial can be understood from these.

The nominal phrase will assume a "totum" feature if it comprises a pronoun or a pronominal adverb (such as *minden* 'all', *az összes* 'same', *mind* 'same', *mindenhová* 'everywhere', etc.), or an adjective with a similar feature: *egész* 'whole'. Collocated in one phrase or one unit delimited by pauses, the adverbial, the object and even the subject with such a feature will effect the preverb so that it holds a prepositive position and cannot be placed postpositively: *A fiú # minden házba bement.* 'The boy entered every house.' *A fiú # minden leckét megírt.* 'The boy has done all his homework.' *Minden fiú # megírta a leckét.* 'Every boy did the homework.' Of course, a verb may take more than one constituent of this kind: *Minden fiú megírt # minden leckét + minden osztályban*. 'Every boy did every homework in every class'. Only the sentence with an adverbial will be examined here from the point of view of its possible permutations:

SVM.

A fiú # bement *minden házba (mindenhová)*.
'The boy entered every house (everywhere)'.

*A **fiú** ment be # minden házba (mindenhová)*.
'It is the boy that entered every house (everywhere)'.

SMV.

A fiú # minden *házba* (mindenhová) *bement*.

MVS.

Minden *házba* (mindenhová) *bement # a fiú*.

MSV.

(*)Minden *házba (mindenhová) + a fiú +* bement.
*Minden házba (mindenhová) # a **fiú** ment be*.

VSM.

Bement *a fiú # minden házba (mindenhová)*.

VMS.

Bement *minden házba (mindenhová) # a fiú*.

Sentences with prepositive preverbs are generally acceptable, but with postpositive preverbs only those constructions are possible in which there is no constituent with a "totum" feature placed together with the verb in one and the same phrase. (Cf. SVM, second example; MSV, second example.) In principle, the variant VSM ought to be correct in the case of a postpositive preverb as well, but the verb would denote progressive action had the preverb been so placed; since the boy cannot enter every house at the same time, such a construction would be incorrect. (Although even with a plural subject such constructions are clumsy: *Mentek be a fiúk minden házba*.) If the preverb is prepositive, then the complement *minden (házba)* may also receive some emphasis.

If both constituents are characterized by a "totum" feature, a postpositive preverb cannot be used.

SVM.

**Minden fiú ment be # minden házba*.

MSV.

**Minden házba # minden fiú ment be*.

"Nil" feature constitutes the opposite of "totum" feature. The former is expressed by negative pronouns, pronominal adverbs (*semmi* 'nothing', *semelyik* 'none', *egyetlen sem* 'same', *senki* 'nobody', *sehova* 'nowhere', etc.). Permutation of the above locative sentence in the corresponding negative form, construed with a negative pronoun, will result in the following variants:

SVM.
A fiú # **nem** *ment be* + semelyik *házba sem.*
'The boy did not enter any of the houses.'
SMV.
A fiú # **semelyik** *házba sem ment be.*
MVS.
Semelyik *házba sem ment be* # *a fiú.*
MSV.
(*)*Semelyik házba sem* # *a* **fiú** *ment be.*
VSM.
Nem *ment be a fiú* # semelyik *házba sem.*
VMS.
Nem *ment be semelyik házba sem* # *a fiú.*
The preverb is always separated from the verb, which is natural since it is always preceded by the particle, *nem* or *sem*. In the variants SVM, VSM and VMS emphasis is placed on the negated verb, in SMV and MVS on the modifier, and in MSV on the subject. (This last sentence is completely acceptable if the negative pronoun *egyik* . . . *sem* is used: *Egyik házba sem a fiú ment be.*)

It is interesting to note that in the case of words like *kevés* 'few' and *nem elegendő* 'insufficient' with "minimum" feature the preverb will be placed postpositively, and considered as having a "nil" feature:

SVM.
(*)*A* **fiú** *ment be* # *kevés házba.*
SMV.
A fiú # **kevés** *házba ment be.*
'The boy entered few houses.'
MVS.
Kevés *házba ment be* # *a fiú.*
MSV.
Kevés házba # *a* **fiú** *ment be.*
VSM.
*Ment be a fiú # *kevés házba.*
VMS.
**Ment be kevés házba* # *a fiú.*

In the variants SMV and MVS emphasis has been laid on the modifier, in SVM and MSV on the subject. Prepositive preverb would not make much sense where a sentence part other than the modifier would be emphasized: *A fiú bement kevés házba.*, (*)*Kevés házba a fiú bement.*

"Few" here designates an insufficient degree, which is not the same as nothing but is still not enough. This places it on a level with *semmi* and it is again this quality that contrasts it with other quantifiers meaning 'few', for instance, with the pronoun *néhány* 'a few, some':

SVM.

A fiú + néhány *házba* + bement.

'The boy entered a few houses.'

A fiú (csak) # **néhány** *házba ment be.*

SMV.

A fiú # bement *néhány házba.*

A **fiú** *ment be* # *néhány házba.*

MVS.

Néhány *házba* # **bement** *a fiú.*

Néhány *házba ment be* # *a fiú (csak).*

MSV.

Néhány *házba* + *a fiú* + **bement**.

Néhány *házba* # *a* **fiú** *ment be.*

Variants with postpositional preverb need no explanation: the element before the verb is stressed. In variants with a prepositional preverb, besides the preverb the word *néhány* 'some' also receives emphasis if collocated with a prepositive preverb, provided it stands before the verb in the given variant that is in an emphatic position. The situation is nearly the same when the numeral *sok* 'many' with "maximum" feature substitutes the pronoun *néhány*.

SMV.

A fiú + sok *házba* + bement.

(*)*A fiú* # **sok** *házba ment be.*

SVM.

A fiú # bement *sok házba.*

A **fiú** *ment be* # *sok házba.*

MVS.

Sok házba # **bement** *a fiú.*

Sok *házba ment be* # *a fiú.*

MSV.

Sok házba + *a fiú* + **bement**.

Sok házba # *a* **fiú** *ment be*.

There is some doubt as to the correctness of some sentences; in any case the context in which to use them ought to be made clear, but this is outside the scope of our study.

Let us now examine types of sentences construed with an adverbial complement, then with an object and subject and having a "totum" feature (for instance *minden, mind*), or a "nil" feature (for instance *egyetlen* 'single', *soha* 'never', *sohasem* 'never', *egyáltalán nem* 'not at all'), or a "minimum" feature (for instance *ritkán* 'seldom', *néha* 'sometimes'), and finally a "maximum" feature (for instance *gyakran* 'often', *nagyon* 'very much'). Since we have seen examples of locatives before, let us begin with the adverbial modifier of time. Sentences with adverbials having the features "totum", "nill", "minimum" and "maximum" will be examined first.

SMV.

A fiú # minden nap (mindig) *megírta* + *a leckét*.

'The boy did the homework every day'.

A fiú # **egyetlen** *nap (soha) sem írta meg* + *a leckét*.

'The boy never did the homework.'

A fiú # **ritkán** *írta meg* + *a leckét*.

'The boy seldom did the homework.'

A fiú # **néha** *írta meg* + *a leckét*.

'Sometimes the boy did the homework.'

A fiú + néha + megírta *a leckét*.

'Sometimes the boy did the homework.'

A fiú + gyakran *megírta* + *a leckét*.

'The boy often did the homework'.

(*)*A fiú* # **gyakran** *írta meg* + *a leckét*.

'The boy often did the homework.'

A fiú # **gyakran** *nézte meg* + *az óráját*.

'The boy often looked at this watch.'

Of the adverbial modifiers of manner, the modifiers of degree can be fairly precisely defined:

SMV.

A fiú # teljesen *befejezte* + *a munkát*.

'The boy has fully performed the work.'

A fiú # **egyáltalán nem** *fejezte be* + *a munkát.*
'The boy has not finished the work at all.'
Az ág # **alig** *tört le.*
'The branch is hardly broken.'
Az ág # **kicsit** *tört le.*
'The branch is slightly broken.'
Az ág # nagyon *(teljesen) letört.*
'The branch is very broken.' (lit.)
*Az ág # *nagyon tört le.*
'The branch is very broken.' (lit.)

The words *sok* 'much' 'many', *gyakran* 'often', *inkább* 'rather' prefer verbs with prepositive preverbs, being semantically related to words with a "totum" feature.

Sentences with an object have been discussed above, yet it is worth while presenting a full spectrum of them:
SOV.
A fiú # minden *leckét megírt.*
'The boy has written all the homework.'
A fiú # **semmi** *leckét sem írt meg.*
'The boy has written none of the homeworks.'
A fiú # **kevés** *leckét írt meg.*
'The boy has written few homeworks.'
A fiú # **néhány** *leckét írt meg.*
'The boy has written some homeworks.'
A fiú + néhány *leckét* + megírt.
'The boy has written some homework.'
A fiú # sok *leckét megírt.*
'The boy has written many homeworks.'

Also the subject may go with adjectives possessing the analyzed features:
SV.
Minden *tanuló* # *elment.*
'All the pupils have gone.'
Egyetlen *tanuló sem ment el.*
'None of the pupils has gone.'
Kevés *tanuló ment el.*
'Few pupils have gone.'
Néhány *tanuló ment el.*
'Some of the pupils have gone.'

Néhány tanuló + elment.
'Some of the pupils have gone.'
Sok *tanuló ment el.*
'Many pupils have gone.'
Sok *tanuló + elment.*
'Many pupils have gone.'
The pauses are marked by the signs # and + only approximately. In reality there are several grades their proper use being dependent on the volume of the sentence, the rhythm of speech, but mainly on the dynamics of the accent. In spite of these factors, I have chosen to apply only these signs. Even they are useful for the formulation of some basis rules. Rule 1 states that a longer pause is to be used before an emphatic element; Rule 2, in turn, prescribes a shorter pause before a milder emphasis, except in cases where the emphasis falls on the first element of the comment which will induce a longer pause; and Rule 3 determines that an emphatic phrase should be followed by a short pause.

2.3. Russian and English Word Order Contrasted with Hungarian

2.3.1. SENTENCES WITH AN OBJECT

Sentences with an object both in English and Russian belong to the SVO type, but while English permits only SVO, that is the basic word order variant, in Russian—as in Hungarian—all six variants are correct.

Let us begin by examining the basic word order of English whose articled variants can be more closely compared with those of Hungarian. The subject may take a definite as well as an indefinite article, and the object may similarly take either a definite or an indefinite article. (Both parts of sentence are expressed by singular nouns.):

SVO.

(i) *The boy is reading the letter.*

A fiú olvassa a levelet.

(ii) *The boy is reading a letter.*

A fiú olvas egy levelet.

(iii) *A boy is reading the letter.*

Egy fiú olvassa a levelet.

(iv) *A boy is reading a letter.*

Egy fiú olvas egy levelet.

The subject takes a definite article in variants (i), (ii), the object is definite in (i) and indefinite in (ii). In variants (iii) and (iv) the subject has an indefinite article, while the object has a definite one in (iii) and an indefinite one in (iv). In connection with Hungarian sentences it has been stated in the preceding chapter that in case of non-emphatic accentuation the mild sentence stress falls on the predicative phrase constituting the second part of the sentence: when an indefinite object is involved it is slightly stressed, while in the case of a definite article the emphasis is rather transferred onto the verb. Similarly in English it is the predicative phrase that receives accent. When the subject is definite the indefinite object is accented, and when the object is definite the verb receives the accent, just as in Hungarian. Nevertheless, what applies to both languages is that when a definite object is involved the object is left unaccented rather than the verb accented; that is, it is rather a case of an unaccented object than of an accented verb.

I have stated in connection with the indefinite subject of Hungarian that when expressed with an indefinite article *(egy fiú)* it is not an altogether unknown boy that is being spoken of but one of some known boys. Such an interpretation is feasible in English as well, since *A boy* comes up as the topic of the sentence (Cf. Firbas 1966, p. 243 ff).

In Hungarian too, a variant construed with an unarticled object is possible, but only in certain contexts with special lexemes, when the subject is definite and the verb accented:

(*)*A fiú* **olvas** *levelet.*

A fiú **olvas** *szakszöveget.*

'*The boy reads (can read) special text.*' (lit.)

In English, unarticled object in the singular mostly results in an incorrect sentence:

**The boy is reading letter.*

(In plural, of course, it is correct to omit the article: *The boy is reading letters,* but here we are dealing only with sentences with a singular object.) Hungarian has SOV word order when the object takes no article:

A fiú levelet olvas.

When the object takes no article, it is irrelevant whether the object of the sentence is definite or indefinite; therefore, sentences so constructed may well be interpreted as having either a definite or an indefinite object. The object with zero article is acceptable from the point of view of communication, it is not determined, and it is precisely for this reason that English usage does not tolerate objects with zero article in the singular. From this it follows that the Hungarian object with zero article can be translated into English as an object with either a definite or an indefinite article (plural object being disregarded here). English is thus able to impart more information than Hungarian because the Hungarian sentence so construed does not make it explicit whether the object is a definite or an indefinite one.

A fiú levelet olvas.

The boy is reading the letter.

The boy is reading a letter.

Here the problems of Russian sentence constructions have to be mentioned. Russian has no articles. This circumstance does not mean that it cannot express the "definite" feature, for Russian also possesses the universal means of expression of the definiteness category, which is the demonstrative pronoun. But the definite pronoun gives expression only to emphatic definiteness:

Etot mal'čik čital knigu.
Ez a fiú olvasta a könyvet.
'This boy has read the book.'
Mal'čik čital etu knigu.
A fiú ezt a könyvet olvasta.
'The boy has read this book.'

When definiteness is unessential, in which case only articles, definite or indefinite, are involved in languages that do have articles, no pronoun is generally used in Russian. We have to say "generally" since we may encounter instances where Hungarian can manage well enough with an article while Russian needs a pronoun.

The Russian examples to follow may have five Hungarian counterparts each if the markedly emphatic variants are left out of consideration:

Mal'čik čitajet pis'mo.
 (i) *A fiú olvassa a levelet.*
 (ii) *A fiú olvas egy levelet.*
 (iii) *Egy fiú olvassa a levelet.*
 (iv) *Egy fiú olvas egy levelet.*
 (v) *A fiú levelet olvas.*

When, however, the sentence stress is also taken into account, and it is supposed that the indefinite object is slightly emphatic or the verb receives an accent because of the definite character of the object, the picture will be as follows:

Mal'čik čitajet pis'mo.
 (ii) *A fiú olvas egy* levelet.
 (iv) *Egy fiú olvas egy* levelet.
 (v) *A fiú* levelet *olvas.*
Mal'čik čitajet *pis'mo.*
 (i) *A fiú* olvassa *a levelet.*
 (iii) *Egy fiú* olvassa *a levelet.*

Accordingly, the written sentence detached from its environment corresponds to five Hungarian counterparts, disregarding sentences with a strong emphasis. At the same time, the spoken sentence proper corresponds to two or three sentences only, which differ from one another mainly in respect of the subject's definite character. In Hungarian the definite character of the subject can be expressed in an explicit way, therefore, word order has a less important part in this language. In Russian the definite, more exactly anaphoric, object may be placed at the head of the sentence while the indefinite subject appears at the end of the sentence.

Knigu čital mal'čik.
'The book was read by a boy.'

Since mainly that object is placed at the head of the sentence which has been mentioned in the preceding context, this phenomenon belongs to the sphere of contextual variants. Here it is mentioned only because the Hungarian article makes it possible for the definite object to stand at the beginning of the sentence even when the object is mentioned:

(Tegnap kaptunk egy érdekes könyvet.) Egy fiú olvassa a könyvet.
'(Yesterday we received an interesting book.) A boy is reading the book.'

Variant:

(Tegnap kaptunk egy érdekes könyvet.) A könyvet egy fiú olvassa.
'(Yesterday we received an interesting book.) The book is being read by a boy.'

In Russian we have to apply the second variant:

(Včera my polučili interesnuju knigu.) (Etu) knigu čitajet mal'čik.

This circumstance warns us that only a thorough comparison of the whole system of actual allocation, that is an analysis of the entire set of variants, may result in a complete picture of the phenomenon examined. Furthermore, besides the active forms the passive ones also require to be analyzed. But first let us cast a cursory glance at the emphatic variants.

In analyzing Hungarian sentences we have distinguished three kinds of emphases: (1) mild emphasis characterizing the basic word order; (2) in all correct variants it is possible to lay a strong emphasis on any of the elements in order to express a contrast; such a strong emphasis presupposes a real or possible contradiction between statements; (3) if the emphasis occurs in a word order other than the basic one, a contrary sentence is not necessary, although a certain contextual correlation is implied. In Hungarian sentences containing an object with an article, emphasis has been shown to prevail in the SOV, OSV and the VSO, VOS variants.

In English only the basic variant is possible; therefore, besides mild emphasis only strong emphasis can be observed. Let us look at sentences with a strongly emphatic subject:

13

(i) *The* **boy** *is reading the letter.*
A **fiú** *olvassa a levelet.*
(ii) *The* **boy** *is reading a letter.*
A **fiú** *olvas egy levelet.*
(iii) *A* **boy** *is reading the letter.*
Egy **fiú** *olvassa a levelet.*
Fiú *olvassa a levelet.*
(iv) *A* **boy** *is reading a letter.*
Egy **fiú** *olvas egy levelet.*
Fiú *olvas egy levelet.*

In Hungarian sentences likewise, emphasis is laid on the subject that goes with the definite or indefinite article, but in connection with the latter we have also shown the variant with zero article *(Fiú...)*, which is obligatorily strongly emphasized and indefinite at the same time. In English the indefinite article of the subject is ambiguous here, as is that of the object above: it may signify both the "indefinite" and the "non-determined" subject.

Of the emphatic variants of the four English sentences only those have been analyzed in which the subject receives emphasis; it is obvious, however, that the verb too, both main and auxiliary, may be strongly emphasized:

The boy **is** *reading the letter.*
The boy is **reading** *the letter.*

In the first example it is implied that someone has previously spoken of the boy not reading the letter; in the second it is implied that someone thinks the letter is not being read by the boy but that he is doing something else with it. In Hungarian the verb consists of one single element; therefore, in both cases, the principal verb is accented:

A fiú **olvassa** *a levelet.*

In turn, Hungarian may use a different word order as well in the first case:

A fiú **nem** *olvassa a levelet.*
'The boy is not reading the letter.'
Olvassa *a fiú a levelet!*
'The boy *is* reading the letter!'

In this example the verb is placed at the head of the sentence; thereby the opposition of the verbs is more explicitly expressed. By separating the verb from the object emphasis has been concentrated on the verb.

Admittedly, we have dealt rather extensively with cases in which the verb receives a strong emphasis, and our reason for doing so is that in the previous chapter no mention was made of the possible antecedents of strong emphasis of this kind. The object too, may be emphasized in English, whether it takes a definite or an indefinite article:

The boy is reading the **letter.**

The boy is reading a **letter.**

In the corresponding Hungarian sentences, however, the verb is not followed but preceded by the object:

*A fiú olvassa a **levelet.**

A fiú a **levelet** *olvassa.*

*A fiú olvas egy **levelet.**

A fiú egy **levelet** *olvas.*

It should be mentioned that the latter example reads much better if its object takes the zero article:

A fiú **levelet** *olvas.*

This sentence is correct even if the letter has been identified in the preceding context, in which case only the opposition of the object is important:

A fiú olvassa *a levelet.*

A fiú a **lapot** *olvassa!*

'The boy is reading the newspaper!'

A fiú **levelet** *olvas!*

'It is a letter that the boy is reading!'

Let us add, by way of completion, a few Russian sentences. In the Russian basic variant there are three possibilities of generating a strong emphasis:

Mal'čik *čitajet pis'mo.*

A **fiú** *olvassa a levelet.*

'The *boy* is reading the letter.'

Egy **fiú** *olvassa a levelet.*

'A *boy* is reading the letter.'

Fiú *olvassa a levelet.* 'Same'

The first example may be paralleled by three Hungarian sentences, if the variations of articles going with the object are left out of consideration, which would result in further parallelisms, except for the conditionally correct pattern: (*)*Fiú olvas levelet.* Let us examine the strong emphasis laid on the object, disregarding here the emphasis on the verb:

Mal'čik čitajet **pis'mo.**

A fiú a **levelet** *olvassa.*

A fiú egy **levelet** *olvas.*

A fiú **levelet** *olvas.*

13*

Unlike in English, a SOV word order can be readily used in Russian in order to make the object emphatic:

Mal'čik **pis'mo** *čitajet.*

It is questionable which of the three Hungarian variants corresponds to this Russian example. In my opinion, it best agrees with the one with the definite article, although an object with zero article is also imaginable in case the species of the object needs to be determined:

A fiú a **levelet** *olvassa.*

A fiú **levelet** *olvas.*

It should be examined, however, what kind of preceding context may have zero article for the object.

There exists in English a special construction with which to make the object emphatic. Let us first accentuate the subject: *the/a boy*, then the object: *the/a letter* of the sentence *The/a boy is reading the/a letter.*, by means of the construction "It is . . . *that/who*".

It is the boy who is reading the letter.

It is a boy who is reading the letter.

It is the letter that the boy is reading.

It is a letter that the boy is reading.

In the first two examples the subject taking the definite then the indefinite article, in the second two the object with the definite and indefinite article have been accentuated by the aid of the emphatic construction "It is. . . that". The sentence following the introductory words "It is" remains unchanged SVO in the first two instances, while OSV is used in the second pair of sentences:

(It is the boy) who is reading the letter.

(It is a boy) who is reading the letter.

(It is the letter) that the boy is reading.

(It is a letter) that the boy is reading.

Translated into Hungarian, similar and equally correct word-order patterns will result:

(Az a **fiú***), aki olvassa a levelet.*

(Az [egy] **fiú***), aki olvassa a levelet.*

(Az a **levél***), amit a fiú olvas.*

(Az [egy] **levél***), amit a fiú olvas.*

Here attention should be paid to the circumstance that English usage applies the OSV word order characteristic of the contextual variants of SOV type instead of OVS which might be expected as natural on the basis of the SVO basic word order. In Hungarian too, the OSV contextual variant is given, apart from the basic word order variant (SVO)

SVO:
(a fiú) aki olvassa a levelet.
OSV:
(a levél) amit a fiú olvas.

It is interesting that the Hungarian examples do not have the OVS word order, whereas this variant is characteristic of the SVO type. It appears that both English and Hungarian have recourse to word order patterns not characteristic of their respective types (SVO), when it comes to cleft sentences with a contextual word order. All this, however, raises the question of contextual variants.

With the last statement we have entered the sphere of contextual variants where first the Russian data offer themselves for analysis. Both the OVS and the OSV variants are possible in Russian, provided one of the elements receives a strong emphasis. Let us begin examination of the OVS variant.

OVS.
Pis'mo čital **mal'čik.**
Pis'mo **čital** *mal'čik.*
Pis'mo *čital mal'čik.*

In initial position the object may be definite, as it may take a zero article in Hungarian; for the moment let us construe the subject with the definite article:

(*)*A levelet olvasta a* **fiú.**
(*)*Levelet olvasott a* **fiú.**
A levelet **olvasta** *a fiú.*
Levelet **olvasott** *a fiú.*
A **levelet** *olvasta a fiú.*
Levelet *olvasott a fiú.*

Here the strong emphasis lent to the final subject is strange in Hungarian since it usually places the accent on the object preceding the verb—in an emphatic position—, while in Russian the subject following the verb is stressed in the SVO word order type customarily allocated the emphatic element to the place after the verb.

In the OSV variant also there is a possibility of accentuating certain elements by laying strong emphasis on them, although we do not think it important to list them here. Instead, we wish to call attention to the circumstance that Hungarian lays primary stress on the subject:

A levelet a **fiú** *olvasta.*
Levelet a **fiú** *olvasott.*
This is possible also in Russian:
Pis'mo **mal'čik** *čital.*
Thê question arises here whether we find an optimal correspondence—optimal from the point of view of usage—between the elements of identical word order and emphasis of the two languages, since in Hungarian OSV word order is used when the subject requires emphasis in a construction beginning with a contextual object, while in Russian—in our opinion—OVS is correct in such instances:
OSV:
A levelet a **fiú** *olvasta.*
OVS:
Pis'mo čital **mal'čik.**
It is only in rare cases and under peculiar contextual conditions that Hungarian places a strong emphasis on the subject standing in final position, and in Russian it is a rare occurrence for the subject standing before the verb to receive a strong accent:
A levelet olvasta a **fiú.**
Pis'mo **mal'čik** *čital.*
This type of word order prevails in Hungarian in the case of double contrast:
A levelet olvasta a **fiú,** *a lapot a* **lány.**
'The boy read the *letter*, the girl read the *newspaper*.'
This is possible also in Russian. But double contrast can be noticed also in the case of OSV: *A levelet a* **fiú** *olvasta, a lapot a* **lány.**, and, therefore, this is not a sufficient explanation for the secondary nature of the Hungarian OV*S* word order. We should rather look for the reason in the field of typology: in the system of Hungarian word order and accentuation, primary stress is lent to the element preceding the verb in the contextual variant.

In contextual word order the most important element of the sentence cannot receive a mild accent. When analyzing the Hungarian data, we found that in the OSV word order the subject receives only a medium emphasis in the case of an object with a definite article, while the object is strongly emphasized in the OVS variant:
OSV.
A könyvet a **fiú** [+ emph.] *olvassa.*

OVS.

A **könyvet** [+ contr.] *olvassa a fiú (nem a lapot).*

It is for this reason that in the case of an OSV word order there is no absolute need for a parallel contrastive sentence to be involved. In Russian the OVS variant does not stipulate the use of a contrary sentence:

(Nedavno pojavilas' novaja kniga. Etu) knigu čitajet mal'čik.

Dealing with contextual variants we have to speak about the passive voice too. Hungarian can manage quite well without a paradigmatic use of the passive voice which is fairly typical of English. Nor has it developed in Hungarian with such a degree of consistency as it has in Russian where it can be formed from imperfective verbs by means of the formative suffix *-sja,* and from perfective verbs in the first place, by means of an auxiliary verb combined with a passive past participle. Russian grammarians do not as a rule regard the passive voice as a paradigmatic usage, although A. V. Isačenko (1960, 362 ff.) has established two sets of paradigmatic expressions in the passive voice. Let us examine a few Russian examples:

(i) *Kniga čitalas' mal'čikom.*

Kniga čitajetsja mal'čikom.

Kniga budet čitat'sja mal'čikom.

In the first column we have imperfective verbs; in the second perfective verbs:

(ii) *Kniga byla pročitana mal'čikom.*

Kniga pročitana mal'čikom.

Kniga budet pročitana mal'čikom.

The first set of examples indicate incompleted action in past, present and future tenses; the second completed actions in all three tenses.

Hungarian also provides two ways of expressing the passive voice (a third being by periphrasis): either by means of formative suffixes or, in the case of perfective verbs, by means of an adverbial participle. It is an important difference between the two languages that the Hungarian passive construction does not tolerate the use of the agent:

(i) *A levél iródott.*

'The letter was written.'

A levél iródik.

'The letter is being written.'

A levél iródni fog.

'The letter will be written.'

(ii) *A levél meg volt írva.*
   A levél meg van írva.
   A levél meg lesz írva.

It is scarcely accidental that Hungarian has possibilities similar to Russian for the formation of the passive voice. Also in Hungarian, perfectivization has reached a markedly advanced stage: the imperfective base verb *(ír)* may be contrasted with its derivative, a perfective preverb *(megír)*, while imperfectivization is comparatively underdeveloped in respect of the aspectual pair *(kiír→φ)* which cannot be formed from verbs taking a lexical preverb. (For more details, see Dezső 1980) From the point of view of word order analysis it is important to note that the patient as the subject of the sentence *(pis'mo, levél)* occupies the first place in the sentence, while the agent *(mal'čik, fiú)* is either missing or if given, is placed in final position in the SVO-type languages. The location of the patient-object and agent is the same as in the OVS word order: patient—verb—agent, but the verb receives a different form of expression: it takes a peculiar formative suffix by which it is transformed into the passive voice. Another difference between an inverted word order with the object in the initial position and a passive construction, is that the passive construction is not obligatorily emphatic while in the former we usually have either an emphasis or a case of contrast:

Hung.
   (i) *A levél íródik.*
   (ii) *A levelet a* **fiú** *írja.*
Russ.
   (i) *Pis'mo pišetsja (mal'čikom).*
   (ii) *Pis'mo piset* **mal'čik**.
   (i) 'The letter is being written (by the boy).'
   (ii) 'It is the boy who is writing the letter.'

By means of the passive construction we may bring about a word order opposed to the active voice where the patient stands in the initial position, this being an indispensable element of the sentence, and the agent, if any, takes the last place.

A detailed analysis of the passive voice in English throws up quite a number of problems. Undoubtedly, paradigmatic columns may be generated from the passive forms by analytical procedure; thus from the morphological aspect English passive voice appears to be most solidly established. On the other hand, when it comes to applying English passive forms in the sentence we come across several stipulations: just think of the difficulties that are likely to arise when we try to carry out the analysis of all possible forms of verbs of sentences containing a subject with definite or indefinite article, or an object definite or indefinite. Many sentence constructions will prove unidiomatic or incorrect when analyzed from the combined points of view of verbal aspect and tense and the definiteness of the subject and object. To this have to be added the semantic features of the verb. We cannot enter into a deeper examination of these questions. Yet in demonstration of the difficulties, it will perhaps be instructive to adduce a few examples.

Passive sentences are correct in general if the subject takes the definite article, while with the indefinite article they are not always correct. This is due to the circumstance that the passive sentence is of a contextual nature as concerns its word order, which means that the patient precedes the agent, although in the given context there is no need for an anticipatory statement containing the anaphoric subject. In general, the subject taking the definite article is usually correct, and so it is with the indefinite article in the second example to follow, if there is an adequate situation:

(i) *The book is being read by a professor* (or: *the professor*).

(ii) (*)*A book is being read by a professor* (or: *the professor*).

Native speakers rejected certain constructions in which both the object and the agent took an indefinite article and the verb was placed in the past tense:

*A book was read by a boy.

In connection with other verbs they accepted such sentences:

A cat was being chased by a dog.

Possibly it has not escaped the reader's attention that we omitted to mention the Hungarian formative suffix *-tatik, -tetik* when speaking about ways of expressing the passive construction in Hungarian. In our opinion to use this element is contrary to present-day Hungarian usage.

Of the contextual variants those are left to be considered which start with a verb: VSO and VOS; in these the verb is placed at the head of the sentence where it receives emphasis both in Hungarian and in Russian. We have adduced only sentences containing a subject with the definite article. (We use past tense in this case, because morphologically there is a coincidence of the present-tense form and the imperative mood: *olvassa*.)

VSO.

Čítal *mal'čik pis'mo.*

Olvasta *a fiú a levelet.*

Olvasott *a fiú egy levelet.*

(*)**Olvasott** *a fiú levelet.*

The use of either the definite or the indefinite article with the object would result in correct constructions, but sentences construed with zero articled object seem doubtful in both instances. Nevertheless it may be correct in connection with some other lexeme in the present tense, provided a contrast of meaning is involved:

Olvas *a fiú újságot.*

'The boy (usually) does read a newspaper.'

But unlike the sentences given above, here a non-concrete action is spoken of. Each of the elements used may take a strong emphasis in Russian:

VSO.

Čital *mal'čik pis'mo.*

Olvasta *a fiú a levelet.*

Čital **mal'čik** *pis'mo.*

Ólvasta a **fiú** *a levelet.*

Čital mal'čik pis'mo.

Olvasta a fiú a **levelet**.

The primary emphasis, however, is placed on the verb. In Hungarian such an emphasis on the noun is a rare occurrence since in it the usual place of the emphatic noun is before the verb.

The VOS variant is less frequent in Russian, coming up possibly in certain peculiar context only:

Čital *pis'mo mal'čik.*

Olvasta *a levelet a fiú.*

Olvasott *egy levelet a fiú.*

Olvasott *levelet a fiú.*

This kind of word order is not unidiomatic in Hungarian, provided the verb receives a strong emphasis as in the VSO variant mentioned before. Of course, a contrastive strong emphasis may be applied in this variant too:

Čital *pis'mo mal'čik.*

Olvasta *a levelet a fiú.*

2.3.2. SENTENCES WITH AN ADVERBIAL

In the domain of sentences with an adverbial those modifiers (M) will be examined here in whose case relations of place, direction, and purpose are expressed by means of a noun and the modifier of manner by an adverb. The following English, Russian and Hungarian sentences will be analyzed, all three representing the SVM variant:

SVLoc.
The boy is walking in the forest.
Mal'čik idet lesom.
A fiú megy az erdőben.
SVDir.
The boy is walking to the forest.
Mal'čik idet v les.
A fiú megy az erdőbe.
SVFin.
The boy goes for the wood.
Mal'čik idet za drovami.
A fiú megy a fáért.
SVMod.
The boy is walking quickly.
Mal'čik idet bystro.
A fiú megy gyorsan.

First the variants beginning with the subject will be introduced. In order to approach the English basic variant of SVM word order, we have to remember that in English the subject as well as the modifier of place and direction may take the definite or the indefinite article; zero article is possible only in connection with the modifier of purpose, which in turn has no variant with the indefinite article, *wood* being a mass noun:

SVLoc.
The boy is walking in the forest.
The boy is walking in a forest.
A boy is walking in the forest.
A boy is walking in a forest.
SVDir.
The boy is walking to the forest.
The boy is walking to a forest.
A boy is walking to the forest.
A boy is walking to a forest.

SVFin.

The boy went for the wood.
The boy went for wood.
A boy went for the wood.
A boy went for wood.

In Hungarian the adverbial complement is absolutely correct with the definite article, which corresponds to *the* in English; the adverbial complement taking the indefinite article *a* can be paralleled in Hungarian by a modifier taking the indefinite article *egy*, or taking no article at all (zero article). With emphases indicated, the sentences will read as follows:

SVLoc.

A fiú sétál *az erdőben.*
A fiú sétál *egy erdőben.*
(*)*A fiú* sétál *erdőben.*

The indefinite article *egy* may be possible, although less convincing in the given example, while the following sentence with the noun *ösvény* 'path' would make sense: *A fiú* megy *egy ösvényen.; further, the word order SVLoc does not suit the adverbial complement with zero article, unless the subject is given a strong emphasis *(A fiú* sétál *erdőben).*

Nearly the same applies to the adverbial modifier of direction:

SVDir.

A fiú megy *az erdőbe.*
A fiú megy *egy erdőbe.*
**A fiú* megy *erdőbe.*

The adverbial modifier of purpose (Fin) can go either with a definite or with zero article in Hungarian, too.

A fiú megy *a fáért.*
A fiú megy *fáért.*

In the preceding Hungarian sample sentences the places where the emphases should be laid have already been shown so as to avoid possible misunderstanding; the same has not been done in the English sentences where both the modifier and the verb may receive emphasis. Let us take the variant with the definite article:

SVLoc.

The boy is walking in the forest.
The boy is walking *in the forest.*

In the Hungarian variants of the SVM type the verb can be made emphatic unconditionally, as has been shown above, while the adverbial complement may be stressed preferably when it goes with the indefinite article *egy:*

SVLoc.

A fiú sétál egy erdőben.

'The boy is walking in the forest.'

A fiú sétál egy parkban.

'The boy is walking in a park.'

From this we might draw the conclusion that it is not the SVM but the SMV variant that is primarily used to make the adverbial complement emphatic; but this variant is impossible in English:

SLocV.

A fiú az erdőben *sétál.*

A fiú erdőben *sétál.*

SDirV.

A fiú az erdőbe *megy.*

A fiú erdőbe *megy.*

SFinV.

A fiú a fáért *megy.*

A fiú fáért *megy.*

Adverbial complements construed with the definite article always result in correct sentences while the correctness of those with zero article is dependent on the specific meaning of the noun used with the adverbial function: *fáért* is correct, but *A fiú erdőbe megy.* is less correct, while *A fiú iskolába megy.* denotes a customary type of action and is, therefore, correct.

The variants SVM and SMV are correct not only in Hungarian but also in Russian. The SVM variant affords possibilities of making slightly emphatic both the adverbial complement and the verb:

SVLoc.

Mal'čik idet lesom.

Mal'čik idet *lesom.*

SVDir.

Mal'čik idet v les.

Mal'čik idet *v les.*

SVFin.

Mal'čik idet za drovami.

Mal'čik idet *za drovami.*

The Hungarian counterparts of these Russian sentences may be in every case construed with the definite article, as seen in the examples given above, with the difference that for accentuating the verb, Hungarian prefers the SVM, and for accentuating the adverbial complement, the SMV word order. If the adverbial modifier takes no article, only the modifier can be stressed in Hungarian SMV word order. This variant is also possible in Russian, but if it is used with no strong, contrastive accent, then it provides an opportunity for focus or medium emphasis to be placed only on the adverbial complement, while the verb may receive only strong accent and only in certain contextual relations marked (*) in the following examples:

SLocV.

Mal' čik **lesom** *idet.*

(*)*Mal' čik lesom* **idet.**

SDirV.

Mal' čik **v les** *idet.*

(*)*Mal' čik v les* **idet.**

SFinV.

Mal' čik **za drovami** *idet.*

(*)*Mal' čik za drovami* **idet.**

Markedly strong, contrastive accentuation will not be examined here in any of the languages involved, since the rules relating to this question have been discussed in the chapter on sentences with an object. On the other hand we have to survey the sentences construed with an adverb, for which the variant SVMod is given in all three languages:

SVMod.

The boy is walking quickly.

A boy is walking quickly.

A fiú megy *gyorsan.*

Egy fiú megy *gyorsan.*

The variant *A fiú megy* gyorsan is also correct, although the mild emphasis of the adverb is more adequately expressed by the SModV variant, unlike in English where only the SVMod variant may be applied with the stresses laid on both the verb and the modifier, SModV being incorrect:

SVMod.

The boy is walking *quickly.*

The boy is walking quickly.

A fiú megy *gyorsan.*

SModV.

A fiú gyorsan *megy.*

In Russian SVMod variant both elements may receive accent without a contrastive emphasis:

SVMod.

Mal'čik idet bystro.

Mal'čik idet *bystro.*

Variant SModV is also correct and both elements may receive mild accent:

SModV.

Mal'čik bystro idet.

Mal'čik bystro *idet.*

The analysis of the contextual variants opening with an adverbial modifier may be commenced with English examples where MSV variant is possible (which was impossible in connection with sentences with an object). In the examples examined the initial position is occupied by an adverbial complement taking the definite article *the*. This, however, presupposes a suitable preceding context which may induce the emphasis to be laid on the adverbial modifier:

(Not in the meadow but) in the **forest** *the boy is walking.*

In the **forest** *the boy is walking (when he hears a sound).*

Still less bound is the adverbial modifier of purpose (Fin) which can more easily be put at the head of the sentence, for instance in the following context:

(I have left my luggage here.) For this **luggage** *I have come back.*

It is a remarkable typological occurrence that English, belonging to the SVO or SVM type of languages, has MSV as its contextual variant which in turn is typical of the SOV and SMV languages. On the evidence of the basic word order, MVS would be sooner expected as a contextual variant in English. Here again we are faced with the same mixed type to whose existence in Hungarian we have pointed above; the SVO basic variant is associated with the contextual variant of the SOV type. As for the Hungarian phenomenon, it can be explained by the circumstance that in it the original SOV type has not been fully replaced by the SVO variant, the change having affected only the basic variant so far. Thus the contextual variant represents the earlier type:

Phase I	Phase II	Phase III
SOV	SVO	SVO
OSV	OSV	OVS

So the process of development has reached the second phase, as against German which has a half bound (half-free) word order and in which development has attained the third stage: SVO. *Der Knabe schreibt den*

Brief. OVS. *Den Brief schreibt der Knabe.* English used to have the same trend of development, but it stopped before it was fully realized, owing to the wear and tear of inflexional suffixes fossilizing the word order in English. In sentences with an object only the SVO variant is possible, except the emphatic variant OSV *(It is the letter that the boy is reading.)* whose word order is characteristic of the second stage of development. There are somewhat ampler opportunities open in respect of sentences with an adverbial complement: apart from the variant SVM, MSV is also feasible without the construction type *It is...that* being involved. The variants SVM and MSV are also characteristic of the second phase.

Hungarian uses both variants of contextual word order beginning with an adverbial modifier: in MSV the subject, in MVS the adverbial complement receives accent:

LocSV.

Az erdőben a **fiú** *megy.*

DirSV.

Az erdőbe a **fiú** *megy.*

FinSV.

A fáért a **fiú** *megy.*

ModSV.

Gyorsan a **fiú** *megy.*

Only those sentences have been introduced here in which adverbial complements are construed with the definite article *a(z)*; those with zero article are similarly acceptable, as shown above. The MVS variant results in sentences as follows:

LocVS.

Az **erdőben** *megy a fiú.*

DirVS.

Az **erdőbe** *megy a fiú.*

FinVS.

A **fáért** *megy a fiú.*

ModVS.

Gyorsan *megy a fiú.*

The difference between the variants MSV and MVS is that while in the former it is the subject, in the latter it is the adverbial complement that receives emphasis; in addition, the emphasis laid on the subject often requires a strongly contrastive complementary statement but that of the adverbial modifier usually does not mean contrast but a simple emphasis being involved. As against this, the situation is different with sentences containing an object, in the OSV variant:

A levelet a **fiú** *írja.*

where the subject usually has only an emphasis, while in the OVS variant a contrastive emphasis is placed on the object:

A **levelet** *írja a fiú.*

Strong emphasis differs from plain emphasis in the context that the former presupposes a contrary statement.

In Russian too, it is the MVS variant that is apt to stand by itself, without the aid of a contrary statement. Depending on the context, the individual elements may receive emphasis, first of all, it would seem, the adverbial:

LocVS.
Lesom idet mal'čik.
DirVS.
V les idet mal'čik.
FinVS.
Za drovami idet mal'čik.

Variants starting with the verb are correct in Russian and Hungarian, but not in English. There are two variants. In Russian VSM is correct without a strong emphasis, and the correct distribution of the emphasis is to the verb:

VSLoc.
Idet *mal'čik lesom.*
VSDir.
Idet *mal'čik v les.*
VSFin.
Idet *mal'čik za drovami.*
VSMod.
Idet *mal'čik bystro.*

The VMS variant is less frequently used, in special contextual conditions. Without a strong emphasis only the verb can be accented:

VLooS.
Idet lesom mal'čik.
VDirS.
Idet v les mal'čik.
VFinS.
Idet za drovami mal'čik.

14

VModS.

Idet bystro mal'čik.

In the sentence *Idet bystro mal'čik* it is possible to lay emphasis on the verb, or rather it is customary to make it emphatic. Hungarian may obtain correct sentences in both of the variants, primarily in the VSM, as shown by the following examples:

VSLoc.

Megy *a fiú az erdőben.*

VSDir.

Megy *a fiú az erdőbe.*

VSFin.

Megy *a fiú a fáért.*

VSMod.

(*)**Megy** *a fiú gyorsan.*

As in the VSM so also in the VMS variant it is the verb in initial position that receives the primary emphasis:

VLOcS.

Megy *az erdőben a fiú.*

VDirS.

Megy *az erdőbe a fiú.*

VFinS.

Megy *a fáért a fiú.*

VModS.

(*)**Megy** *gyorsan a fiú.*

While the variant VMS is a rare occurrence and comes up in exceptional contexts only, the variant VSM is likely to be needed every now and then. Sentences with an adverbial complement have rather strong contextual implications in both variants, and are, therefore, less frequently used.

Part 3

Theoretical and Methodological Problems of Typology

3.1. On Theoretical Questions

INTRODUCTION

It is useful to clarify some notions connected with the topics discussed in details in order to avoid possible misunderstanding and to set the problems in a broader framework.

I shall not discuss the complex relationship between ideology and linguistics. This would be outside the scope of this discussion, but the questions raised by me have a direct or indirect relationship to philosophy, and through philosophy to ideology. The concepts both of ideology and philosophy can be understood in various ways and even when they are interpreted in the same way, different aspects can be emphasized. It seems to be useful therefore to clarify those aspects of these notions which have particular relevance for the discussion that follows. Ideology is "a set, a system of ideas and views in politics, law, philosophy, ethics, esthetics, or religion costituting a superstructure over basis. Ideology is determined by economic relationships as by its final cause but it is relatively independent. This means that the laws of the development of economy affect ideology, not directly, but through a chain of other factors. Ideology depends on the set of ideas and views accumulated earlier; on the affect of other ideologies with which it co-exists" (see Kondakov 1975, 189).

Linguistics may be directly or indirectly connected with different aspects of ideology but only those connected with philosophy are relevant in this paper. The concept of philosophy differs in various schools. Its Marxist definition is well known (Kondakov 1975, 639) and it is not necessary to repeat it here. Since the most general laws of the development of nature, of human society, of thinking and of cognition are the subject matters of philosophy, "dialectic materialism is the universal methodology underlying all special methodologies which apply and elaborate their own more specific methodologies" (Kondakov 1975, 348). The methodologies of various sciences have very much in common as well as having their own specific features. This common core of methodological problems is a special field of investigation. It is more specific than the universal methodology of philosophy but is more general than the methodology of individual sciences, in our case, that of linguistics. It is apparent that the methodology of linguistics has an important philosophical aspect and here lies its connection with ideology.

As in any field of ideology it is relatively independent but also depends on the common core of ideas and views accumulated earlier. It is this aspect of the methodological foundations of linguistics that is usually highlighted. But the elaboration of philosophical—methodological problems "has particular importance in transitional periods when linguistics in general and, especially theoretical linguistics, is at a critical period" (Panfilov 1977b, 3). The examination of the methodological problems of general typological, comparative linguistics is even more important because its basic problems have not yet been elaborated.

The philosophical questions of linguistics can be divided into two cycles: ontological and methodological problems (Cf. Panfilov 1977b, 4—14, for detailed discussion). Among the questions of methodology Panfilov mentions those which are of special interest in the discussion that follows: problems concerning the adequacy of linguistic theories to language and the relationship between methodology and methods in linguistics. "In particular, one of the important aspects of this problem is the question as to the role of formal methods in the investigation of language and their relationship to substantive *(soderžatel'nyj)* analysis, questions concerning the limitations of application and that of heuristic value of formal methods in linguistics" (Panfilov 1977b, 11).

In the following discussion I shall examine the linguistic side of some fundamental methodological problems of comparative linguistics with regard to philosophy, especially to the methodology of science.

3.1.1. ON THE NOTION OF COMPARATIVE LINGUISTICS

One can find in any handbook on general linguistics chapters on the classification of languages, on the comparison of languages dealing with the comparison of unrelated and related languages. The comparison of unrelated languages may have no restriction concerning the languages to be compared and will result in typological comparative linguistics serving as a basis for various kinds of restricted comparison. Contrastive linguistics must be founded on general typology and usually compares only two languages. Its optimal procedure takes into consideration the typological characteristics of the given languages based on general typology (Cf. 3.4). The comparison of related languages has two aspects: the identification of elements: sounds, morphemes and lexemes and the comparison of linguistic structures. For a long time the first aspect was dominant, and the second aspect has been coming to the foreground only in this century. In my view, the comparison of the structure of related languages can be carried out with respect to their typological characteristics. Comparison can be restricted to a linguistic area including both related and unrelated languages. It highlights structural similarities.

What has been said so far implies an assumption: general typology dealing with universals and types can and, if it is necessary, must be complemented by the characteristics of individual languages and the latter are based on the former. No restriction of typological comparison is accepted: typology cannot be restricted to types because they cannot be explained without an underlying invariant and typology must 'go back' to individual languages in order to check itself and be useful for the 99 % of linguistic investigation.

In my examination of the notion 'comparative linguistics', I did not speak of the classification of languages, I mentioned it only as a possible title in a handbook, and a misleading one, I must add. Linguistic comparison cannot be confined to a specific procedure, to one stage of research: to classification. It compares linguistic structures and assumes theory as complete and exact as possible in order to explain the unity and diversity of human language. Both completeness and exactitude are important, but I must emphasize completeness, because it has been disregarded in linguistic theory.

Typology as general comparative linguistics studies human language in its unity and diversity. This explains the necessity of the reconsideration of the relationship between synchrony and diachrony. Today, most linguists are far from their rigorous separation suggested by Saussure. But typology needs more than that: it studies human language from the earliest reconstructed stages of proto-languages to present-day languages and requires a panchronic view of language combining synchrony and diachrony in a dialectic unity suggested by Jakobson. Such a view meets the optimum and maximum requirements of Marxist philosophy of science. Svidersky (1965, 137 ff.) differentiates extensive structures "characterized by common relations of coexisting states" and intensive "structures characterized by states that follow one another". The former are studied from synchronic, the latter from diachronic aspect in linguistic typology. Panchronic typological analysis studies synthetizing structures. Svidersky demonstrates them by space, time and space-time structures of physics and says: "one of the objectives of the analysis of extensive and intensive structures is to find their underlying structure, in comparison with which they appear only as individual aspects or specific phenomena. The study of the general characteristics of synthetizing structures of this kind is a new objective of great theoretical significance. Methods of solving the problem have not yet been made clear; it is doubtless, however, that the common, obligatory criterion of any synthetizing structure is the dialectical unity of constancy and mutability, in which the leading and determining role is played by mutability" (Sviderskij 1965, 139).

It is clear that such a synthetizing, panchronic view of human language gives deep insights into the nature of human language but its requirements are very high, maybe, too high even at present. It was only Jakobson's phonological theory that could cope with it.

3.1.2. ON THE RELATIONSHIP BETWEEN METHODOLOGY OF SCIENCE AND THE THEORETICAL FOUNDATIONS OF TYPOLOGY

On the Methodology of Science. Typology, as general comparative linguistics, studies the system of human language, formulates its regularities on various levels of abstraction: rules of individual languages, those of types and universals. Linguistic typology has its theoretical foundations which I shall examine later. Here, it suffices to say that it has specific characteristics of an individual science, those of linguistics and characteristics more general, shared with those branches of other sciences which make comparison and study types. The latter belong to a higher level of abstraction, to that of methodology of science. There is a set of specific problems of typological comparison common to sciences dealing with types: general sociology, psychology etc. (Hempel and Oppenheim 1936, Hempel 1965, Greenberg 1973). Linguistic typology compares various linguistic systems and faces problems common to many sciences studying systems. They are, or, rather, must be generalized in system theory on the level of methodology of science.

Thus, methodology of science generalizes the problems of individual sciences, formulates its theories, the results of which can be used by these sciences in the formulation of their theoretical foundations. The degree of elaboration of various problems is different, e.g. the questions of type are less studied than those of system. Nevertheless, methodology of science can help comparative linguists, typologists in the clarification of their problems. The specific problems of individual sciences cannot be neglected: linguistic systems, linguistic types have also their own characteristics. At present, the emphasis on common properties of various sciences is more important.

Methodology of science has its partial theories. They can more or less be independent of any philosophical paradigm. Marxist philosophers point out that system theory proposed by von Bertalanffy (Bertalanffy 1968) is compatible with Marxism but cannot be identified with it. Dialectical materialism itself can serve as a basis for the elaboration of a system theory or any other theory of the same level (Cf. Lektorovskij and Švyrev 1971, 150). The theory of typology had been elaborated on the basis of logical positivism (Hempel—Oppenheim 1936, Hempel 1965), but a Marxist theory of typological comparison can be formulated.

Thus, theories of methodology of science are interposed between those of individual sciences and philosophy. This middle level of generalization may be lacking and a direct contact between individual science and philosophy be established. In the twenties and thirties R. Jakobson leaned directly upon phenomenology when characterizing the system of language (Jakobson 1972, for Jakobson's relation to phenomenology see Hollenstein 1973) and the Marxist analysis of the system of language has not been based on Bertalanffy's system theory (Solntsev 1971). Nevertheless, the development of methodology of science will result in theories of middle level based on various philosophical schools or more or less independent of them.

There are requirements that any theory must meet. Hempel criticised the first variant of system theory because of the lack of a clearly formulated theory (Hempel 1951). Marxist philosophers pointed out that even its later variant does not produce a "theory in the proper sense of the word, only a certain sum of methodological and substantive propositions" (Sadovskij 1972, 82). Therefore, it has a hypothetical character and it can produce but a heuristic model (Lektorovskij and Švyrev 1971, 150). Its structure, objective and metalanguage were also critically examined (Sadovskij 1972).

The questions of type were examined by Hempel and Oppenheim (1936) criticised by Greenberg (1973) and Hempel reconsidered this problem in the sixties (Hempel 1965). Nevertheless, typological comparison has not been elaborated in detail. It is necessary to elaborate its problems on the level of methodology of science based on Marxist philosophy by joint efforts of philosophers and experts of various sciences. But, there are important statements in Hempel's article that seem to be acceptable to scholars with any philosophical background: the examination of type cannot be restricted to classification, it must reach the level of theory and result in typological constructs. This has important implications for the study of linguistic typology: it cannot discard theory, it must have theoretical foundations, construct theories on high level of abstraction. When doing this, it must take into consideration the recent development of linguistic theory. These are not only requirements of methodology of science, they are dictated also by the development of linguistic typology, as I will show later.

Since typology has been an empirical discipline, this new stage of its development requires the reconsideration of its foundations: theory, method and laws in typology. Their study can be carried out by only taking into consideration the recent theoretical foundations of linguistics, but the specific problems of typology neglected by linguistic theory necessitate the use of the results of methodology of science.

On the Theoretical Foundations of Typology. Since the theoretical foundations of typology highlight the theoretical foundations of linguistics from the viewpoint of typology, one should clarify the latter in order to arrive at the special problems of typology.

Theoretical foundations of linguistics consider and reconsider the fundamental problems of language and linguistics. They contain statements about the system of language as a whole, about its functions, about its sub-systems as parts of the whole system, about theory and method in linguistics, about linguistic laws, about synchrony and diachrony, etc. Statements and principles of the theoretical foundations are based on a general theory of science which is understood by me as having ontological, gnoseological and logical components, i.e. not reduced to the problems of logic. I am not going to analyze such basic notions of the theory of science as system, structure, element, function and their application to language and reflection in various linguistic theories.

The theoretical foundations of linguistics were outlined by Humboldt, a part of them was clearly formulated by Saussure, and refined and developed by the Prague scholars, especially by Jakobson (Cf. Jakobson 1972). They are in constant change and development. Any new theory of language has to deal with the questions of the theoretical foundations of linguistics. I do not think that a detailed justification of the notion of theoretical foundations is required (Zvegincev 1973, 233 ff. for illustration).

The theoretical foundations of linguistics are not identical with any specific theory of language. 'Specific theories' of language formulate the problems of theoretical foundations in their own way and usually do not cover all of them. Specific theories formulated with maximum exactness and capable of shaping the approach to linguistics are called 'paradigmatic theories' (Kuhn 1970). There are mutual stimuli between theoretical foundations and specific or paradigmatic theories. Theoretical foundations of linguistics change under the influence of paradigmatic theories. Paradigmatic theories attempt to cover more and more of the theoretical foundations. One of the criteria for the evaluation of paradigmatic theories may be according to their coverage of theoretical foundations. (Another one is the coverage of a substantive base of linguistics, see below.)

Besides the theoretical foundations of linguistics and specific or paradigmatic theories there is a set of partial theories attempting to explain the sub-systems of language (e.g. aspect, case, theme–rheme theories). They have two faces: they are theories, but they explain substantive generalizations of limited scope. Partial theories are usually disregarded by the theoreticians of language. Since they are theories, they are based on the theoretical foundations of linguistics. At present, typological research focuses on sub-systems and hence partial theories are essential for it.

The empirical base of linguistics contains the facts of individual languages and those of typology based on the former. If the empirical base of typology will be described and explained, this will result in substantive foundations. In my opinion, its optimal form is a substantive universal grammar. However, the scope of substantive universal grammar and that of substantive foundations may not be the same: the former may not cover the whole of substantive foundations.

The distinction between empirical base and substantive foundations has not been formulated explicitly in theoretical linguistics. I think its relevance is apparent to typologists. It is supported by general methodological considerations. Marxist philosophy differentiates between empirical and rational knowledge. "Empirical knowledge is knowledge obtained on the basis of experience *(opyt)* the results of which are transformed into the forms of primary generalizations of various degrees, first of all by means of such procedures as induction and analogy. Empirical knowledge is completed by rational knowledge which acts together with empirical knowledge, on all levels of the cognitive process, and applies notional devices, in the process of investigation, and transforms the results into deeper generalizations" (see for a detailed discussion Kondakov, 1975, 685).

It is clear that the difference between empirical base and substantive foundations is relative because no empirical knowledge exists in pure form but the present stage of typological research calls for deeper generalizations, for substantive foundations.

The empirical base and the empirically oriented partial theories are closely connected. They can be opposed to the theoretical foundations of linguistics and paradigmatic theories. The notion of substantive foundations is essential for typology because they have to explain the general laws governing the empirical base incorporating the results of partial theories. It is clear that substantive foundations of typology are very important both for the theoretical foundations of linguistics and for specific, paradigmatic theories because they must consider them.

The theoretical foundations of typology highlight the theoretical foundations of linguistics from the point of view of typology and complete them with the specific problems of typology. The theoretical foundations of linguistics are or, maybe, should be abstract; they disregard the various aspects of language. It was H. Paul who specified the theoretical foundations of linguistics of his time in order to make them applicable to the historical comparison of related languages. I think it is necessary to fulfil the same task in regard to typology, of the synchronic and diachronic comparison of the languages of the world. The clarification of the problems of typology is necessary for two reasons: to establish typology as a well-organized aspect of linguistic investigation in its own right and to adopt the results of typology into empirical, exact and formalized linguistic descriptions. I think that one of the main difficulties in the incorporation of the results of typology into linguistic descriptions is its shapeless, diffuse state. Since typology is one of the aspects of various sciences, the study of the theoretical foundations of typology should account for the methodological problems of typology in the framework of the methodology of science. The latter is needed for another reason also: the status of typology has not been clarified and the theoretical foundations of linguistics simply do not give satisfactory answers to various specific problems of typology. Hence comes a rather natural conclusion: one should ask for an answer on a level underlying the foundations of individual sciences in the methodology of science.

What are the problems of the theoretical foundations of typology? Instead of a full list I shall mention those I am going to comment on in the analysis that follows (3.1. and 3.2.).

(i) Typological investigation raises the problems of theory, its level of exactitude and scope of application.

(ii) The analysis of the method will deal with the analytic and synthetic approaches.

(iii) The problems of laws in typology will be examined with special regard to the rules and principles underlying a set of rules and to their typological status (universals, types).

3.1.3. ON THE EMPIRICAL BASE AND PARTIAL THEORIES: ORDERING OF MEANINGFUL ELEMENTS AND TOPIC-COMMENT THEORY

The empirical evidences of sub-system typologies show that they meet at several points; a greater or lesser number of connections can be stated to exist between them, which sooner or later, makes it necessary to account for them within a broader framework, e.g. the relationship between aspect and word order types (in Hungarian), the role of aspect in the use of the ergative (in Georgian), or in the use of the partitive (in Balto-Finnish) and the relationship of aspect and case systems to determination, etc. (see Part 1 and 2). If the theories of two or more sub-systems can be restated within a theory of a larger scope, this makes it possible to assert more general principles and to explain more types. Thus, one arrives at one of the most difficult problems of present-day typology, to complex types: certain typological phenomena occur jointly in various parts of the system of language. It is necessary to find certain explanatory principles which are general enough to encompass the various sub-systems of language and to fit in a more general theory.

Thus, in typology, the investigation of sub-systems necessarily leads up to a large set of substantive generalizations effecting grammar and, beyond it, the whole language system, and to the integration of partial theories covering an ever-growing part of the empirical base.

An example is in place here which is capable of illustrating the whole process, but, thus far, it merely refers to possibilities.

Greenberg, in his classic article (1963), outlined the word order types of simple sentences and the implications existing between them and the connection between the word order of the sentence and the attributive nominal group as well as the place of prepositional, postpositional elements joining the nouns. The explanation of the interrelationships of various word order variants and of various types can be carried out within the framework of a theme-rheme theory. Then theme-rheme theory, originally explaining the positions that words occupy in the sentence, has turned out to be in direct contact with the theory and typology of sentence structure and with typological invariant structure. Therefore, it exerts an influence on the selection of terms of the invariant structure and, through it, of syntactic theory (for instance, the theory must contain a category like 'subject', 'agent' or a feature like 'active'). Thus, theme-rheme theory in the framework of a more general theory of communicative organization of sentence can be applied in the explanation of ergative and nominative types of sentence structure: the active and ergative languages have subtle morphological means to express the central part of the theme: the *subjectum*, or deep subject. The nominative languages mark the central part of the rheme: the *objectum* or deep object (Part 1). Theme-rheme theory affects the selection of case suffixes and hence the case systems. Thus, theme-rheme theory has a large scope of application. Here I shall confine myself to the problems of order and examine an other direction of its extension: from sentences to word groups and to the order of morphemes.

Both the word order of subordinate clauses and that of non-finite constructions can easily be derived from the sentence; furthermore, it is instructive from the diachronic typological angle, for the word order of the latter is more conservative, e.g. in German and in English the word order type of subordinate clause may differ from that of the main clause and represent a more archaic typological stage. Theme-rheme theory, however, can and must be extended to explain the word order of a new collocation, that of the attributive nominal group, on the level of the noun phrase.

Thus, the range of application of the theme-rheme theory expands, its principles will be valid on a larger scale, but, at the same time, they will be more 'vacant': the order of the sentence and the noun phrase will be connected only by entirely general principles. Such are the two principles of the order of the *rectum* and *regens: regens post* and *ante rectum:* for example SOV and AN can be observed in Hungarian on the basis of the principle *regens post rectum*, e.g. *levelet ír* 'letter writes', *szép lány* 'nice girl'. That such principles may be created will be understood if the relationship between the sentence and the noun phrase can be demonstrated by showing that the latter can be derived from the former and that it can be parallelled by clauses and non-finite constructions. The rules of word order reflect the degree of dependence of these structures: a more or less specific variant of sentence word order is characteristic of subordinate clauses, the word order of constructions containing non-finite forms is also linked more closely with that of the sentence, whereas the word order of attributive nominal groups is considerably more independent. Moreover, we could follow these lines up to the problems of the word, but that would lead us too far (Part 2).

I think that the given example has clearly demonstrated that the connecting and explaining of typological facts has to lean on a more and more comprehensive theory.

The greater validity substantive generalizations achieve, the more it becomes obvious that they themselves can be derived and fit into a theory of a larger scope. Although the theory accounts for the generalizations, it cannot be deduced from them; moreover, they often come into being independently of each other. Word order typology and theme-rheme theory have come to existence independently of each other and the process of their linking is now going on.

The distance between theory and substantive generalizations is not always so great, but there is, undoubtedly, some gap between them. The theory serving to give explanations of generalizations necessarily contains more than what is manifest in the generalization. There is an essential methodological difference between the two: generalizations represent induction, whereas the principle derived from the hypothetical construct is deductive. The former is not regarded as a law by Shaumjan who represents an extreme position (Šaumjan 1971, 125).

It is apparent from the above analysis of the general tendency of typological research that the aim of theoretically oriented investigations is the creation of an interpreted theoretical system on various levels of abstraction. It has to satisfy some basic requirements of the methodology of science by "(a) specifying a list of characteristics with which the theory is to deal, (b) formulating a set of hypotheses in terms of those characteristics, (c) giving those characteristics an empirical interpretation, which assigns to the theory a specific domain of application, and (d) as a long-range objective, incorporating theoretical systems, as a special case, into a more comprehensive theory" (Hempel 1965, 171).

Let us consider briefly these requirements in connection with the above example. In the case of a typologically relevant topic-comment theory, if we want to apply it to the sentence, we obviously need characteristics like 'comment' or 'rheme', 'topic' or 'theme', 'focus' and 'emphasis', which have no universally accepted specification and empirical interpretation for the time being and difficulties must be faced at this point, even though the various conceptions have an essential intersection in this respect.

The inaccuracy of the characteristics makes difficult the verification and application of hypotheses formed with them as well as the empirical interpretation of terms. Further difficulties arise if a theory which claims to be valid for sentences of any language, i.e. for a vast area of application, is illustrated only by the data of only a few languages, and the empirical interpretation is not satisfactory even there. Word order typology, whose foundations were laid by Greenberg, renders assistance in this. Greenberg formulated the typology of syntactic word order in terms of subject, verbal predicate and object, which, in the given form, are valid for nominative languages, although they can be reformulated, considering the theory and typology of sentence structure, to meet the requirements of ergative languages. The categories subject, verbal predicate and object have a significant intersection in all languages even though they do not precisely correspond to each other. That is why they should be interpreted in every language and they themselves also belong to the metalanguage of observation (see below). Beside these terms Greenberg also makes use of the concept of basic word order, which can only be defined as contextually unmarked word order within the framework of a topic-comment theory. For that matter, topic-comment theory requires that, besides word order, sentence stress and pause also be taken into account; therefore, word order typology must be supplemented by the typological data of stress and pause (Dezső—Szépe 1974).

Topic-comment theory is in great need of empirical interpretation. The starting point for this is provided by word order typology, and the latter also claims the "assistance" of topic-comment theory. Topic-comment theory explains, for instance, why OSV and OVS are secondary word order variants in relation to SOV and SVO: this ensures that the O mentioned in the context can be placed at the beginning of the sentence, although there is no sufficient explanation at our disposal as to a secondary variant, SVO, of VSO basic word order.

Let us go no further into the comparison of topic-comment theory and word order typology. This much, perhaps, will be sufficient to claim that

a) partial theories and typological generalizations necessarily complete each other;

b) the characteristics of partial theories need specification, even if no claim for formalization is put forward;

c) the prerequisite of empirical interpretation is the working out of an appropriate metalanguage.

If we wish to connect the topic-comment theory of the sentence with a similar analysis of the word groups or units smaller than the word, within an extended topic-comment theory, the properties of the new theory and its empirical interpretation have to be redefined accordingly, and the relationship between the components of the extended theory is also to be clarified. And then, on the basis of this, general topic-comment principles can be defined capable of explaining Greenberg's implications existing between the order of elements in the sentence, in the noun phrase and in the word. Thus far, no attempt has been made to produce a topic-comment theory of such a large scope. There is still a long way to go from statements concerning the universal and type rules of typology to the incorporation of all this in a theory.

No doubt word order typology and topic-comment theory followed different paths and, therefore, the integration of empirical statements and theory is more difficult. The task is perhaps simpler in the theory of case systems, which was worked out by L. Hjelmslev: he defined the basic terms of theory, the semantic features, and interpreted them against languages of different types when forming hypotheses. But a further fundamental task arises here: the morphological theory of case paradigms must be connected to syntactic theory if we want to integrate it in a more complete grammatical theory. In principle a possibility exists for this within an extended case theory. I attempted in Part 1 to make the first steps in this direction, but it does not seem to be an easy task to connect "case categories" in the deep structure with surface cases. Here the joint treatment of syntagmatic and paradigmatic aspect, i.e. the transition from syntax into morphology, causes the problem.

Seeing all this, it is no wonder that formal grammatical theories claiming the highest degree of exactness were not yet able to cope with either task, namely that of incorporating topic-comment or theme-rheme theory and that of case system theory and especially the typologically relevant variants of these. The typological interrelations, however, which exist between topic-comment, case theory and other partial theories of grammar, demand that these should be incorporated into a unified theory.

Such a research framework makes it possible for us to encompass a larger area of the typology of sub-systems and to reckon with partial theories as well as to make use of theoretical statements and principles indicative of the relations existing between them and affecting the basic questions of grammar. The theoretical coherence of such a research programme is of a lesser degree than that of paradigmatic theories encompassing the whole of grammar and, in addition, it does not prescribe formal methods.

3.1. 4. ON THE THEORY: FROM PARTIAL THEORIES TOWARDS SUBSTANTIVE FOUNDATIONS OF TYPOLOGY

On the theory.

No understanding of the relationship and perspectives of the development of typological investigations and linguistic theory is possible if one overlooks the fact that scientific theory as well as the theory of linguistics have entered a new stage of development. It is a striking fact that, especially at the beginning of a new era, science does not develop in a simple, cumulative manner, but changes affecting the basic principles of its theory also take place.

It is characteristic of typological investigations that they have to combine a broad empirical basis with a theory, as general and exact as possible and capable of matching it; therefore, the beginning of a new era, which will gradually affect the whole of linguistics, will make its effects felt in typology more and more intensely.

The linguistic aspect of this epoch-making change has been fully analyzed by V. A. Zvegintsev (1973, 27 ff). Below, I shall take into consideration his work in dealing with problems relating to typology.

Any theory claiming to encompass the whole of language system is specific with regard to philosophy, and even system theory. A theory of the previous age can be characterized as follows: "it can be defined as a system of generalized knowledge explaining various aspects of reality. ...it postulates that generalized knowledge (in the form of laws) is based on a certain sum of impersonal observations and facts and is independent of probabilistic characteristics. . . Such a theory, in fact, forms a closed system" (Zvegincev 1973, 37—38). As opposed to this, today, "a theory is the system of such hypotheses that are corrected by practice, . . . it has probabilistic character and its validity is proved or refuted by further research. It is the goal of every theory to serve as a basis for the exhaustive description of its object, without contradictions" (Zvegincev 1973, 38).

It is more correct to call the specific theory the theory of language here, whereby it can be distinguished from partial theories describing individual sub-systems of language, e.g. grammar, or, within it, syntax or, within the latter, case systems or the system of topic-comment rules. In optimum cases the theories of narrower sub-systems are based on those of broader systems. Zvegintsev quotes as an example of this that the theory of the Slavic case system should be based on a general case system theory, which, in turn, rests on a theory of grammar based on a theory of language system relying on language theory. This hierarchy of partial theories, in practice, does not follow such an unbroken line, or more exactly, the relationship between theories is interrupted and becomes uncertain.

Any theory must satisfy the basic requirements of the methodology of science mentioned above (Hempel 1965, 171).

On paradigmatic theories. Typological analyses handle hosts of facts which serve for them as a starting point. As opposed to this, formal analyses are deductive, which is characterized by J. H. Greenberg, from the viewpoint of typology, as follows: "Ideally, by means of an a priori logical analysis of certain class phenomena, a scheme is developed which exhausts the logical possibilities. This scheme is then applied to empirical data" (Greenberg 1973, 21). In comparison with typology, the empirical base of a formal theory is narrower. Greenberg writes about this as follows: "The analytic approach tends to concentrate on one or very few examples studied in detail which becomes the initial stimulus for detailed conceptual analysis in order to arrive at a logically consistent structuring" (Greenberg 1973, 22).

It must be added, however, that investigators of individual languages have the same feelings towards typology as the typologist has towards a formal theory: typology reduces the rich diversity of individual languages, restricting it to such general characteristics as reveal little about the peculiarity of a given language. It contents itself with analyzing a small number of typologically relevant data of a given language and contrasting them with those of other languages. If, however, the typologist wants to characterize a language in detail, for example its case system, he has to take into account a lot of incidental phenomena, too, which are irrelevant from the typological viewpoint, and, moreover, inexplicable. Obviously, the point in question here is the various degrees of abstraction.

Further difficulties arise from the viewpoint of typological investigations: although the axioms of a formal theory are universally acceptable, the concepts of a given theory can only be interpreted within the framework of the theory, and it is necessary only for the last line of the formalized derivation to lead up to the empirical base. The empirical base, or more exactly the level of observations, is represented by the facts of the given language. Typological rules operate on a level above that of the facts of the given language and they are not manifest in the derivation itself. It is necessary to have a peculiar reconstruction of derivation, therefore, to render it typologically analyzable. Attempts have been made to transform the set of rules of generative grammar into another set relevant from the typological point of view (Birnbaum 1970). In generative grammar, deep structure is supposed to be stratified in a special manner to enable the linguist to grasp typological rules explicitly (see Birnbaum 1970, 19 ff). Therefore, the typological layer, i.e. the set of typological rules, has to be rendered explicit within the framework of formal theories.

The elaboration of the theoretical foundations of typology creates the exact basis for this. It has to be mentioned here that the analysis of the role typology played in the Prague school of linguistics, in glossematics, is important from this angle. The latter had been the most exact linguistic theory before generative grammar, and various views were presented both as far as its evaluation of language theory and that of typology is concerned (Zvegincev 1973, 42—46, Birnbaum 1970).

From partial theories towards substantive foundations of typology. Formal grammatical theories have to account for the substantive generalizations of typology, and they must incorporate the types of sub-systems, as was pointed out by J. H. Greenberg (1973, 53—54). We are still far from this. Sure enough, a bi-directional process will have to be taken into account here: substantive generalizations of a larger scope will arise, their formulation will be more exact, and formal theories will be typologically more substantial, encompassing more and more from the substantive foundations of typology.

A framework for partial theories, too, would be a formal grammatical theory, but its embedding into a theoretical construct can be carried out only from the aspect of the given formal theory, and only the inner development of the theory can lead up to it. This is significantly promoted by the elaboration of partial theories as exactly as possible. For the time being, the typologist has on the whole to face such partial theories that do not form part of a broader coherent theory, e.g. case system theories, aspect theories, theme-rheme theories, etc. One of its causes can be found in the circumstance that coherent, though not formal, grammatical theories, which, however, claim to be exactly formulated, do not contain partial theories either, for their typological component has not yet been worked out.

Let us disregard the point of view of paradigmatic theories and examine the integration of partial theories as an internal process towards the substantive foundations of typology. The typologically relevant theories of various sub-systems are necessarily built up from hypotheses explaining the existing types. In the course of the verification of hypotheses the data of languages known so far will confirm, refute, or—most frequently—modify them. For example, L. H. Hjelmslev built up the typology of case systems on the basis of numerous languages, and explained them in the framework of an exact partial theory. His case system typology seems to be correct. It needs refinement and it must be posited in broader framework and be connected with other partial theories, e.g. that of determination. It will contribute to new substantive foundations of typology formulated in a coherent and exact way, although the latter will not reach the exactness of paradigmatic theories.

The paradigmatic theories are also interested in a typology of this type. Their development and their application to concrete investigation made it clear that the mass of facts can be reliably explained by formalized theories only through appropriate generalizations made by typology. Thus a theory of paradigmatic level does not have to face an unorganized mass of facts and jump to conclusions easily refutable by new facts not accounted for.

Substantive foundations of typology must be shaped according to the requirements of the theoretical foundations. By now typology is considered as a conglomerate of facts and statements of universals or typological validity. My main point in the whole discussion that follows is that it is wrong both from empirical and theoretical considerations. The clarification of the theoretical and substantive foundations of typology is not merely an obsession of theoretically minded linguists, it is a requirement resulting from the typological research in progress. Therefore, it will have an impact on the general strategy of typological investigation. The increasing results in the study of various subsystems result in generalizations of wider and wider scope and require explanations based on partial theories and their combination within theories of a wider sphere of application. The substantive foundations have an impact on the theoretical foundations of typology as well as the development of linguistic research determined the development of the theoretical foundations of linguistics. I consider it important to emphasize this aspect, but another one cannot be neglected either: a theory is never a mere result of the impeti coming from inductive research. The internal development of theoretical thought plays an important role here. These two factors will often be confronted in the discussion that follows.

The substantive foundations of typology will be formulated in a substantive universal grammar. This optimal form presupposes a considerable development of both theoretical and substantive foundations of typology. It is a long way to go but not so long as it seems to be at the present state of typology.

3.1.5. ON THE RESEARCH PROGRAMME:
TYPOLOGY AND PARADIGMATIC THEORIES

It is clear from the previous examination that the future studies based on the theoretical foundations of typology will only have a certain degree of exactness and a lower level of constructing a theory. Although it will be one of its advantages that it will encompass a large area of phenomena and that it will have a broad empirical base.

One of the important questions of the future development is the relationship between exact but non-formalized typology and formal, paradigmatic theories. In order to comment on this problem a brief analysis of a formal system and of a research program is required.

The general properties of the formal system can be characterized as follows: "If axiomatization and the exact determination of logical means parallels with the fact that the notions and expressions of a given theory are substituted by symbolic signs, scientific theory becomes a formal system. The usual intuitive reasoning concerning content is substituted by derivation in formal systems (the basis of which is constituted by certain initial expressions) and according to precisely fixed rules, and from the viewpoint of the realizations of these it is not necessary to take into account the meaning and sense of the expressions of the theory" (Kurjajev

1971, 58). This definition of formal theories was quoted only to make it evident what a significant distance separates typological studies from the requirements of a formalized system. In the course of the elaboration of substantive foundations the distance between the two becomes less and less, but the gap between them could only be bridged by a very strong formal theory, in which one could arrive at all the empirical facts by means of derivation and which would incorporate into itself the statements of the partial theories. This is too distant a possibility for the time being.

There is a possible interrelationship between paradigmatic theories, too, but perhaps, all the more so between substantive foundations of typology and paradigmatic theories. In investigations belonging to the former some notions and procedures of formal theories can be made use of (e.g. base structure, transformations). They reveal essential aspects of language structure and language activities, with which a description of language has to reckon, irrespective of the differences between modes of description. Besides, formal theory is not confined to the formalization of the already existing substantive attainments; in addition it uncovers the interrelationships of these and obtains new information. All this has to be taken into account in non-formal research, too. Syntactic paradigms could be quoted as examples. They were proposed by R. Jakobson who had in mind the formal and substantive results of generative grammar (Jakobson 1972, 78). Incidentally, this is the normal way of development in science.

Of course, the notions and procedures of a paradigm can only be generalized if this does not lead to eclecticism and if the consequences following from the application of the notions are also considered. The requirements of this cannot easily be determined, but it definitely requires a certain isomorphism between theories and may necessitate certain modifications. The interpretation of non-formal procedures in a formal theory can be studied better (e.g. the application of distinctive features in generative grammar). Some of the procedures of formal theories are widely applied, e.g. transformations, but so far no attempts have been made at the generalization of the instructive results of these. At any rate, the application of the concepts of the base structure and of transformations requires a typological conception aiming at synthesis.

Generative grammar is the dominant formal theory in linguistics at present, and in our view it can certainly be considered a paradigm in the sense in which Kuhn generally uses this notion (Kuhn 1970, 10 ff). However, justified the critical remark that paradigm is not rigidly defined may be, its essence is clear and its criteria match generative grammar. With Kuhn we find the emphasis of the science organizing role of paradigm essential, but as far as the general conception of science development is concerned, Lakatos's views are closest to ours (see Lakatos 1970, for the analysis of Lakatos's conception from the viewpoint of dialectical materialism see Švyrev 1971 and the work of Akčurjan and Mamčur 1972).

According to this, the constant development of science is determined by a research programme, which is realized by a whole series of theories. Therefore, I assume the plurality of theories and reckon not only with the diachronic series of theories following each other, but with their synchronic series, too. This does not mean that the research programme is realized by synchronic series of theories with equal success. There are dominant theories (although the importance of competing theories naturally varies). Individual contradictory facts do not yet invalidate the applicability of a theory, they only refer to the necessity of revision and as a result of a revision the predictive force of a theory may considerably be enhanced (see Mamčur 1971, 76). These statements concerning science history, generally accepted today, cannot be overemphasized, for in linguistics a strong fluctuation can be observed either in the form of theoretical monism or that of the immediate rejection of theories confronted with contradictory facts.

If one accepts that the development of linguistics realizes a "research programme", then the question arises how paradigmatic theories and typology are related to it. Paradigmatic theories must investigate the pivotal points of this programme, and development will necessarily be greater in the investigation of problems which can be examined in formal paradigmatic theories. Studies built on substantive foundations of typology prepare the possibility for a given group of problems to get into the research programme of paradigmatic theories. The significant results accumulated this way compel paradigmatic theories to incorporate them, but this can only be done if in their inner development they attain competence for this. The relationship between syntactic typology and paradigmatic theories could be quoted as examples.

Certain results of grammatical typology, primarily J. H. Greenberg's research into the nature of universals, became widely known in the sixties. But even generative grammar, the dominant paradigmatic theory, could not do anything with typological problems. In the future, however, it can be hoped that the tendencies of development of typology and paradigmatic theories will meet. Typology can contribute to this by the substantive analysis of sub-systems under investigation and by the clarification of its theoretical foundations.

The question arises what will be the relationship between typology, non-committed to a specific theory, and typology realized in paradigmatic theory. Obviously, the two will not be identical with respect to their vital problems: the empirical basis of the former will be broader, that of the latter will be narrower, the exactness of their method, however, will shape to the advantage of paradigmatic theory.

The other problem which arises is: how the typological descriptions of different paradigmatic theories analyzing identical linguistic sub-systems are related to one another. Non-formal typology secures an identic substantive base for them and provides them with certain terms from the metalanguage of observation. Individual paradigms, however, describe partial theories within the framework of the given theory using its notions and methods. This leads to necessary differences in the description. It is more important that general theories incorporate partial theories into the whole of the theory in a special way and, hopefully, reveal different connections and make different predictions possible.

Unfortunately, all these are only more or less plausible assumptions for the time being, for I have no material proving this, no typological description of a partial system carried out in different paradigms and on the basis of an identical empirical basis is at our disposal. John Lotz planned to have a generative, stratificational and tagmemic description of a certain sub-system of a language (that of Hungarian) made on the basis of an identical empirical material in order to see concretely which theory and to what degree is suitable for the project "The Languages of the World".

Typology has never been homogeneous, but in the absence of exact formulations differences have not been so sharply delineated. By means of exact description these differences will be much sharper and various views will confront one another more precisely. This development will take place at the expense of the quasi-unity of typology.

If the principle of plurality which allows for more linguistic theories within a research programme is accepted, typology will not be an exception to this rule. The plurality of theories has doubtless to be taken into account in the successive aspect, but presumably in the not too distant future in the simultaneous aspect, too.

3.2. Method, Metalanguage and Laws

3.2.1. ON THE METHODS AND APPROACHES

Stepanov's book on linguistic methods (1975) and Greenberg's mono-graph (1973) on the method of typology makes it possible for me to touch on the question only in brief. First I shall only dwell on the relationship between theory and method with respect to typology.

In the history of linguistics, method often played a pivotal role; the appearance of some objective method initiated great turning points: let it suffice for me to refer here to American descriptive linguistics. Method was not followed by the shaping of a clear-cut theory; moreover, descriptive linguistics significantly reduced the existing theoretical problems.

Taking into consideration these historical experiences Zvegintsev writes that "if science begins to develop from method, this renders science of 'poor calibre', for methods are generally oriented towards the solution of a well defined task... The result is that the whole of science becomes a set of partial problems and will contain partial theories [the theory of the case, syllable, word, etc.] not united by a common principle" (Zvegincev 1973, 56). Of course, certain conceptions about the object of the investigation underlie all methods and these define them, but they "do not follow the conscious aim of establishing a theory for the cognition of the object" (Zvegincev 1973, 58). The method of the neo-grammarians was described in detail by H. Paul who outlined the conceptions about language, which was linked with this method, though he himself did not create a language theory. The unity of method and theory was first realized by L. Hjelmslev—according to Zvegintsev—but method de-termined theory with him, as Hjelmslev "thought that theory could be derived from the methodological principles" (Zvegincev 1973, 43). In ideal cases, just the reverse process has to take place; "the derivation of method from theory can be regarded as the norm when the former does not occupy an autonomous, independent position" (Zvegincev 1973, 56).

It is not characteristic of typological investigations to follow an elaborate method, although a set of methodological procedures is applied in typology, too, but the conscious elaboration of these has not yet reached the stage which historical-comparative linguistics reached in H. Paul's classical book or descriptive linguistics in Z. Harris' famous work. The first step towards the working out of the methodology of typology was made by Greenberg in his work entitled *The Typological Method*. If we consider the two classical works mentioned above to be two types of methodology, typology is in need of a methodology along the extended lines of H. Paul's work. A methodology as detailed as the one worked out by Z. Harris could hardly be set up in typology on the one hand, and it would have to provide much more information on the object studied than is available with Harris, on the other. This does not mean that H. Paul's work should be regarded as a pattern, far from it, the peculiar object of typology necessitates a new type of methodology.

The peculiar subject of typology requires the creation of a methodology just as it happened in the case of historical and descriptive linguistics. This stage of development is unavoidable.

The work of both Paul and Harris was very significant in the shaping of linguistic methods, but, beyond this, they also contributed to the further investigation of the theoretical questions of linguistics, for they contained implicitly and even more or less explicitly essential hypotheses concerning the whole of language. Saussure's work can hardly be conceived without Paul, and Chomsky was the discipline of Harris. This does not mean that, from the viewpoint of theory, methodology must necessarily play the role of thesis and serve as a basis for an antithesis.

In typology the elaboration of methodology is in a more advanced stage than the formulation of its theoretical questions. In this it follows the general pattern demonstrated by the history of linguistics. The impact of methodology on the theoretical basis can be expected. A possible negative influence, however, can be balanced at the present stage of linguistics when theory has a prominent role.

Talking of the more concrete treatment of method, mention must be made about the relationship between induction and deduction. Typology is considered by many a discipline applying induction and collecting data, although Greenberg, disagreeing with Bloomfield, who was an adherent of inductive generalizations, pointed out in the introduction to the *Universals of Languages* (IX): "However, it seemed also to be generally agreed that the method of science is both inductive and deductive. The formulation of generalizations attained by inductive examination leads to higher level hypotheses from which is turn further generalizations may be deduced. The latter must then be put to the test of empirical validation." Induction is evidently limited in typology by the fact that all the languages of the world cannot be encompassed; therefore, induction can be applied only to a representative sample of languages, which is to be chosen on the basis of a general knowledge of the world's languages and not by chance (Ferguson 1971). Non-professionals are usually sceptical with respect to this, for they are reluctant to believe in the possibility of choosing such a sample. But it is possible, although extensive knowledge is required to carry it out. J. H. Greenberg stated the syntactic implicational universals on the basis of 30 languages. The writer of the present paper was not sure either whether this was possible and checked it in several hundreds of languages and, in fact, only certain corrections were necessary (the most important of them being the setting up of a fourth type, VOS, whose range, however, is geographically limited).

Induction is necessarily followed by generalizations affecting both the sub-system under investigation and the interrelationship between sub-systems. In turn generalizations must be explained within the framework of a partial theory and a hypothesis must be set up, from which generalizations can be explained and deduced. Thus, for example, Greenberg's first universal that the subject precedes the object in the basic word order (Greenberg 1963, 61),—which, in fact, is valid only in a modified form— can be explained within the framework of a theme–rheme theory. The aim of further typological investigation is no longer only the analysis of the generalizations, but also the verification of the hypothesis set up and the conclusions drawn but not yet analyzed against the background of facts following from the hypothesis. J. H. Greenberg's classical article triggered off a chain reaction which advances not only and not so much towards further facts, but theoretical hypotheses.

Hypotheses unite the two stages of theory: that of exact and formal theory. Deduction must also play a significant role beside induction in typological investigations, whereas in a formal theory, deduction is the main hero and, with it, hypothesis. Abstract theory is built up deductively, certain universal structures and elements are accepted as axioms, and facts are reached by means of certain operational rules and can thus be derived deductively (Zvegincev 1973, 99, where generative grammar serves as an illustration). Facts, however, do not necessarily agree with the conclusions drawn, therefore, the so-called 'problem-situation' comes into being and a new cognitive cycle is started: a new hypothesis is developed to solve the 'problem-situation', its impact on the whole theory is studied, the revised theory is checked against new facts.

Such a procedure differs markedly from the one outlined above and used in typology, because deduction has a fundamental role in a formal theory. In typology, however, the role of induction is very important and it is supplemented by deduction.

Formal theory, in principle, encompasses the whole of grammar operating with its deductive procedures and creating its concepts within it. Exact typology, even if it succeeds in uniting the partial typologies in universal grammar, will not dispose of a formal system and its concepts will not be explicit enough. No doubt in non-explicit, or less explicit, concepts "the non-rigorous definition of concepts is compensated by their being more meaningful and deep" (Šaumjan 1971, 145). The existence of the exact form of typology in the age of formal theories is also justified by this substantive richness.

Talking of typology, one must not forget about its heterogeneous nature, namely the circumstance that its procedures extend from the inductive generalization of facts up to the creation of typological theoretical constructs.

An essential determining factor of typological method is its analytic or synthetic character. The use of this pair of concepts is not unified, so we have to explain what is meant by them.

Both notions belong to gnoseology but they can be interpreted in linguistics and language typology. Analysis starts from the facts, examines them, arrives at wider and deeper generalizations. Synthesis presupposes analysis, starts from generalizations and from them arrives at facts. The principal task of cognition using synthesis is that it must create an internal and organic unity of the essence discovered analytically and brought into prominence by abstraction with all the components, relations and interrelationships of the object, at all stages of its development (Bogdanov 1964, 122 ff.). Analysis and synthesis figure here as an epistemological pair of concepts, and this is what we need first and foremost. One can formulate the two approaches in a way relevant to typology. Analysis moves from the phenomena of individual languages through generalizations of types to universals. Synthesis starts from the universal invariant reveals its representation in types and from them moves to individual phenomena. It should be clear from what has been said so far that the part of typological investigations revealing the elements and relations of linguistic sub-systems is of an analytic character. The more a typologist aims at bringing into existence a theory as comprehensive as possible, the more synthesis becomes dominant in his research.

Such formal grammatical theories as generative grammar are supposed to be of synthetic character because the derivation starts from a universal layer and proceeds to the phenomena of individual languages. In Marxist epistomology, analysis is complemented by synthesis and induction by deduction in empirical sciences, and synthesis is based on results of analysis, it contains them. Therefore, a synthetic procedure in formal theories can only be regarded as synthesis from an epistomological point of view if it is based on the results of analysis and takes into account the generalizations of the latter. Typological synthetic procedure should be precisely of this type. In that case the results of typology integrated into formal and exact theories will have a great heuristic value.

There is a contradiction between a claim of universality of various theories and the neglect of typology. I think universality cannot be achieved only by the study of individual languages. The application of a theory to the description of individual languages is natural insofar as individual languages are the object of the bulk of linguistic investigations. From the viewpoint of the further development of theory, however, it would be essential to take into account the results attained by typology. It seems to the typologist that the typological status of the linguistic data appearing in the final phase of the deduction and illustrating theoretical assumptions is not clear; for instance, the individual properties of English or some other language do not get separated from what is really general. It would be more proper if investigations having a theoretical goal were checked by the result of typology, by its substantive foundations. Of course, all this is significant if investigations aim at arriving at substantive statements.

Analysis and synthesis pose a substantive problem, which is one of the basic problems of present-day typology. There are typological analyses which start from the data of a certain representative sample of individual languages and generalize these data into types. Furthermore, they look for universal implications existing between various types and single out complex types from the comparison of the types of various sub-systems. This route leads from the individual to the type, and from the types towards the universal implication without specifying the invariant underlying types and explaining universal implications. This is not sufficient. Full analysis capable to promote synthesis requires the clarification of universal invariant because synthesis can start only from a universal invariant underlying types and move from types to individual phenomena.

The notions of analysis and synthesis can be correlated with those of semasiological and onomasiological approaches proposed by E. Coseriu. From a semasiological point of view grammar is described "von Ausdruck zum Inhalt" and from an onomasiological aspect "von Denkinhalt zum Ausdruck" (Coseriu 1975, 59). The first attempts of the integration of typology in the form of complex types proposed by Skalička and Greenberg had analytic character and dealt with forms from a semasiological point of view (3.3.1.) The integration of typology in a universal grammar can be done by an onomasiological approach as it is proved by the proposals concerning universal grammar. At the same time they apply synthesis (3.3.). One of the major criteria of the two types of universal grammar is the dominance of induction or deduction.

Our analysis of the integration and application of typology will show that these methodological notions of the theoretical foundation of typology are relevant not only to typology but also to the description of individual languages.

3.2.2. ON METALANGUAGE

The metalanguage of linguistics was discussed by J. H. Greenberg from the point of view of a typologist (Greenberg 1970b). I shall examine it in the framework of the approach to typology outlined above. Since Greenberg's article deals with the basic issues of this problem, a brief presentation of the problem with some comments will suffice here.

I prefer to separate the substantive and the epistomological aspects of the problem. When dealing with the problem of metalanguage this means a separation of the substantive phenomena one is describing from the language one uses for the description.

The description of individual languages examines the phenomena of the language in question. It is presented in sentences consisting of terms of observation language. Such sentences can be understood more or less by linguists of general training because they contain terms that can be interpreted by the community of linguists. Such a consensus is possible because all languages are variants of human language. At the same time these descriptions will use more specific terms (such as 'noun

class', 'ergative case', 'possessive suffix', 'objective conjugation' etc.)
which are less familiar or unfamiliar to linguists outside the circle of
experts of the given language. Because of the specific phenomena of
individual languages meant by both kinds of terms, their interpretation
will, of course, vary in the descriptions of individual languages. One of the
reasons for this variety is in the language itself: the 'noun' in Hungarian
differs from that in English, e.g. the first has a rich inflection and
postpositions, the second has prepositions and no inflection. Another
reason is explained by linguistic tradition that can often be traced back
also to structural differences, e.g. in Hungarian grammar the 'object' is a
noun in the accusative, and there is no distinction between direct and
indirect object as in Russian or English. This leads us to the function of the
accusative: the noun in the accusative is usually an object, while the
accusative in Russian is the case of direct object and direction (Part 1).

Nevertheless, the language of observation of individual languages
can very well be understood if a small set of specific terms and
complementary interpretation are given, and it "seems to provide a
language which is neutral in relation to the various schools and their rival
analyses, or between members of the same school when presenting
different analyses" (Greenberg 1970b). "It consists of statements regard-
ing individual languages which rest in some reasonably direct way on a
body of observations, that is, it consists of observation statements"
(Greenberg 1970b, G5). A more detailed analysis of observation statements reveals that they are the results of generalizations on the level of the
given individual language and their language is a variant of an observation
language reflecting important achievements in the theoretical reasoning of
linguistics (Greenberg 1970b, G5—G10).

Studies in typology and grammatical theory use the terms mentioned
above in different ways, if they use them at all. They mean 'noun', maybe
'object' as universal and the 'accusative' as a typological term, which are
general enough to account for the phenomena of various languages. A
general understanding of the terms of individual observation languages is
based on the existence of meta observation language used in typology
and grammatical theories. The interpretation of his terms bridges the gap
between universal or typological terms and those of individual languages.
This is true, but if typologists want to formulate universals and typological
rules in the meta observation language, they must revise its terms because
their unique understanding and interpretation is far from being satisfactory.

Greenberg examined the statements made in observation and meta observation languages from the point of view of their analytical or synthetical character. This sophisticated problem has philosophical implications and goes beyond the scope of linguistics. My main concern here is the nature of the terms of meta observation language.

The metalanguage of observation of typology should have the same terms with the same interpretation in the vocabulary of all typologists. What we have now is only a consensus on basic terms. A common language is not simply a question of agreement on terms and their interpretation, it can only be a consequence of a consensus on the fundamental problems of typology.

The meta observation language is important also for linguistic theories. There is a substantial difference between the theoretical foundations of typology and formalized or exact theories, and it has an impact also on the terms used in them. The term 'noun' in typology should be general and abstract enough to be interpreted in the individual observation languages. The same holds for the term 'noun' in an exact or formal theory. In addition to that, this term will have a specific context in a theory which more or less differs from one theory to an other. It is not arbitrary because it reflects the "substantive" context of language, more or less known to linguists and systematized in typology. The latter will support or question the use of a term in a theoretical context. The term 'noun' serves as an example. It figures in the standard generative derivation in "traditional" places, its use is supported by our knowledge of language, but in the first variant of an applicative generative model the 'noun' figured with verb, adjective and adverb at the top of the derivation, its context was unusual and needed explanation. I do not want to deny the relative freedom of a theoretical construct from the observed facts (Greenberg 1970b, G9, G13) and establish a simple relation between the two. If one claims that a stratification of derivation from a typological point of view is desirable, then the interrelation between "substantive" processes and their reflection in theoretical constructs should carefully be studied.

I have highlighted the dependence of a theoretical construct on the substantive properties of language, because it was the point I specifically wanted to make. It would, however, be misleading without calling attention to the role of theory in opening new insights into the structure of language which may lead to the reconsideration of the substantive basis of typology.

In the foregoing analysis the term of the metalanguage of typology was considered as a whole and in *abstracto*. There is no use in analyzing the individual terms, but some classes of terms do need special attention. The parts of speech belong to the apparent candidates for typological terms and their interpretation in individual languages seems to be feasible. They are elements of linguistic structure, and no description of a system is possible without the terms of its elements. The same holds for the terms of structures, like 'clause', 'phrase' etc., composed from these elements by rules. The functional terms of both surface and deep structure are far more problematic, such categories as surface 'subject', 'object' or "deep case" terms as 'agent' are the terms in question. They are indispensable in a functional approach because one can form sentences of high explanatory power by using them. Therefore, one should attempt to clarify rather than discard them.

The deep case categories have their roots beyond language in the categories of human activity. They are of relevance to linguistics, and their linguistic interpretation is possible. They belong to a set of terms of a higher level and of broader application that have or need linguistic interpretation (e.g. base, derived structure) used both in the metalanguage of typology and in theoretical constructs.

3.2.3. RULES AND PRINCIPLES: TYPES AND UNIVERSALS

In analyzing the regularities of typology I shall briefly touch upon the concept of 'law'; the role of rules and principles in describing structures typologically; the questions of universals and types; and, finally, I shall make remarks about universal grammar.

The Question of Law

In order to have a closer look at the various laws (rules, principles, types, universals) occurring in typology, the broader conception of law has to be established as our starting point, by which the essential, constant, general and necessary relations of phenomena are meant in Marxist philosophy. They can be classified according to their structure and range of validity.

As far as their structure is concerned, they can be dynamic, expressing simple phenomena manifested in reality and freed from incidental phenomena associated with them. Therefore, dynamic laws express simple and direct causal relationship. Statistical laws have a more complicated structure; they are characterized by the fact that, given external effects, the initial state of the system cannot determine unambiguously and cannot prescribe all its further states. Dynamic laws disregard incidental phenomena, whereas statistical ones take into consideration and sum up the effects of homogeneous, and among other things, incidental phenomena, revealing the complex determination underlying them. A statistical law always forces its way through the mass of homogeneous and incidental processes and manifests itself as a resultant of these processes (Pilipenko 1965, 49—50).

In the history of linguistics, phonetic laws were the classic examples of dynamic laws, but then they needed some modification and although they cannot be conceived as statistical laws, they seem to be less consistently valid than the Neogrammarians believed (for the history of this problem see Kovács 1971). Probably the types of laws can be considered ideal types as well. There are ideal dynamic and statistical laws: with the former the simple causal relationship between the two states can easily be revealed, whereas with the latter, the causes cannot be uncovered on account of their manysidedness.

Typological changes, for instance typological changes of word order, are brought about by numerous factors, but it can perhaps be assumed or surmised that there are fundamental causes or such that are more essential than others. For the transition from type SOV to type SVO, for example, the change in the nature of aspect in Finno-Ugric languages may have played an important role. In Hungarian, which is at a transitory stage of this change, the basic word order SOV cannot be used with perfective verbs, so word order SVO must be resorted to, since it is applicable both with perfective and imperfective verbs. The role of aspect can also be observed in other languages with two alternative types of word order, but it does not necessarily mean a relationship between a given aspect and a given word order (for instance, perfective aspect and SVO), but, rather, it means that until the aspect gets morphologically fixed, the word order also contributes to its expression. A similar cause may have been behind the Slavic SOV→SVO typological change, but there, with the establishment of the perfective aspect, the duality of word order types became superfluous and disappeared. In Hungarian, the development of the perfective

16*

aspect was accompanied by the establishment of the articles and, in contemporary Hungarian, the object is used without an article in SOV and it has either a definite or an indefinite article in case of SVO. There is no article in the majority of Slavic languages, and that is why it could play no role, but the question is more complicated, for the means of expression of definiteness are different in Slavic languages. It is not sure that a certain structural "cause" necessarily underlies all changes in word order typology. Several factors have possibly taken part in the change of language structure, without any of them playing an outstanding role.

Causes triggering off changes have been dealt with so far, rather than the processes themselves which are characterized by having a certain trend, for they manifest themselves only statistically in transitory periods. One of the reasons for this is that the structure of sentences and the semantics of the verb play a role in the typological change and, beyond this, the new type makes its effect felt to a varying extent (Cf.: the change in English word order; Shannon 1964, Palmatier 1969).

Dynamic laws are for the most part related to changes of elements or groups of them (e.g. changes of open vowels into closed or vice versa), rather than to the changes of structures. Statistical laws, however, are related to both, but, perhaps, more typically to structures. Jakobson called attention to the statistical nature of structural changes and not only from the linguistic, but also from a general methodological point of view (Jakobson 1953, 227—228).

Structure itself is a type of law (of determination). Structure reveals an intricate relationship among elements. Structures can be relatively stable or unstable, for instance in a period of great diachronic changes (e.g. the system of phonemes in Hungarian, in the 12th—14th centuries). In the course of changes, the variability of elements and sub-systems can be of a different degree. It may be revealed in the analysis that certain parts have a greater role in the change, but it is also possible that no difference can be found between parts in this respect. In the latter case, the 'principal' cause cannot be uncovered, and the dynamic factor is negligible, so we face a statistical change. After the termination of the change, as a result of a comparison between the original and the resulting structure, the 'aims' of the change are revealed (Cf. Jakobson 1953, 227—228). This, however, does not mean that changes take place without stages where certain structural laws can be asserted, even if only with statistical validity. In contemporary Hungarian, for example, the dual word order SOV and

SVO represents a stage of the change SOV→SVO. The same holds true for the Hungarian mixed word order, SOVM and SMVO. Transitory types can also be observed, for example an SVO basic word order and an OSV contextual word order at one stage of development in English, but this will be handled together with typological changes.

Rule and Principle, Type and Universal

"The construct of '*type*' is, as it were, interposed between individual language in all its uniqueness and the unconditional or invariant features to be found in all languages" (Greenberg 1973, 179). Types determine certain characteristic features of linguistic structures from the analytic point of view, synthesis singles out, from the viewpoint of the derivation of these structures, rules that generate these characteristic features. Thus, the basic SOV word order is characterized, from the analytic angle, by the fact that the verb figures at the end of the sentence, while the subject stands at the beginning of it, before the object. In a contextual word order, it is the object that is shifted to the beginning of the sentence and the verb remains in its place. In ergative sentences the centre of the theme (the *subjectum*) is in the Ergative if the verb denotes action proper, and the centre of the rheme (the *objectum*) is in the nominative or in an absolute case: $N_{erg}+V+N_{nom}$. But typological structures can also be characterized by rules which generate them, or more precisely by rules which assist in establishing the features characteristic of the type in question, for the rules that generate the structure may include typologically irrelevant ones, too.

To quote an example, the basic word order of the A word order main type is to be constructed by a typological rule which places the subject (S) before the object (O). With Greenberg this figures as a universal (Greenberg 1963, 61):

A': S+O

In main type B the order of the two is reversed:

B: O+S

Within main type (A), 3 typological rules place the verb at the end of the sentence, between S and O, or at the beginning of the sentence:

1: SOV   2: SVO   (3): VSO

In a contextual word order, in the sub-types of types 1, 2 and 3, the A" rule is in operation and it shifts the object before the subject:

A": O+S

Then the above typological rules can be applied, which place the verb at the end, in the middle or at the beginning:

1′: OSV   2′: OVS   3′: VOS

The third type, however, includes another sub-type, too, in which the contextual word order is SVO, so the order of S and O is identical with that of the basic pattern, and the verb comes between the two parts of sentence, and so it differs from any other word order variant in that it has two special rules.

The two rules of main type A, A′ and A″, together with the typological rules, have created several variants of word order types. Their number is greater in reality, for these are also valid for sentences having more complements (object and adverbial), which I shall not analyze here. Rules applied in creating structures containing various constituents, but of the same type, can also be labelled as 'typological principles'. Limits of types restrict the validity of typological principles, whereas no such restrictions are imposed on universal principles. If, returning to the previous example, we approach the surface from the universal layer of deep structure, we meet the following universal principle. If the sentence to be constructed is not marked from the point of view of the text, i.e. no passive construction has to be applied and no contextual word order variant is necessary, the theme (or if the theme consists of several elements, the centre of the theme: the *subjectum*) is represented by the argument of the predicate marked as 'active' if the noun is marked as 'living': Hung. *A fiú sétál* 'The boy is walking', *A fiú írja a leckét* 'The boy is writing the homework'; if no noun marked as 'living' occurs, the centre of the theme will be represented by a non-living 'active' argument: Hung. *A szél süvít* 'The wind is whistling', *A szél fújja a fellegeket* 'The wind is blowing the clouds'; irrespective of whether or not the verb has other complements, too. In the course of further derivation, the subject created by means of this universal principle is in the ergative case in languages marking the theme, whereas it is in the nominative case in nominative languages marking the rheme, as in the Hungarian example above.

This example also helps in the further elucidation of the concept of 'type', for sentences of ergative languages are not only characterized by the use of the ergative, even if the rules producing the theme are considered, so the *subjectum* of non-active verbs can be in the dative, etc., but the use of the ergative is an indispensable rule of ergative sentence construction.

To use an epistomological expression, the quality of the ergative type is determined by the use of the ergative. The *subjectum* can be expressed by the dative in nominative languages, too, as in Hungarian: *Péternek van kalapja* 'Péter has a hat' but it can never occur in the ergative. That is why the use of the dative is not an obligatory criterion of ergative languages, but it is not characteristic of nominative languages, either.

The previous word order types also have a variant, VSO, which is characteristic of type 3, being its basic word order, but it is not characteristic of type 2, though it occurs occasionally. It is still less characteristic of type 1 and, in fact, very rarely occurs with it:

    1: SOV   2: SVO   3: VSO
       OSV   OVS   VOS
       VSO   VSO

That is to say, type 1 is characterized by having the verb at the end of the sentence, whereas it is in the middle in type 2 and at the beginning in type 3, and so it can be seen that the VSO variant violates mostly the principle concerning the place of the verb in type 1, and type 2 is less affected.

The complex type is, supposingly, characterized only by certain general principles, or by an intersection of them. Such are the two principles *regens ante rectum* and *regens post rectum*, which connect the word order types of the sentence and those of the nominal group. The principle *regens ante rectum* unites the basic order of the three sentence word orders and one of the word order types of the attributive nominal group, as the dominant word is always placed before the word dependent on it (the dominant word in boldface the dominated word in italics)

    SV*O*   **N***A*
    VS*O* and **NN**$_\mathrm{g}$
    V*O***S**

This principle assumes that the verbal predicate and the word qualified are dominant, which is acceptable. The principle *regens post rectum* acts contrary to the former. It is the basic principle of the following sentence word order and nominal group:

    S*O***V** and *A***N**
               N_g**N**

This principle highlights the object and the verbal predicate, so it completes the above principle determining the place of the subject: the S precedes the O in the basic word order in main type A by stating that the verb goes before the object as a dominant element in types 2 and 3: SVO, VSO, but follows it in type 1: SOV. Only this second principle has to be taken into account in the order of the attribute and the word qualified, for instance: NA and AN. If the principle whose task is to determine the place of the subject is called the 'thematizing principle', the one responsible for the order of O and V as well as the attribute and the word qualified can be called the 'rhematizing principle'; since the attribute of a nominal group conveys new information, just like the object in the sentence, it can be regarded as a representation of the rheme.

I find it essential to emphasize the importance of rules and principles, for in sentence typology—in accordance with the analytic approach— resulting structures have been the main target so far, and not rules and principles creating them.

The above examples are, at the same time, illustrative of types and universals, too, but we would like to dwell on both of them separately later, though it will not be our task to go into detail, since both are exhaustively treated in various papers (Greenberg 1966, 1973, Jarceva 1975, Sgall 1971, Birnbaum 1974, Bell 1971, Hockett 1963, Kiparsky 1968, Kroeber 1960, Roždestvenskij 1969, Ulmann 1963, and Voegelin 1956). We should like to pick out just one question: the relationship between types of primary and secondary structures having the same deep structure. Let us consider an example here. The basic word order in a Hungarian sentence containing an object, as mentioned above, depends on the aspect of the verb and on whether the object has an article or not. If the verb is not perfective and the object has no article, the basic word order is SOV:

  1: *A fiúk tévét néznek.*
  'The boys are (the) TV watching.' (lit.)

If the verb is perfective and the object has an article, the basic word order is SVO:

  2: *A fiúk megnézik a tévét.*
  'The boys will watch the TV.'

Several other problems arise, but let us disregard them and look at these two sentences when they figure as clauses:

  1: *A szülők azt mondták, hogy a fiúk tévét néznek.*
  'The parents said that the boys were (the) TV watching' (lit.)
  2: *A fiúk jöttek megnézni a tévét.*
  'The boys have come to watch the TV.'

The dual word order of Hungarian consistently runs through the basic word order of the main clause, the subordinate clause and the construction with the infinitive. In numerous languages, however, differences in the typological rules of word order can be witnessed in the subordinate clause and the main clause (e.g. in German and in English), and the typological rules exhibited by the construction with the infinitive are also different from those of the main clause (e.g. in Russian). The nature of typological differences is also interesting: in these Indo-European languages, which are at an advanced stage of their development from the SOV type to the SVO, the SVO type manifests itself more consistently in the main clause than in the subordinate clause or in infinitive constructions. Thus, a certain relationship can be observed between the primary or secondary character of the construction and the extent of the typological change: typological changes make their effects felt sooner in primary constructions than in secondary ones.

This is not characteristic of Hungarian, or perhaps, not yet, for a similar phenomenon can be observed between the basic word order of the main clause and its contextual word order. The SOV basic word order can equally be accompanied by an OSV and an OVS contextual word order.

SVO:

A fiúk megnézik a tévét.

'The boys will watch the TV.'

OSV:

A tévét a fiúk megnézik.

OVS:

A tévét megnézik a fiúk.

If the verb is not perfective, there is a difference of emphasis between OSV and OVS:

OSV:

*A tévét a **fiúk** nézik.*

OVS:

*A **tévét** nézik a fiúk.*

In German, only OVS would be possible in reverse word order. This set of problems poses several others. In Russian, OSV is applied primarily in contextual word orders, if the subject is a pronoun:

OSV:

Televizor oni smotrjat.

'The TV they watch.' (lit.)

Sentences in which pronouns figure as subjects are also secondary, for the noun is substituted by a pronoun on the basis of the situation or context.

These secondary constructions of different nature illustrate expressively and concretize typologically R. Jakobson's assumption that a double code can be observed in diachronic change, here in the typological change (Jakobson 1953, 227). The new type represents the main code here, which is a property of primary constructions, secondary constructions exhibiting the old one. The typological change concerning the word order is characterized by the circumstance that it is in primary constructions that it prevails first, though, supposedly, it emerged there as a non-dominant construction. Thus, Hungarian only occasionally had SVO as a variant of SOV, accompanying and expressing the initial stage of actualization and perfectiveness. The present dual word order established itself afterwards.

Diachronic typological changes can be attested in other languages, too, in the form of both a dual and a mixed word order. Mixed word order is characteristic of sentences having four elements. Thus, in accordance with what has been said above, the basic Hungarian word order places the object either before the verb or after it: SOV and SVO. Further complements either follow the type of the position of the object SMOV and SVOM, the resulting sentences being of a pure type, or they deviate and form a mixed word order SOVM and SMVO (where M is adverbial).

The above examples shed light on the abundance of patterns in the syntactical (word order and other) typology of languages. Order can only be achieved if, through the consistent application of rules, pure types are set up, which can perhaps be found in reality, too, but their significance lies in the fact that 'non-pure' constructions are compared with them. This leads up to the problem of etalon i.e. of a construct used as a base for comparison where pure types figure as such (Birnbaum 1970; Uspensky 1968). Pure types as a structure of etalon are established only on the basis of universals and rules characterizing types. In the case of individual languages individual rules can co-occur or even harmonize with them, but only if these do not belong to a different type. We have imperceptibly passed over to diachronic typology from synchronic, but not by chance. Typology is characterized by panchrony, i.e. the peculiar unity of synchrony and diachrony.

In philosophy *universals* are characteristic of the whole eternally moving material whereas language universals are peculiar regularities, which determine development of a given set or class of phenomena, in our case, that of language (Pilipenko 1965, 40 ff.). *Linguistic universals* serve as a basis for the non-universal typological rules in syntactical derivation, and they can yield the realization of a relationship even more general than themselves, and may, for example, connect language to thought. We are less concerned with this external aspect here, however essential it may be from some other angle (Chomsky 1968 and Kacnel'son 1972).

The categories of system and structure theory predetermine the possible occurrences of types of universals in language: universal elements (constituents, features), universal structures and universal implications (Dezső 1979 for a detailed account).

Universal elements in syntax can be universal parts of speech, universal semantic and grammatical features. The former mark the semantic cognitive and functional features of the basic parts of speech (verb, noun), and the latter the features of the predicate and its arguments (e.g. 'annimate', 'active', etc.) forming the deep structure. The analysis of universal features and within the confines of this the clarification of the universal character of features is not trivial, either, but even more important is the study of relations and structures formed by means of them and the elucidation of their role in syntactic derivation. I should like to mention here that categories created by means of cognitive-functional features, like the agent, patient and instrument of the action are generally applicable to the characterization of human activities; their role is rather essential in the analysis of work and can be found in the works of Marx, too. However, they play a special role in the linguistic reflection of reality; they determine thematization, the case of the centre of the theme, i.e. *subjectum*, and that of the rheme, i.e. *objectum*, etc. (see above). Theme and rheme form a pair of categories leading from the universal layer to the layer of types. They are supposedly the basic categories of all linear messages, just as the sentence is merely one variant of the basic structure of communication (Jakobson 1970, 437—439).

Perhaps universal implications are those variants of universals which are most specific to language. Universals can best be studied on the basis of the classical works of J. H. Greenberg (1963 and 1966). Their single prerequisite is the universal character of implications. The question whether they can be established between elements, structures, or variants of structures and whether they are universal or type phenomena calls for further study. It is believed to be one of their shortcomings that the mere existence of an implication does not provide explanations and it is necessary also to uncover the structures they are related to, and the relations must be accounted for by means of principles which are taken from some theory (see Kacnel'son 1972, 10). Implications, however, are of great significance even so, for they pose questions which demand an answer, an explanation; and the question need not necessarily contain instructions concerning the answer. The fact that Greenberg's classical article has carried out this task is proved by the existence of the vast amount of literature, aiming at their extension and interpretation.

With implications we go beyond the range of universal elements and structures, as implications establish contact among type phenomena, too. Their strongest variant is the one setting up implication relations between types of various structures, for this evokes a generalization of the greatest degree in the exploration of structures connected with implications and it is this that requires the most comprehensive theory as a background of the explanation (such as implications between the sentence, the nominal group and the word).

The substantive component of a grammatical typology must include all the implications in one way or another, and the explanatory power of a theory can be judged according to its capacity for explaining them.

Thus, implications embrace the whole of typology. Typology can be divided into a universal and a typological component, the former containing universal elements and structures, the latter containing types, but such a division cuts typology into two parts gratuitously, for the two complement each other organically. Any attempt to restrict typology to the investigation of types only, and to separate universal elements and structures from it and refer them to the theory of grammar would be equally fallacious.

3.3. Integration of Typology: Towards Universal Grammars

The clarification of the theoretical foundations of typology is necessary to integrate typology in a cohorent way. This is the condition of its application in descriptive, historical comparative and contrastive studies. At present, typology consists of dozens of books and of a great number of articles. The nontypologist, i.e. 99 % of linguists, has only these fragments at his disposal. He can make use of typology, if he finds a study matching his field of investigation, but it is not easy to discover it in the ocean of linguistic literature. For the descriptions of individual languages and their comparisons, an integration of typological information currently available, is badly needed. The task of integration is enormous, both from the theoretical and substantive point of view, but it must be done.

There have been attempts to integrate typology in the last decades and I can review only some of them.

Dealing with such a complex task as the integration of typology, methodological problems are of great importance: the questions of theory: partial theory, specific theory, those of method: analysis and synthesis, induction and deduction, the problems of law. (They were examined in chapters 3.1. and 3.2.)

The integration of typology may be restricted to the statements of the observation of co-existing facts in various sub-systems without their theoretical explanation. These are the complex types revealed in an analytic approach by induction. Three proposals on complex types will be presented: Klimov's contentive (Russ. *kontensivnyj*) types, Greenberg's types formulated by Lehmann, and Skalička's types. Induction is their dominant method, but deduction also plays an important role in their discovery and specification. The methodological statement that analysis and induction play the major role here must not mislead the reader as to their importance for typology. They challenge typologists: they ask for explanation covering a wide range of phenomena. The large literature connected with Greenberg's universals apparently proves this: these universals have been refined and extended and there are hypotheses for their explanation.

Another form of integration of typology is universal substantive grammar. Its approach combines analysis with synthesis. From the study of individual languages the investigations in universal grammar arrived at generalizations at universal level and from them came back to individual languages. They have worked out theory and methodological devices to do that. Universal grammar is of two types. These differ in the role played by induction and deduction. In the first type induction has a great role, in the second deduction is more important than in the first type. The conception of the Leningrad group on typology respresents the first type, and Keenan's proposal on universal grammar the second. They also differ in their objectives and in the role of theory. In the first type the description of a series of sub-systems and partial theories explaining them are in the focus. In the second type, the whole of grammar is the primary objective and there is a specific grammatical theory underlying the conception. The first type studies the "positive" rules against the background of a calculus, in the second type the constraints are the major form of typological law. As a result of synthesis the first type arrives at concrete languages, the second at possible human languages.

These are ideal types. There are and will be proposals on universal grammar which are transitory in nature. Even the conceptions to be examined do not represent these two types in pure form. But this is usual in any typology.

There is no gap between complex type and universal grammar: analysis can be completed by synthesis and be explained by a theory, e.g. there is a tendency towards universal grammar in the new versions of Klimov's contentive types.

This chapter examines the proposals on complex types (3.3.1.) and the two types of universal grammar (3.3.3.—3.3.5.) I inserted a section on Hjelmslev's general grammar which is interesting as a forerunner of universal grammar and some major problems raised in it, are to be answered in the study of universal grammar in the eighties (3.2.).

I shall deal with the problems of substantive universal grammar. The questions of formal universals and formal universal grammar are beyond the scope of my book because they require the analysis of the development of generative grammar and a new field of theoretical problems.

3.3.1. ON COMPLEX TYPES

Typology in the second half of the last century was dominated by morphology, but it also studied the phenomena of the syntax of morphological categories. The morpho-syntactic approach was particularly well demonstrated in Misteli's book (Misteli 1890), which has been neglected, or underestimated, by the linguistic historians. In this century, the complexity of type was very clearly formulated by Sapir (1921), whose conception of type includes morphology, word formation and the semantics relevant in their analysis.

Development towards complex types was one the major tendencies of typology in the 20th century. I cannot examine this trend in a historical perspective. I will highlight only three conceptions of complex types resulting from the main trends of typology in the sixties and in the early seventies:

1) contentive types based on the Soviet development of typology, especially on Meshchaninov's works and formulated by Klimov,

2) ordering types based on Greenberg's universal and formulated by Lehmann,

3) Skalička's complex types.

The order of their presentation is motivated by my approach from syntax to morphology and phonology: the complex types of sentence structure are followed by the ordering rules; Skalička's morphologically oriented types will be my last topic. Their historical development followed a rather converse order.

The presentation of complex types will be very brief and far from complete. I want to justify my claim that the proposed complex types complement each other to a great degree and there are important implications among them which must be taken account of by typology today.

Ergative complex type will be examined here in G. A. Klimov's formulation (Klimov 1974, 259—263) but the conception goes back to the 30's, to I. I. Meshchaninov. Ergative type has four major obligatory criteria:

a) a formal opposition of transitive and intransitive verbs,

b) ergative sentence structure,

c) ergative case or ergative suffix of the verb, or both, for making ergative construction,

d) SOV basic order.

There are frequentals occurring in ergative languages: classes of nouns, singulative and plurative verbs indicating one or more objects, an important role of *Aktionsart*, inclusive and exclusive 1st plural, the lack of infinitive etc. Maybe, that some of the criteria a)—d) will turn out to be non-obligatory and to be considered as frequentals.

Klimov's recent book characterizes active complex type (Klimov 1977), which is close to ergative type but is more consistent in marking the subject and, therefore, is more clearly opposed to nominative type marking the object. Klimov summarized his results in a proposal on "contentive" typology. It clarifies the relationship between the various types mentioned above, and the lack of them in languages which are neutral from this point of view. Contentive typology highlights the dominance of lexical classes and their effect on grammar. Klimov deals with a wide range of phenomena, and even a brief presentation of his "contentive" typology would lead us far (Klimov 1976). I must notice, however, that his proposal is one of the most ambitious attempts at the integration of typology along the lines of complex types.

The *ordering types* are based on Greenberg's classical article (1963) and are formulated in various versions. I shall present a modified variant of Lehmann's criteria (Lehmann 1974, 15—20) complemented by mine (for details see Part 2 of this book). The two types labelled by me as *regens post rectum* or dominant after dominated (briefly OV) and *regens ante rectum* or dominant before dominated (briefly VO) will be given in two columns.

A) The order of phrases
    a) relation of object to verb:
      OV   VO
    b) comparatives:
      (N) A Conj N   (N) N Conj A
    c) relative constructions:
      Relative N   N Relative
    d) adjectival constructions:
      A N   N A
    e) genitival constructions:
  N_{gen} N   N N_{gen}
B) The order of analytic and synthetic words:
    f) interrogative and negative verbal modifiers:
      V neg inter   inter neg V

g) postpositions and prepositions:
N   Postp   Prep   N
h) prefixes and suffixes:
N—suf   pref—N

The order of phrases clearly shows the effect of the two principles: *regens post rectum* and *regens ante rectum*. In word order the subordinated element follows or preceeds the main element (see Part 2 of this book for an explanation of the difference).

The above two complex types treat the phenomena of syntax. The third complex type concentrates on morphology. V. Skalička has formulated his complex types in various ways. I shall present the last variant (Cf. Skalička 1974). Only two types will be examined.

Agglutinative type has the following characteristic:

a) richness of inflectional suffixes,
b) limited homonymy and synonymy of inflectional suffixes,
c) weak differentiation of word classes,
d) restricted word order,
e) no grammatical gender,
f) verbal nouns, adjectives and adverbs instead of subordinate clauses,
g) developed system of consonants,
h) word formation by derivational morphemes.

Inflective type has the following criteria:

a) synonymy of inflectional suffixes,
b) homonymy of inflectional suffixes,
c) bisematic morphemes *(serv-orum)*
d) the sole inflectional suffix of an individual word (einzige Endung des Einzelwortes),
e) strong differentiation of word classes,
f) free word order,
g) grammatical gender or other systems of noun classification,
h) subordinate clauses instead of verbal nouns, adjectives and adverbs,
i) the dominance of vowels instead of consonants,
k) word formation by classes of words *(asinus—asina, Esel—Eselin)*.

The complex types presented above more or less complement each other. Ergative and nominative types deal with the structure of sentence and the morphological representation of the predicate, *subjectum* and *objectum*, i.e. with the generalized subject and object. The ordering types define the basic principles of the arrangement of the elements in sentence, clause, phrase and word. Agglutinative and inflective types deal with the general principles of the morphological representation of sememes both in inflection and derivation, and with the characteristic of word classes. They also include criteria of ordering, especially those concerning its freedom and the formal representation of subordinated propositions.

Ergative type has SOV order as one of its criteria. It is, therefore, connected with OV type of ordering. In earlier versions of Skalička's types, agglutinative type had SOV order as one of its criteria and inflectional type had SVO order among its characteristics. In the present version they are lacking, but inflectional type has verbal prefixes, a *VO* phenomenon, among its criteria.

I think one can consider the link between OV type and agglutination as a frequental. Thus ergative type is frequently connected with OV type and with agglutination.

Nominative type may be complemented by the principles of both OV and VO types and use both agglutinative and flective ways of morphological representation.

Complex types represent the first stage of the integration of typology which highlights the links of various sub-systems. The core of each complex type, however, is one of the sub-systems. The chain of complex types combines the various parts of grammar and thereby contributes to the integration of typology. The emphasis on the relationship between various parts of grammar is an apparent advantage of complex types, but the lack of clarification of the structure of sub-systems themselves is its disadvantage, particularly in the earlier versions.

The integration of typology is inconceivable without an exact description of sub-systems, without the clarification of their formulation based on an exact theoretical foundation. This requires a new approach to typological investigation which had its antecedent in Hjelmslev's *grammaire générale* and leads us to the recent developments in typology.

3.3.2. HJELMSLEV'S GRAMMAIRE GÉNÉRALE:
A FORERUNNER OF UNIVERSAL GRAMMAR

Hjelmslev's *Principes de grammaire générale* has been neglected because of his later works which represent the mature form of a new structuralist theory. It was followed by his *La catégorie de cas* with the subtitle: *Étude de grammaire générale* thus indicating the link between the two works. I am interested here in *Principes* as an approach to general grammar and not as it was an earlier version of Hjelmslev's theory. His *Principes* raises the questions of the theoretical foundation of linguistics: synchrony, diachrony, and panchrony, form and function and the fundamental problems of grammar: the relationship between syntax and morphology and especially those of morphology: grammatical form, grammatical category, grammatical function and the system of grammar. Even brief analysis of Hjelmslev's early theory goes far beyond the scope of my examination because a comparison to the later version of his theory and its place in the theoretical context of the twenties would also be required. *Principes* can be considered not only as an early version of Hjelmslev's theory, as a prelude to his *Prolegomena*, but also as a theoretical foundation to his general grammar which was followed by his *La catégorie des cas*, to mention only one of his content oriented studies.

In Hjelmslev's view grammatical theory and typological research form two aspects of general grammar. This is so natural that he deals with the questions of typology but little in *Principes* and the same is true of general grammar in *La catégorie des cas*. What is important to note is that the clarification of theoretical foundation precedes the analysis of the empirical base. The latter is followed by a return to theory in Hjelmslev's later works.

In *Principes* his requirement of a panchronic theory deserves special attention: "Il est établi que la grammaire scientifique est avant tout d'ordre panchronique" (1928, 106). The empirical base of typology must be studied from the point of view of such a theory. Types are complex and he highlights the "constraints" on the combinations of types: "Les types existants et constatés contiennent, chacun, certaines combinaisons de certains faits, et ces combinaisons de ces faits sont donc possibles; mais il est hors de doute qu'il y a d'autres combinaisons — des mêmes faits ou bien de faits différents — qui ne seraient pas possibles en matière linguistique. Le système linguistique peut revêtir certains types. Mais il ne peut pas appartenir à un type quelconque. La variété s'arrête. Elle a ses limites." (1928, 292). In the context of the twenties he pays special attention to historical linguistics and reconstruction. Both observe only symptoms instead of general principles. He quotes Sapir: "These symptoms are being garnered in our descriptive and historical grammars of diverse languages. Some day, it may be, we shall be able to read from them the great underlying ground-plans" (1921, 152—153). Sapir looks for

17*

principles explaining both synchronic and diachronic phenomena. They belong to general grammar according to Hjelmslev who highlights their importance for diachrony: "Il nous semble certain que, les principes de la grammaire générale un fois posés, ils peuvent fournir à la linguistique diachronique et reconstructive un appui très heureux et aussi très nécessaire" (1928, 292). One may question Hjelmslev's view of diachrony: "La grammaire diachronique n'existe pas; elle n'existe qu'en tant que juxtaposition de plusieurs états synchroniques." (1928, 292—293), but his panchronic approach to general grammar demonstrated in the next quotation is very important: "Et la grammaire reconstructive, ... ne pourra se réaliser qu'en tenant compte de tous les faits synchroniques du monde, des faits panchroniques de cet ordre, bref, des résultats de la grammaire générale." (1928, 293).

In his preface to *La čatégorie de cas* Hjelmslev writes: "Cette étude servira à fair voir comment nous voulons entendre la grammaire générale. Il faut abandonner selon nous la distinction entre morphologie et syntaxe aussi bien que la division de la linguistique en une partie comparative et une partie générale. Par un procédé synthétique, il faut embrasser l'ensemble des faits." (1935, III). Here, one may question how far morphology can be merged with syntax. Note, in addition, that Hjelmslev was more specific about the relationship between comparative and "general" linguistics in his *Principes*. However, as a result of his study of case systems, he can clarify the relationship between the study of general grammar and that of individual languages: "Etant une étude de grammaire générale, ce travail n'a pu traiter que d'une façon forcément incomplète de détails particuliers propres à chaque état de languge pris à part. Les faits particuliers ne sont apportés qu'afin de les voir à la lumière d'un principe totaliste. Nous espérons qu'un tel travail pourra jeter les bases à des recherches de grammaire spéciale. Nous sommes persuadé que celles-ci sont impossibles sans une théorie générale." (1935, III—IV). His analysis of cases starts from the criticism of earlier theories, then he outlines his theory and demonstrates by an examination of the types of case systems represented by various languages.

Unfortunately, Hjelmslev's study of case systems was not followed by a series of studies in general grammar and no general grammar was written. The goal formulated by Hjelmslev was far more closely approached in phonology by Trubetzkoj and Jakobson. There is no room to examine their conception of general phonology and show the differences between Hjelmslev's notion of general grammar and the Prague School that is: [+ trans. + in]; while *po* + acc.: 'horizontally to the upper limit' general phonology. It will suffice to mention that both are theoretically oriented and panchronic. In my view, however, the Prague linguists could more precisely formulate the relationship between synchrony, diachrony and panchrony. Theoretical foundations, the study of types, and that of individual languages are more interrelated, the empirical base of their theory is far broader than that of Hjelmslev's. I want to emphasize these advantages of the Prague school because they are relevant today.

3.3.3. FIRST TYPE OF UNIVERSAL GRAMMAR: THE LENINGRAD APPROACH

The Leningrad group described the typology of causative constructions, that of diathesis, and, at present, studies the typology of sentences with subordinate propositions in the role of one of the arguments (subordinate clauses, non-finite constructions etc. on the surface). In its approach the analysis of a set of individual languages results in typological generalizations and in a partial theory of the given sub-system. Analysis is followed by synthesis: they describe the individual languages with in the framework of a synthetic conception proceeding from universals to the regularities of individual languages.

The sub-systems examined by the Leningrad group are closely connected and the partial theories are in the process of integration. Their approach is based on Russian structural linguistics but is not the application of any specific grammatical theory. Induction precedes deduction which is their basic method. Typological laws were formulated in "positive" rules in the study of causative constructions. This was complemented by a calculus in the study of diathesis.

The Leningrad conception does not formulate the structure of the whole of universal grammar as Keenan does (3.34.). Therefore, my analysis must be confined to a sub-system of grammar, to diathesis on the basis of V. S. Khrakovsky's recent article "Diathesis" (1980).

The treatment of the diathesis in Khrakovsky's article clearly shows the procedure from analysis to synthesis, from the data of individual languages to a typological construct and from it back to concrete languages. My presentation of the conception will be restricted to some basic issues of the Leningrad conception. Diathesis can briefly be defined as the correlation between the semantic and syntactic presentations of predicate structures (Khrakovsky 1980, 2, and Part 2 in this book).

In the semantic presentation, called semantic object, the arguments of the verb have their semantic roles with different semantic weights. There is a hierarchy of roles according to their weights. E.g. Russ. *davat'* 'to give' has three roles with different weights in a hierarchy (1 = who, 2 = what, 3 = whom). The problem of roles (or deep cases in American terminology) is not clarified. Khrakovsky is ready to accept Apresjan's approach establishing 25 roles, based on the analysis of Russian verbs. The problem of weight is connected with the questions of grammatical relations, e.g. in the above example the subject has number one and the highest rank in the hierarchy and the direct and indirect objects have lower ranks and less weight. In the earlier versions of the Leningrad theory the grammatical relations were highlighted, in the recent version they are excluded from the formulation.

The major concern of the Leningrad theory is the obligatory arguments of the predicate, called roles, but the non-obligatory constituents called attributes, are also considered if they are relevant from the point of view of diathesis.

Thus, the typological analysis of the syntactic and semantic structures of individual languages has lead us to a theory which deals with the correlation of semantic and syntactic "objects". In synthesis a calculus is applied in order to connect the semantic "object" of universal nature with the syntactic "objects" of languages: "it is possible to consider the hierarchically ordered and theoretically unlimited set of semantic variables A, B, C, D . . . as the first essential object for the establishment of the calculus of diathesis. This set includes roles and attributes which take an obligatory syntactic position in at least one of the constructions formed by the given lexeme." (Khrakovsky, 1980, 19). The calculus relates the semantic object to the syntactic "object", which is "the hierarchically ordered and theoretically unlimited set of syntactic variables: 1, 2, 3, 4 . . . which include actants and circumstants being obligatory in at least one of the constructions formed by the given lexeme." (Khrakovsky 1980, 22). The actants are usually the subject and objects, the circumstants are adverbials in individual languages. The calculus will not be analyzed here because its technical problems are beyond the scope of our presentation. I shall give a very simple example of the calculus for the· diathesis of transitive verbs (requiring a direct object) with two actants:

(A = 1) (B = 2) *Vnuk* (A) *razorval rubašku* (B)
'The grandchild tore the shirt.'

(A = 2) (B = 1) *Rubaška* (B) *razorvana vnukom* (B)
'The shirt is torn by the grandchild.'
(A = X) (B = 1) *Rubaška* (B) *razorvalas'*
'The shirt is torn.'

From a static point of view all diatheses are equal, from a dynamic viewpoint the first is the basic one, the rest are derived.

The Leningrad theory of diathesis has been applied in the description of dozens of concrete languages (see *Typologija passivnych konstrukcij* 1974, *Diatezy i zalogy* 1975, *Satzstruktur und Genus verbi*, 1976, *Problemy teorii grammatičeskogo zaloga* 1978, *Zalogovyje konstrukcii* 1981).

The problems of diathesis are closely connected with those of sentence structure, subordinate propositions replacing an argument (subordinate clauses, non-finite constructions) and word order. There are two other sub-systems which have been studied by typology and must be related to these sub-systems; these are determination and aspectuality. These sub-systems of grammar, however, require the reformulation and extension of the Leningrad theory.

3.3.4. SECOND TYPE OF UNIVERSAL GRAMMAR: KEENAN'S PROPOSAL

The presentation of Keenan's proposal will be misleading from the point of view of the whole of his conception and his studies. His proposal (Cf. Keenan 1978) is the result of his analytic research of the various sub-systems of numerous languages. This analytic and inductive background will not be reflected in the following presentation of his proposal, but its novelity lies precisely in its deductive nature which implies induction in typology.

The principle goal of linguistic theory is to define the notion of 'possible human language' (PHL) according to Keenan (Cf. Keenan 1978, 1). This determines the objective of universal grammar: "Universal grammar... presents a conception of language universal... universals determine constraints on the form and substance of Possible Human Languages. But it does not conceive of universals as properties which all PHLs have... Rather... are characterizations of the regularities in the ways languages differ from one another. Structures which vary from language to language, as surface structures do, are among the primary object of study in Universal grammar." (Keenan 1978, 90).

The structure of universal grammar consists of four parts (Cf. Keenan 1978, 94—95):

1. *Syntactic inventory* UG must define the set of possible grammatical categories and lexical items from which any PHL may draw its stock.

2. *Semantic inventory*

   a) UG must define the set of meaning representations which are possible interpretations for items in the syntactic inventory.

   b) UG must define a meaning function M which associates with any item in syntactic inventory the set of possible meaning representations it could have.

3. *Choice Constraints*

   UG must define the constraints on the choice of elements from the syntactic and semantic inventories which we must follow in constructing a PHL... these constraints determine, and are empirically established by patterns of cross-language variation, and constitute language universals.

4. *Principles of Variation*

   UG must specify principles which allow us to predict what types of variation are possible across languages and what types are not. The principles of variation apply to the syntactic inventory in order to construct further categories and possible lexical items not actually attested in a known language.

In my view the most interesting part of Keenan's conception are the choice constraints which are instructions "how we may chose from the universally available elements in the syntactic and semantic inventories to form a PHL" (Keenan 1978, 96). The various types of choices follow each other and determine the structure of universal grammar which consists of 1. A set of common properties, which all languages have as determined by the obligatory independent choices and 2. A set of independent optional properties determined by the optional independent choices and 3. A set of dependent choices. (Cf. Keenan 1978, 110.) Keenan formalizes the dependent choices by a kind of decision three (Cf. Keenan 1978, 108 ff.). I shall give an example of dependent choices following an independent optional choice:

"First Option: Assigning overt case-marking to intransitive subject (S_i).

Yes: Then we must subsequently choose to overtly case-mark transitive subjects (S_t).

No: Then we subsequently have the option of overt case-marking S_t." (Keenan 1978, 107.).

This brief characterization of Keenan's choice constraints could perhaps show how typological rules and their combinations are formulated in constraints. In the given example an optional, i.e. type rule, is connected with an implication: "if in a language the intransitive subject has overt case-marking, then the transitive subject has overt case-marking as well." The lack of case-marking of intransitive object has no implication concerning the transitive subject. Many similar implications can be found in the typological literature. Keenan formulates them in a systematic way in his universal grammar.

Obligatory independent choices create an incomplete language because they will be followed by optional independent choices which add or do not add certain properties and create a rather large number of different partially constructed languages. They are still incomplete because further properties must be added by dependent choices in order to arrive at a possible human language (Keenan 1978, 106).

3.3.5. ON THE TWO TYPES OF UNIVERSAL GRAMMAR

After my brief presentation of the two proposals on universal grammar the reader probably has the feeling that they are so different that no reasonable comparison is possible. A more detailed description of the two conceptions would complete and clarify many points but would not bring them closer because of the major differences in the basic issues. My aim cannot be the discovery of the similarities in their formulation. I can only show some basic differences and similarities from a methodological point of view, disregarding the details of their structure and of their procedures which are really different.

The basic differences between the two types of universal grammar can be summarized by the following criteria.

Universal grammar of type 1:

a) the object of investigation is the sub-system of languages analyzed in subsequent studies,

b) in the method induction plays a prominent role,

c) it formulates partial theories and extends them incorporating other partial theories,

d) typological laws are formulated as rules against the background of a calculus,

e) synthesis arrives at the sub-systems of concrete human languages.

Universal grammar of type 2:

a) the subject of investigation is the whole grammar,

b) in this method deduction has a prominent role,

c) a specific theory of grammar underlies the formulation of grammar,

d) constraints are the major form of typological laws,

e) synthesis arrives at possible human languages.

The two conceptions analyzed cannot be considered as the only possible realizations of the two types of universal grammar. On the one hand, they have properties not obligatory for the given type of universal grammar, on the other, there can be conceptions which are formulated not only in a different way but are of transitory nature. The Cologne approach differs from both the Leningrad conception and Keenan's proposal not only in the details of formulation of universal grammar, but also in the criteria proposed above, e.g. it shares the prominent role of induction with the Leningrad conception, but in principle, its subject is the whole of grammar and it formulates its theory accordingly (Seiler 1980).

The two conceptions presented above have important similarities despite the differences in their formulation. Both of them correlate syntactic and semantic "objects" from an onomasiological point of view proceeding from content to expression (Coseriu 1975, 59). In Keenan's proposal the semantic and syntactic inventories are among the major parts of grammar. In the Leningrad conception the essence of diathesis is the correlation of the semantic and syntactic objects. The elements of both objects are studied as far as it is necessary for diathesis: roles and attributes in the semantic presentation; actants and circumstants in syntax.

The structure of grammar is shaped by the subsequent application of constraints and rules and makes typological stratification in both conceptions possible. In Keenan's proposal the obligatory constraints create the universal part of a possible human language. Then it is completed by optional independent choices resulting in partially constructed languages. These constraints correspond to type rules. Dependent choices are then added in order to arrive at possible human languages. The specification of their typological status requires the clarification of the relationship between the possible and concrete human languages and is beyond the scope of this analysis.

In the Leningrad conception the formulation of the various rules is less explicit. But the structure of grammar implies universal semantic rules followed by universal syntactic rules leading to those of individual languages.

These common properties of the two conceptions are important because they are suspected to be general properties of any universal grammar. The fact that the Cologne approach faces the same problems and solves them in its own way, supports my claim. The relationship between semantics and grammar and between the universal and the non-universal components are formulated in an explicit, exact way in the Cologne theory (Seiler 1978).

At the end of my analysis I must mention some fundamental questions which require an answer concerning the two conceptions of universal grammar. These questions follow from the nature of these two types of approaches and are not connected with the peculiarities of the given conceptions.

In the first type of universal grammar the major problem is the integration of sub-systems and of partial theories into a complete universal grammar. From a substantive point of view the relationship between sub-systems must be considered. A methodological problem arises in connection with the form of the whole of grammar: can its form be shaped as a sum of sub-systems? If not, how will the new form of the whole grammar effect its parts and their previous description from the point of view of substance and form?

If we shall have two universal grammars as the result of the investigation of two types of approaches and they will explain the same set of facts, then the two types of universal grammar are equal from the point of view of descriptive adequacy. But this fact does not imply that they have the same formal explanatory adequacy, if one of them is on a higher level of formalization. Therefore, the formal aspect must be an important aspect of investigation of universal grammar of type 1.

So far, I was concerned with the integration of typology, with universal grammar. My other major concern is the application of integrated typology, of universal grammar in the study of individual languages and their comparison. In the studies of the Leningrad group, the typological characteristics of individual languages play an important role. This cannot be said about Keenan's studies, and it is not clear to me, how the possible human languages can be related to concrete human languages or how their typological characteristics can be given.

3.4. Application of Typology: Characteristics of Languages and Contrastive Studies

3.4.1. HUMBOLDT AND THE TYPOLOGICAL CHARACTEROLOGY OF INDIVIDUAL LANGUAGES

In the second half of the 20th century typological characterology (this coinage means a discipline studying the typological characteristics of one or more languages) has been thrust into the background in research practice, and even more so in the examination of the theoretical problems of typology. In an analysis of the latter it is advisable to return to Humboldt, who raised these questions in an essentially up-to-date manner.

Outstanding personalities in the history of various disciplines could formulate requirements of a theoretical nature which subsequent generations cannot realize or can only realize fragmentarily in the practice of research. A century or even more may pass before their conceptions can serve as a basis for a scientific research program—naturally on a more advanced level, relying on the results arrived at in the meantime.

Humboldt was such an exceptional personality, and there is considerable literature on his typological views (of recent works cf. Coseriu 1972, Ramat 1973, and Telegdi 1970, whose approach is closest to the one adopted by the present author).

For Humboldt, general linguistics is essentially a comparative discipline of linguistics. It is however important to add that the "object of Humboldtian general linguistics lies, therefore, in a difference of languages; on the other hand, the recognition of the difference presupposes a comparison, and can present itself only through it, as its result (Telegdi 1970, 234). It is essential to specify what is meant by the second statement here in relation to the subject of general linguistics and comparative language studies, for it functions as a borderline towards the general grammar of the 18th century, which considered the diversity of languages superficial and incidental, and assumed the existence of a universal grammar underlying them. Universal grammar, the universal features of languages are of course essential from the viewpoint of comparative language study, but, as opposed to general grammar, Humboldt emphasized the need for a systematic understanding of the specific properties of individual languages. For Humboldt, the description of individual languages was the goal of linguistics, while the scholars of general grammars regarded as science only the investigation of the general characteristics of language. As the properties of individual languages are incidental, they considered them as 'techné' rather than science. The Humboldtian conception of general linguistics could transgress the view of general grammar because it discovered the importance of examining types which created the link joining the universal properties of language with its specific properties.

No detailed analysis of Humboldt's views can be attempted here: it is significant to note that for Humboldt language meant unity, by which he basically meant that language is a system, and he was diametrically opposed to general grammar, which aimed at the examination of (universal) elements only, and took no cognizance of language as a system. Humboldt's systemic view of language went unnoticed for nearly a hundred years. This is even more true to another of Humboldt's fundamental insights, namely that language is essentially an activity: "He relates languages to the faculty of mankind to create languages, which means that he considers them to be creations, in which this ability manifests, explicates, expounds, and unfolds itself, while the comparison of languages serves for him to encompass as to methods and volume of the ability from which they derive" (Telegdi, 1970, 229). The product of activity is secondary for him, and his conception concerning this essentially differs from that of his great successor, de Saussure, for whom language is primarily a closed system, linguistic activity being thrust into the background, and it is only in the second half of the 20th century that linguists have received to the Humboldtian view. The recognition that language is a system is necessarily accompanied by the proper notion of linguistic form: "By linguistic form (in the Humboldtian sense of the word) one must therefore understand the 'method of language creation', i.e., the law according to which a community incessantly creates, 'generates' its own language" (Telegdi 1970, 230). Humboldt's view of linguistic form is, therefore, closely connected with his entire conception, and it is very difficult to identify it with any contemporary conception. Perhaps this is the Humboldtian concept, which most depends on he theoretical context, and can be interpreted only with difficulty when isolated from it. This had led to a number of misunderstandings of which one is connected with generative grammar. "The Humboldtian 'Sprachform' is thus not a structure whose proper reproduction is generative grammar but a principle (more exactly a living 'Drang' that creates this structure and its details, in so far as it manifests itself through them and unites them into a whole)" (Telegdi 1970, 235).

Humboldt's conception, I believe, unites several aspects: In Humboldt's principle of activity linguistics is not separated from psycholinguistics, language being closely bound up with thought. His conception of language is essentially functional, for he considers language in its communicative function. Linguistic activity is directed at the expression of thought, and 'thought' is used here in the broad sense of the word, denoting the message to be conveyed, as well as some other things, although it is not exactly defined or interpreted. The division between the psychological and the linguistic study of language came about some time later, although they are still closely intertwined as a result of the work done by one of Humboldt's followers, Steinthal. The Humboldtian linguistic form does not assume rule—wither abstract or concrete—but rather a general principle creating the structure of language, which, if one intends to remain faithful to Humboldt's entire conception of language, is primarily of a typological nature and means something like a complex type in contemporary typology, except that its manifestation in individual languages and its expression is not explicit.

With Humboldt, typology is not yet divided into two approaches, one aiming at a classification of languages into types and the other intending to grasp the peculiarities of individual languages on the basis of the former. In the course of later progress, it has mainly the first tendency, i.e., the classification of languages into types, that developed markedly. It was this field whose typology achieved more and more significant results: from morphological types to syntactic ones and from simple types to complex ones. Incidentally, morphological types came to be regarded to a certain extent as complex morphologico-syntactic types in the 19th century. Humboldt's approach, however, was characterized not only by this but also by the endeavour to characterize individual languages in the unity of their typological and individual properties, through the principle creating their form.

This is the point to which one must revert today, but it must be further developed so that typology may be applied to the descriptive and historic examination of individual languages. It is insufficient only to establish what types languages belong to since it is also necessary to understand the specificity of individual languages.

If the relevant aspect of Humboldt's conception is summed up in present-day terminology, from the viewpoint of today, it can be established that Humboldt considered language primarily an activity and, in this respect, his view was at variance both with universal grammar and de Saussure's conception. In the description of individual languages, it was of crucial importance for him to take into account the universal and typological laws of languages, but, according to him, both kinds of laws manifested themselves as a particular whole in the individual properties of languages. Accordingly, linguistic form and linguistic structure must be interpreted as the fundamental principle of creating individual languages which is unique in the case of every language, but in which the general and typological laws of language also manifest themselves. (On the latter see Telegdi 1970, 236, footnote 13.) It is essential to add that for Humboldt linguistic form is a method of creating languages, a law, a procedure with which language is created (Cf. Telegdi, 1970, 28). Thus, Humboldt's conception is basically a synthetic one, in which emphasis is laid on creating linguistic forms. This is the idea that brings Humboldt's views so close to trends in modern linguistics. In spite of the imprecise interpretation, Chomsky is right in part in pointing out that Humboldt was a precursor of the synthetic view of language and that the generative approach is connected with Humboldt's views only as one version of the latter approach. Examining Humboldt's conception raises problems which are the recurrent basic questions of linguistic science and which are accounted for in a variety of ways. An analysis of his views is made especially opportune by the fact that he has placed comparative language study at the centre of his research and his views are closely bound up with a conception of linguistic theory that aims at creating linguistic structures. Necessarily, further developments in typology did not go along the way indicated by Humboldt.

3.4.2. TYPOLOGICAL CHARACTEROLOGY AFTER ONE HUNDRED AND FIFTY YEARS

Obviously we can make no attempt here at surveying the progress of research in general linguistics and typology during these one hundred and fifty years. A general characterization of the advance made in the typological approach, however, is indispensable for the linguist to understand what the current typological characterology must be like.

The empirical base of typology, i.e. the typological generalization of individual languages developed gradually though unevenly, at a slower or quicker pace. In the 19th century, just as in the whole of linguistic science, morphology was predominant, but those familiar with the typology of this period know that morphology-based syntactic descriptions relating to the use of morphological forms abound in the works of Misteli, Winkler, and Fink, and Skalička's morphological terms of types extend over morpho-logico-syntactic phenomena (Misteli 1893, Winkler 1887, Finck 1910, Skalička 1935). Syntactic analysis, however, emerged only in the thirties and forties of the 20th century with Meščaninov and his disciplines (for its mature version see Meščaninov 1963), but did not spread until the second half of the century. Nowadays syntax-based typological research has come to the foreground. This is, however, a result of conceptual change, which derives from the fact that the analytic approach has been supplemented by a synthetic one seeking rules for creating sentences and word forms.

The methodology of typological investigations was characterized by the analytico-taxonomical method which centred around the technique of forming words. This is how it is generally interpreted and, on the whole, this interpretation holds water. In reality, however, this was supplemented by a number of other morphological and morphology-based syntactic generalization as early as the 19th century. These were not formulated clearly as classificatory criteria because they could not be integrated into the classificatory framework. Classification became complex with Sapir and came to be formulated explicitly, preparing quantification in the early works of Greenberg. The earlier criteria based classification involving elements was replaced by the typological characterization of the sub-systems of syntax, or morphology and syntax in the Prague School and the Soviet school during the thirties of the century.

In this connection the interpretation of the pivotal concept of typology (i.e. type) also undergoes a change: the simple type is replaced by the complex one, which states the coexistence of the properties of several sub-systems. So far such a conception of type only records phenomena but does not account for them. Indeed, this could not be done, since the examination of types is not supplemented by a theory or hypothesis, which could explain the jointly observable features. Besides, typology usually remains within the limits of sub-systems, and even if there exists a typologically relevant theory, as for example Hjelmslev's case theory, it does not go beyond the limits of sub-systems. Today there are possibilities in principle for theories of sub-systems to become connected and integrated. In reality the sub-systems of grammatical typology are not integrated into a uniform explanatory theory, although attempts at this have been made (Klimov 1977).

The emergence of typological characterology and the typological characterization of individual languages was made possible by a more precise interpretation of the concept of type and the formulation of the mixed type in addition to the pure one—mainly in the Prague school (Skalička, Mathesius). Current and future research in typology must make further attempts for the Humboldtian approach to be applied on a higher level of development.

Typologists face great tasks in concrete research, namely in the examination of typologically hitherto unrevealed sub-systems of grammar. This, however, must take place on a higher level. We cannot be content with merely recording facts in revealing the typology of sub-systems, but must account for them on the basis of a partial theory, and the information thus obtained must be integrated into the whole of typology, and finally partial theories must come to form parts of a fairly complete theory. This helps typology to go beyond the empirical level proper and, what is more, beyond the classificatory level to attain a theoretical level yielding typological constructs (Hempel 1965), which are accounted for by principles based on theories.

In order to bring typological research to such a high level, one must necessarily elaborate the general theoretico-methodological questions of typology, and clarify the theoretical basis of typology. The concepts of typology, the application of linguistic theory, methods and laws in typology must be examined in terms of the recent achievements of linguistic theory. In the comparative study of cognate languages this was carried out a hundred years ago by H. Paul. The foundations for an analysis of non-cognate languages were laid by Humboldt. The next period was characterized by the typological chapters in Gabelentz's work (Gabelentz 1891), which, however, cannot be compared to Paul's book as regards either exhaustiveness or impact. Even so, there was an eighty year lapse between those and their paper sequal (Kacnel'son 1972, Greenberg 1973), which has started a new move of research.

There is a significant change under way in the manner of approach: analysis is being supplemented by synthesis; i.e. the derivation of linguistic

18

constructs, which will take one to a higher level of abstraction using the results of the analysis. This is again something not unprecedented. It was Gabelentz (1891) who, following Humboldt, formulated the analytic and synthetic approach clearly but the synthetic approach did not become a research procedure until the second half of the 20th century. It should be noted that, from the viewpoint of the methodology of science the derivation of sentences and morphological units can be described as synthesis only if the results of analysis are also taken into account and if a fairly complete picture of language and linguistic activity is given.

It is impossible to establish types in typology without thorough knowledge of the underlying universal invariable. The investigation of types was supplemented in the sixties by an examination of universals which led only to universal implications between types (Greenberg 1963) but the typological investigation of universal invariable underlying the types of individual linguistic sub-systems is a quite recent development. If we consider the requirements treated above, this research proceeds from universals towards types, encompasses the whole of grammar and may yield a universal grammar in the not too distant future.

All this will be significant from the viewpoint of the synchronic and diachronic investigations of individual languages, i.e. from that of the overwhelming amount of linguistic research, if it is supplemented by a characterization of the present state and history of individual languages. Such a typological characterology must be based on general typology. Attempts at this have been made both by typologists and students of individual languages, language families and groups.

For Misteli, individual languages illustrated only types and for this reason merely the characterization of languages of the pure type could be considered. Skalička's aim was to characterize individual languages and language families on the basis of complex types—with a view to the fact that one language usually represents several types (Skalička 1935).

It is here that the discussion of an interesting aspect of Humboldt's comparative linguistic analysis can be resumed again, namely the investigation of the principles which are relevant to individual languages and explain their rise and present form. The last quarter of this century will have to face the task of constructing a research programme to realize Humboldt's conception. Its basis is provided by a completely reformed general comparative linguistic discipline which began with Humboldt but which could be formulated in detail only in our age.

3.4.3. A BRIEF TYPOLOGICAL CHARACTERIZATION
OF RUSSIAN IN COMPARISON WITH HUNGARIAN

Process, or, to use another term, dimension, is a fundamental notion here. Unfortunately, there is as yet no uniform definition of this notion. A process, which will be the term employed here, represents the formation of the types of grammatical sub-systems from an invariable basis by means of various formal devices, as a result of the application of a system of rules including cardinal principles of great explanatory power. Processes that create sub-systems fulfil a certain function, as parts naturally have their functions in the whole.

The representation of such processes can be successfully achieved if it satisfies the needs of exact typological description, of which the following are singled out:

a) description of the invariable object in typological terms which are sufficient for the derivation of grammatical objects representing various types;

b) objects obtained as a result of the application of derivational rules have the following characteristics:

(1) there is a calculus, i.e. a system of rules that help to create all resulting objects from an initial object, with principles that create types;

(2) there are means of formal expression, with the help of which resulting objects are formed.

In a typological characterization of individual languages the description of types irrelevant for a given language is reduced and the typological description is supplemented by language-specific rules and means. Here some individual processes will be represented so far as these will be indispensable from the viewpoint of Russian and Hungarian, but most of the specific phenomena in these languages will not be considered. Below an elementary characteristics of Russian will be given in the framework of the following processes.

(a) the primary organization of the sentence: ergative and nominative construction;

(b) the actualization of the nominal and verbal components of the sentence: determination, aspectuality and tense;

(c) diathesis: active, passive, elliptical sentences;

(d) theme and rheme: their expression by word order, sentence stress and special morphemes;

19

(e) the morphological expression of syntactic components: analytic and synthetic words, agglutination, inflection, etc.;

(f) the structure of nominal paradigms: case systems.

The division of the uniform process of sentence formation inevitably leads to a division of complex interrelations within sub-systems of the sentence, which at the same time modify the picture. This is traditionally the case in linguistics. For example the subject functions in a sentence, but the grammar singles it out for the sake of analysis. Undoubtedly, when individual processes are considered, one must constantly keep in mind their interrelations. Besides, it must be borne in mind that in the formation of sentences there are primary sentences starting off various processes. In an extremely simple sentence like *Petr pišet pis'mo* ('Peter is writing a letter'), one simultaneously faces a nominative construction, a primary or zero diathesis, a primary theme-rheme division, unmarked determination and aspectuality. Yet, the given distribution of processes is motivated by the fact that the primarily formed sentence is a starting-point for the rules of secondary diatheses, and that each diathesis has its own rules of theme and rheme. Therefore, one group of processes has to be preceded by another and each process has its own principles and types distinguished from others. Determination and aspectuality contain auxiliary information which is relevant in the primary formation of the sentence and is taken into account in subsequent processes. There is no need to justify the fact that complex propositions are singled out and are introduced after the processes of the simple proposition. The explanation for the fact that morphological processes proper are placed after syntactic ones is that the impact of syntactic factors on morphological ones is considered to be more important than the reverse connection, but one must not in any case disregard the impact of morphology on syntax.

As has been noted above, in the description of processes it is indispensable to describe the universally invariable object of syntactico-semantic nature, the rules of derivation (calculus), the object obtained as a result of the application of the rules. It goes without saying that the present description can only partially meet these requirements: invariable objects will be characterized in brief, with major principles singled out and major types outlined.

The universal underlying structure of syntactic derivation consists of the predicate and its arguments, which are divided into actants and circumstants, i.e. obligatory and free arguments. Semantico-grammatical features of predicates and arguments are taken into account but no detailed account of them can be attempted here. Only features which will be necessary later in the analysis are touched upon here. Dynamic and stative as well as transitive and intransitive predicates are differentiated among others (incidentally, there is considerable disagreement concerning the naming of various kinds of predicates and features). Dynamic predicates have primary actant which possesses the functional feature of activity, while a non-active primary argument can be found with stative predicates; intransitive dynamic and stative predicates: *Devuška tancuet* ('The girl is dancing'), *Devuška krasiva* ('The girl is nice'); transitive predicates: *Petr pjot vodu* ('Peter is drinking water'), *Petr vidit vodu* ('Peter sees the water'). Circumstants express place, tense, instrument, etc. Some auxiliary information on tense, aspect, determination, etc. must also be contained in a universal invariable structure, since it is indispensable for the derivation of various types.

What features must a universal invariable structure contain? An enormous amount of information ought to be taken into account, and be analyzed both from empirical and theoretical aspects. This problem can be solved in the course of typological investigations.

For a typologist, this structure serves for the derivation of types and it must contain the amount of information that is indispensable for this purpose and nothing but this information. The features themselves are defined by means of abstraction in the course of typological investigations, in which not only overt but also covert categories are taken into consideration. The following example is familiar to Slavists: 'totality' is the common feature of 'Slavonic' type aspect, and although it does not coincide with any of the partial features of aspectuality, the latter can be derived from it.

Formation of primary sentences. In the derivation of simple sentences, the process of primary sentence formation plays a prominent part. But, as was noted above, a primary sentence represents a zero diathesis as well and in this way serves as a point of reference for rules of diathesis. Besides, it is neutral from the viewpoint of the process of theme and rheme and its elements are placed in accordance with the basic rules on the word order and accentuation of an initial diathesis. It is advisable to unite the processes of diathesis and theme-rheme in the complex process of communicative organization or functional perspective but to examine them separately. The first term is to be preferred since the second has a specific connotation which associates it with the the conception of the Prague school.

19*

Communicative organization and the semantics of the predicate jointly determine which actant will become the subject and which one the object; for instance, in the basic communicative organization of dynamic predicates, the active argument becomes the subject, while the non-active will function as the object: *Petr pišet pis'mo* ('Peter is writing a letter'). The subject *(Petr)* is the theme or topic, whereas the object *(pis'mo)* is the rheme or comment, or at least is part of the rheme. In primary sentences, the relationship between the subject and the theme as well as the one between the object and the rheme are typical. It is necessary to recall that the terms subject and object are from the metalanguage of typology and can function as subjects or objects in individual languages.

It is this kind of sentence derivation that the typology of sentence formation is linked with, distinguishing topic-prominent languages, which stand in contrast to subject-prominent languages, with an intermediary group of topic and subject-prominent as well as neutral languages (Cf. Li-Thompson 1976). There are a number of well known subject-prominent languages. Topic-prominent languages have a morphologically marked theme (topic) and lack a set of rules which are connected with the subject in 'subject-type' languages. It must be noted, however, that in subject-prominent languages, like Hungarian, features characteristic of topic-prominent languages can also be observed (Kiss 1981).

The formation of actants in the sentence can be controlled by two principles: (1) the object, or the centre of the rheme is marked, (2) the subject, or the centre of the theme is marked. In nominative languages it is the object that is marked, and even the semantic features of the verb can be reflected in the formation of the object by means of various case endings. *Petr rešaet zadaču* ('Peter solues the task'), *Petr ždet pis'ma* ('Peter is waiting for the letter'), *Petr rad pis'mu* ('Peter is glad to the letter' /lit./), etc. The subject has the unmarked form.

In active and ergative languages it is the subject that is marked and the semantic features of the predicate can be reflected in its formation. If the predicate is dynamic or active the active argument or the agent appears in the ergative case, while other cases mark subjects in case of other predicates, the object being unmarked. Within this main type one can distinguish active languages which mark the subject of all verbs from ergative languages where the subject of intransitive verbs is not marked. Instead of esoteric examples from little known languages, the active sub-type will be illustrated by pseudo-Russian examples: Russ. *Petrd pišet stat'ja*, 'Peter is writing the article', *Petrd tancuet* 'Peter is dancing', where *d* is a fictitious case suffix.

The marking of the active subject is an inalienable feature of ergative languages, unencounted in nominative languages, although the subject of a non-dynamic verb may also be marked in the latter, leaving the object unmarked, e.g. Russ. *U Petra jest' šljapa*, Hung. *Péternek van kalapja* 'Peter has a hat', where the subject assumes the genitive or the dative case, while the object the nominative (cf. Serbo-Croatian: *Petar ima šešir*, Russ. *Petr imeet šljapu*).

Apart from this specific sentence structure with corresponding rules of marking by means of nominal and verbal morphemes, the ergative type also implies the formal opposition between transitive and intransitive verbs as well as the basic word order of SOV. In ergative languages one can observe the frequent occurrence of nominal classes, nouns (singularia or pluralia tantum) denoting one or more than one object respectively, the important role *Aktionsarten* play, the inclusive and exclusive 1st person plural, the absence of infinitives, etc. (Klimov 1973, 259—263). That is why ergative languages represent a complex type with a number of frequentals.

Primary sentence formation is an extremely complex process. As a basic link in the derivation of sentence, it is bound up with cognitive processes on the one hand, and with morphological processes, on the other (Cf. Panfilov 1977). No attempt whatever will be made here even to sketch the contours of this complex interrelationship.

The question of division into sub-types will be touched upon. Ergative and nominative languages are divided into sub-types which are established on the basis of the expression of the predicate, subject and object, and of the role of aspect and determination in it. Sub-types of ergative languages will be neglected here. The partitive sub-type of nominative languages alone will be considered. In Balto-Finnic languages the subject is expressed by the nominative or the partitive case, while the object by the accusative or the partitive. The total subject or object represented by a nominative or accusative is regarded as definite, the verb being perfective. Indefinite or partitive subjects or objects are collocated with non-perfective verbs. In Lithuanian the partitive subject or object is expressed by the genitive case. In Slavonic languages only traces of the partitive-genitive have been preserved. In Hungarian representing the total sub-type this correlation is unknown. The fact that the partitive sub-type is on decline in Slavonic languages is accounted for by the occurence of the 'overt' category of aspect, similar to Hungarian where the absence of the partitive sub-type is due to the occurrence of the 'overt' category of definiteness. Wherever neither of these categories developed, their function was taken over by total and partitive case endings. Illustrative examples will be given from Finnish together with their Hungarian equivalents and Russian translations:

Pietari osti leipää.
Péter evett kenyeret.
Petr jel hleb.
'Peter ate some bread.'

The Finnish accusative *(livän)* corresponds to a verb with a perfective prefix in Hungarian and Russian, and a noun in the accusative preceded by the definite article in Hungarian: *a kenyeret* or a noun in accusative in Russian.

Pietari osti leivän.
Péter megette a kenyeret.
Peter s'jel chleb. (definite)
'Peter ate (has eaten) the bread.'

The Finnish partitive case corresponds to the accusative of the Russian noun and to the accusative of Hungarian noun with zero article *(kenyeret)*. The perfective prefixes *meg-* and *s-* are not added to the verb in Hungarian and Russian, respectively.

The Russian sentence *Petr s'jel chleba* 'Peter ate/has eaten some bread' with a perfective verb and the object in the genitive expresses a perfective action directed to a part of the object.

The partitive sub-type encompasses a wide range of constructions as can be testified by a comparison between Estonian and Russian. (Pjall et. al. 1962 and Part 1 of this book). The remains of the partitive-genitive in Russian represent considerable difficulties for Hungarian learners of Russian, for partitive constructions are missing in Hungarian.

Although the questions of primary sentence formation have been analyzed in some detail nothing has so far been said about 'circumstants' expressing place, time, etc. by means of nouns and adverbs. Their typology is not yet worked out, the typology of case systems deals with this range of problems—on the paradigmatic level. This is clearly insufficient, for one must also take into account languages possessing no case system. The means of expressing adverbials in Russian and Hungarian, however, have been elaborated on a semantic basis in detail, which greatly facilitates their typological analysis (Cf. Pete 1973, 1976). The expression of adverbial relations in English and Hungarian has been studied along similar lines (Keresztes 1975). These works provide some support for typological analysis. This has had to be noted first of all in order to point to the relevance of contrastive research in typology (for details see Deže 1982a).

On aspectuality and determination. In Balto-Finnic languages, in Lithuanian, in Slavonic languages and in Hungarian the same type of aspectuality can be observed. It has received a clear-cut shape in the Slavonic aspects. Aspectual pairs are formed by two cycles of rules; perfectivization and imperfectivization: *pisat'* ('write' /imp./) → *napisat'* ('write' /perf./) *perepisat'* '(rewrite' /perf./) → *perepisyvat'* ('rewrite' /imp./). In Lithuanian and Hungarian only perfectivization exist: Hung. *ir* ('write' /imp./), *megír* ('write' /perf./), there being no imperfectivization. In this way they represent only aspectuality, without the category of verbal aspect, which implies highly developed morphological means in both perfectivization and imperfectivization. This type of aspectuality is contrasted with another one represented by English, Swahili and some other languages, which manifests itself in two series of the temporal forms of dynamic verbs expressing activity in process and out of process: *Peter was reading the book. Peter read the book.* Types of aspectuality have implications concerning the system of tenses and *Aktionsarten* (on typology see Comrie 1976, on the comparison of Russian and Hungarian see Bihari—Tyihonov 1968, Deže 1982a).

Balto-Finnic and Slavonic languages as well as Lithuanian lack articles, whereas Hungarian has definite, indefinite and zero articles. The presence of articles provides a solid formulation on which to group some languages into one type, in which, apart from universal demonstrative pronouns expressing 'emphatic' determination, there is also an article for the expression of 'non-emphatic' determination. Both types of languages, those with and without articles, are further divided into sub-types according to what features of determination are conveyed by what formal means. In spite of valuable general works (Moravcsik 1969, Krámský 1972, Majtinskaja 1969), no clear picture of these features has yet been drawn and with the exception of the article the devices of determination have remained little studied.

Determination is also connected with aspectuality, as was pointed out above. The link between determination and grammatical number is also known, and here only one generally neglected factor will be considered: the attitude of the speaker. In aspectuality the role of this factor is taken into account, but sometimes only with some reserve, as a non-systemic factor. In the typology of determination and number, one must distinguish between languages which consistently apply their

marking from those that use them only when the speaker considers it
necessary to express them for his own purpose in communication. It goes
without saying that the freedom of the speaker is limited by a number of
factors. For example, in the Hungarian sentence *Péter újságot olvasott*
'Peter newspaper read' (lit.) it is not known whether Peter read one or
more than one newspaper, or whether the newspaper were already known
or not. If he thinks it necessary, he will communicate for example that he
read one definite newspaper: *Péter olvasta az újságot.* If, however, he
highlights aspectuality by the help of perfective preverb *meg*, he must
express number and determination: *Péter elolvasta az újságot, Péter
elolvasott egy újságot* 'Peter read (has) read the/a newspaper' where
determination is expressed by definite or indefinite articles *(az,
egy)*.

On parts of the sentence. No mention of the parts of the sentence was
made when processes were enumerated, as they must be considered to be
the result of a number of processes. As is well known, parts of the sentence
like predicate, subject, object, adverbial are distinguished in all languages.
Grammars of various languages, however, differ greatly in their ways of
drawing a borderline between parts of the sentence because they link these
categories with the peculiarities of their expression in the given language.
This side of the question does not concern typology. There are, however,
phenomena which do not depend on the peculiarities of individual
languages and their grammatical traditions. In nominative languages, for
example, there is a remarkable agreement in the definition of the predicate
and the subject, but no consensus can be encountered in the definition of
objects and adverbials. In the majority of grammars, including grammars
of Russian direct and indirect objects and adverbials are distinguished. In
Hungarian grammar there are only direct objects and adverbials. It would
be an error to consider the latter division as just a whim of Hungarian
grammarians. Tradition chose only one of the possible solutions, which
can be conceived as the formal expression of sentence constituents. Even
the examples quoted above suffice to show that Hungarian has objects
expressed by the accusative even in cases where Russian and other
languages use other oblique cases. If, with a view to the Hungarian case
system, this analysis were extended to other cases and other parts of the
sentence as well, the Hungarian accusative expressing a primary object
would turn out to stand in clear-cut contrast to other cases expressing
adverbials and secondary objects. The division into direct object and
adverbials, the latter comprising secondary objects too, could be effected

on such a basis. Naturally, not all details concerning the parts of the sentence in Hungarian are determined by the case system. From the point of view of the present author, it is more important that the Hungarian case system represents a special type, and that the division into parts of the sentence is motivated by typological factors.

If in nominative languages there are also constructions typical of the ergative type, problems of defining the subject and object arise. The sentence Russ. *U Petra jest' mašina* and Hung. *Péternek van kocsija* ('Peter has a car') can be given a twofold interpretation: *U Petra* and *Péternek* will be the subjects, while *mašina* and *kocsija* the objects or vice versa. In the second case, the subject will be represented by the part of the sentence that is expressed by the nominative *(mašina, kocsija)*, but then a strange primary order of subject and object is obtained where the subject appears in sentence-final and the object in sentence-initial position. Since Hungarian grammarians pay more attention to morphological means than to word order, they chose the second solution. But then the parts of the sentence in individual languages do not correspond to universal categories, according to which the actants *U Petra* and *Péternek* are subjects, but *mašina* and *kocsija* object, as in the Russian sentence *Petr imeet mašinu*. (On the typological question of parts of the sentence see Čleṇy 1972, Deže 1982.)

The communicative organization of the sentence: diatheses, theme and rheme. The primary rules of communicative organization are applied in deriving primary sentences. Secondary rules change primary sentences in accordance with the context, situation, and the goals of the speaker. It is advisable, nevertheless, to consider primary and secondary rules jointly.

The system of rules on diathesis precedes the rules on theme and rheme: each diathesis has at its disposal theme–rheme rules of its own, but so far typology has studied the word order rules of complete active sentences only. The process of diathesis is less familiar under this term. In addition to complete active sentences, it encompasses incomplete active and passive sentences as well. Diathesis is meant as the interrelation between the arguments of the underlying invariant structure and the various parts of the sentence. Complete active sentences show a primary interrelation which changes when one of the arguments is omitted from the sentence or their interrelation in passive sentences is altered (cf. Tipologija 1974, 13), e.g. *Petr pišet pis'mo* ('Peter is writing a letter'), *Pišet pis'mo* ('/He/ is writing a letter'), *Pis'mo pišetsja Petrom*, ('The letter is being written by Peter'), etc. From the viewpoint of typology passive voice represent the most important derived diathesis. The primary formation of the sentence, however, may exclude the possibility of the emergence of passive constructions: topic-prominent languages do not have passive sentences or their role is marginal (Li—Thompson 1976, 467). It may very well be case that the absence of the passive in a number of languages is closely bound up with their topic-prominent properties. Hungarian also belongs to this group. In the majority of languages the agent is missing in passive sentences. If passive exists in a language, one has the following opportunities for passivization: the subject of the passive sentence can be the direct object, the indirect object or even the adverbial depending on the language, e.g. Eng. *Peter gave the book to Paul*, Russ. *Petr dal knigu Pavlu;* Eng. *The book was given to Paul*, Russ. *Kniga byla dana Pavlu;* Eng. *Paul was given the book (by Peter)*, Eng. *Somebody slept in the bed*, Russ. *Kto-to spal v posteli*, Eng. *The bed was slept in*, Russ. **Postel' byla spana* (lit.).

In languages with no passive, the interrelation between actants and parts of the sentence is expressed by some other means, e.g. verbal predicates have a double base with a transitive and an intransitive variant, Hung. *nyit* 'open' (tr.), *nyílik* 'open' (intr.) and word order is free, as in Hungarian and topic-prominent languages (Kiss 1981).

Parts of the sentence in the basic diathesis may be ordered on the basis of four types of rules. They are well known and it is sufficient to enumerate two variants:

(1) SOV   (2) SVO   (3) VSO   (4) VOS
     OSV   OVS   VOS   or   SVO

In the basic order in types (1) to (3) S precedes O, and in type (4) it is the other way round. In the secondary order of the categories in question, O precedes S, with the exception of one of the sub-types (3). For types (1) and (2), the characteristic position of the verbal predicate is at the end or in the middle of the sentence.

Russian belongs to type (2): *Petr pisal pis'mo*, but it has free word order, which allows 6 variants. Hungarian too has free word order, but there the basic orders may be SOV: *Péter levelet írt* 'Peter letter wrote' (lit.), if the verb has imperfect aspectuality and the object has no article, but also SVO: *Péter írta a levelet* 'Peter wrote the letter', if the object has a definite or indefinite article and or if the verb has imperfective aspect.

Word order rules themselves are insufficient for the typology of the theme and rheme. They must be supplemented by rules of sentence stress. Unfortunately these rules are little known. Data from a large number of languages of type (1) testify to the principle of pre-verbal stressing, when the nominal part of the sentence immediately preceding the verbal predicate receives sentence stess: XV (where X is a stressed part of the sentence). If this place is taken by an unstressable element that cannot be removed from its place, the stressed part of the sentence (X) precedes this element: XYV, where Y is an unstressed element. When in the case of free order the verb is not placed in sentence final position, the principle of pre-verbal stress is preserved, e.g. in Hung. *Péter levelet irt* 'Peter letter wrote' (lit.), **Levelet** *irt Péter* 'Letter wrote Peter' (lit.). The part of the sentence following the verb is not stressed in Hungarian (VY), but in some languages it may have contrastive stress (VX).

In languages of type (2) the principle of postverbal stressing is applied: the part of the sentence immediately following the verb or some other element receives sentence stress: VX: *Petr pisal pis'mo*, VYX: *Petr pisal pis'mo Pavlu*. In languages with free word order the part of the sentence preceding the verb may also be stressed, usually for contrast' sake: *Petr* **pis'mo** *pisal*.

On the basis of word order and sentence stressing rules it will be possible to elaborate the typological rules of theme and rheme. A comparison of data from languages of various types demonstrates that the same configuration of word order and stressing fulfils different functions, whereas the same function is expressed by means of a different configuration, e.g. Russ. *Pis'mo pisal* **mal'čik** ('The letter wrote a boy' /lit./) has its Hungarian counterpart in *A levelet egy* **gyerek** *irta* (Cf. Part 2 for more detail).

The linearization of parts of the sentence, words making up phrases and morphemes within words, i.e. the order of elements in grammatical units follows two typological principles. They have various names, here the old latin names will be used: the principle of *regens post rectum* and that of *regens ante rectum*. Greenberg's universals, which layed the foundations of the typology of word order were formulated on the basis of these principles. The principles themselves, however, had been well known before. Some of them will be enumerated here, with illustrative examples from Hungarian and Russian:

A) Word order of phrases

    a) the relationship between the object and the verbal predicate: OV: *levelet irt*, 'letter wrote', VO: *pisal pis'mo* 'wrote letter'

    b) attributive constructions expressed by participial phrases: (N + Participle) + N *a levelet iró fiú* 'the letter writing boy' (lit.); N + (Participle + N) *mal'čik pišuščij pis'mo* ('boy writing the letter').

c) attributives expressed by adjectives: Adverb + Adjective + N:
csodálatosan szép lány '(a) wonderfully nice girl' (lit.); N + Adverb +
Adjective: *devuška udivitel'no krasivaja* ('/a/ girl wonderfully nice' /lit./).

d) possessive attributes expressed by nouns in the genitive: N_{gen} + N: *a
fiú kalapja* 'of the boy hat' (lit.) N + N_{gen}: *šljapa mal'čika* 'the hat of the
boy'.

It is clear for all speakers of these languages that the Hungarian word
order may also be VO, while in Russian a participial phrase may precede a
noun, and an adjective usually takes its place before a noun. In Hungarian
the principle of *regens post rectum* is observed consistently enough,
whereas in Russian this principle is enforced together with the principle of
regens ante rectum.

B) Order of analytic and synthetic words

   e) postpositions or prepositions:

az iskola **mögött za** *školoj* '*behind* the school'

   f) suffixes and prefixes: *téved-***és-ek-et** 'errors', **pere***vesti* '*trans*late'

Here it must be noted again that the principle of the postposition of
auxiliary morphemes and words is consistently observed in Hungarian
and that in Russian suffixation is also highly developed. All this is not a
result of mere chance. In Hungarian, like in languages of the type SOV, the
principle of *regens post rectum* is consistently observed. The principle of
regens ante rectum is consistently applied only in languages of the type
VSO, while languages of the type SVO are inconsistent. In the case of
Russian, one must also reckon with the fact that the type SVO is the
result of a relatively late development. In an originally SVO language like
Swahili, the principle of *regens ante rectum* is more consistently adhered to
(Cf. Part 2).

On morphological processes. With the analysis of the complex types of
linearization the field of morphology has been entered and the order of
morphemes in analytic and synthetic words has been touched upon. The
principles of the agglutinative, inflective and isolating expression of
grammatical meanings in morphemes and their integration into words are
well-known. Nor is it necessary to treat in detail the analytic or synthetic
shaping of words. It is however indispensable to touch upon the
paradigms, namely the case and inflectional systems. Russian a primarily
inflective language and Hungarian a primarily agglutinative one, have
different types of case and inflectional systems. The case system of Russian
belongs to type 1, while that of Hungarian to type 2 (Cf. Hjelmslev 1935,
1937, and Part 1). From the viewpoint of general typology the data of the

two languages under analysis here would suggest the conclusion that inflective languages have a case system of type 1, whereas agglutinative languages a case system of type 2. The problem is much more complex. The relationship between inflective and agglutinative techniques as well as case systems is not clear as yet. The sole assumption of reasonable likelihood here is that agglutinative languages may have a case system of type 2, while inflective languages may have case system of type 1 or lack that.

Some basic information on the complex range of problems connected with the two types of case systems will be chosen here.

Type 1 is adequately represented by Russian, while for type 2 Hungarian may serve as apt illustration, though the picture is less clear in the latter case. In type 1, cases express objective as well as adverbial meanings, whereas in type 2 some cases express (basic) objective meanings but others—adverbial ones. In addition, adverbial meanings expressed in Russian by the same case with various prepositions are expressed in Hungarian by means of various case suffixes.

e.g. acc. *stol* (object), acc. *asztal-t* 'table'

   v + acc. *stol*   illative *asztalba* '*in (the)* table'

   na + acc. *stol*   superessive *asztal-ra* 'on (the) table'

Three Hungarian cases correspond to the Russian accusative with or without a preposition. This demonstrates why the Russian case system consists of six cases, while the Hungarian one of twenty cases (there is no consensus because of defective cases). It is of course a question of principles rather than number: in Russian the principle of the joint expression of objective and adverbial meanings is in force, as opposed to Hungarian where the principle of the separate expression of these meanings holds. This principle is at work in agglutinative languages which have only a small number of cases with adverbial meanings and a great number of postpositions as well as in agglutinative languages with a case system of type 3 (e.g. Tabasaran) in which even the meanings expressed by postpositions in Hungarian are conveyed by case suffixes whose number may reach fifty. Such a development of a principle is open for all languages in which postpositions are collocated with an unmarked case, usually the genitive and the transformation of postpositions into a case suffixes is possible.

The 'simple' Russian case system is realized in three declensions, and each case is expressed by various suffixes in the singular and the plural, so that each case is as a rule represented by six suffixes. In addition to

declinations, the phonetic shape of the last vowel of the stem is also taken
into account, which further increases the number of variants. In addition
to the synonymy of case markers, their homonymy can also be observed.
The 'complex' system of Hungarian cases, on the other hand, is expressed
by uniform suffixes in both singular and plural, and have only phonetic
variants, in compliance with the phonetic shape of the stem. The forms of
the dative in the two languages are compared below (with no claim to
completeness, for details see Deže 1982a):

Russ.

singular I. *škol-e, tët-e* II. *dom-u, kon'-u*, III. *ploščad-i*
plural I. *skol-am, tët-am*, II *dom-am, kon'-am*, III. *ploščad'-am*
Hung.

singular: *iskolá-nak, néni-nek*
plural: *iskolá-k-nak, néni-k-nek.*

Apart from morphological features, complex types, as worked out by
Skalička, also rely on syntactic, derivational and phonological features;
that is why they characterize language systems in the fullest possible way.
This brief survey of the grammatical typology and characteristics of two
languages is concluded here by the enumeration of a number of features
characteristic of the inflective and agglutinative type (Cf. Skalička 1974,
18—19).

The inflective type:

    a) synonymy of case endings
    b) homonymy of case endings
    c) strong differentiation of word classes
    d) grammatical gender or some other classification of nouns
    e) free word order
    f) subordinate clauses instead of deverbative noun phrases
    g) predominance of vowels over consonants

The agglutinative type:

    a) abundance of case endings
    b) limited homonymy and synonymy of case endings
    c) weak differentiation of word classes
    d) absence of grammatical gender
    e) bound word order
    f) deverbative noun phrases in place of subordinate clauses
    g) highly developed system of consonants

If the present analysis were complete and if complex propositions
were also dealt with, one could note in connection with feature f). that

although both languages have subordinate clauses as well as deverbal noun phrases, subordinate clauses are of later development in Hungarian, and Russian participial structions were secondarily introduced under the influence of the literary language. Skalička's criterion c) is also correct: in Russian, parts of speech are well distinguished, while in Hungarian there is no clear boundary between nouns and adjectives. A consideration of the phonological criteria would stretch the frames of the present paper too far. They are only given as an illustration of complex typology as worked out by Skalička (1974).

3.4.4. TYPOLOGY IN DESCRIPTIVE GRAMMARS

This brief survey is far from complete: it has taken into account elements of a characterization of two languages. It has had a twofold aim: to direct the typologists' attention to the fact that their results become common property if they are made use of in descriptive and contrastive grammars of individual languages, and to convince scholars interested in individual languages that their descriptions based on typology may be important to a great number of linguists who are not specialists in other languages. The unifying force of typology may be contrasted with the process of isolation, as a result of which linguistics is transformed into an unfortunate conglomerate of separate fields of investigations. I do not mean by this that typology is the only consolidating factor of the discipline; I firmly believe, however, that it helps linguistics to reach a higher stage of development.

The object of descriptive grammars will continue to be the system of a given language in its specificity. It is not a question of returning to general and rational grammar but of explicitly formulating typological laws relevant for a given language, for they have great explanatory power, serving as a source for the establishment of a considerable number of though naturally far from all individual features. Since no language in general represents a 'pure' type, it is necessary in characterizing an individual language to consider all the types that manifest themselves in the given language. Other types can be briefly noted.

Contrastive grammars are based upon descriptive grammars, and knowledge of the system of the languages contrasted is assumed. However, the focus of attention in such grammar is transferred to a comparison of two language systems. The mere fact that different types and sub-types are probably reflected in the system of two languages requires a broader and more detailed presentation of typological information than the characteristics of one language only. In addition attention must be paid to the individual properties of contrasted languages. A contrastive grammar is not the .amalgamation of two individual grammars. This would give rise to voluminous grammars. A contrastive grammar must contain those parts of the systems of two languages which have explanatory power as a result of the comparison itself. For example, in a contrastive grammar of Russian and Hungarian, the principles of the case systems and inflections of the two languages must be included, an enumeration of the formal variants of the case endings of Russian declination, however, should not be incorporated into this contrastive grammar, with the exception of those that can be better understood on the basis of a comparison with Hungarian.

Authors of descriptive and contrastive grammars can, however, blame typologists for the fact that the typological information is scattered in hundreds of publications and is not generalized. Certainly their claim is justified. The integration of typological knowledge is indispensable even for the typologists themselves. Only a generalization of the results attained by typology will create the necessary conditions for the writing of typological characteristics of individual languages. These characteristics will then serve as an optimum source for the application of typology in the description and comparison of individual languages.

3.4.5. THE RELATIONSHIP BETWEEN THEORETICAL AND APPLIED CONTRASTIVE STUDIES

This question and the next one (3.4.6.) will be examined in the context of contrastive linguistics in Yugoslavia. An examination of the problems of contrastive studies connected with Serbo-Croatian entails the analysis of the actual problems of the theory and application of contrastive linguistics in general. This is the case since the contrasting of Serbo-Croatian with other languages started in the form of projects involving many scholars and there were very few similar attempts in the world. Yugoslavian contrastive linguistics has maintained the role of an avant-garde even today. Its results, especially those of English-Serbo-Croatian project, are known all over the world. In addition, the contrasting of the national languages of Yugoslavia with each other and with the world languages taught in Yugoslavian schools will result in such a diversity of contrastive studies that Yugoslavia can be considered as a laboratory of contrastive research in which the theoretical and methodological problems can be studied under excellent conditions.

The richness and diversity of Yugoslavian contrastive studies makes even their brief description impossible, and I must restrict even my comments to some theoretical and methodological questions approached by me from the point of view of a participant in the Serbo-Croatian-Hungarian contrastive project who is also a typologist.

I accept the proposal of the Polish scholars who define two types of contrastive linguistics: theoretical studies and applied studies. I am, of course, aware of the fact that the majority of the studies can be posited in the continuum between these two poles. In my opinion this division is important for two reasons: contrastive studies can be characterized with the help of these two "ideal" types and it calls the attention to the importance of both theory and application. The definition of these two poles, therefore, forces scholars to consider both theory and application in a systematic way. At present I think it is necessary to call the attention to the role of theory from the point of view of application.

The dichotomy of the two types of contrastive studies will be quoted from the book "An Introductory English-Polish Contrastive Grammar": "Theoretical contrastive studies give an exhaustive account of the differences and similarities between two or more languages, provide an adequate model for their comparison... Theoretical semantico-syntactic contrastive studies operate with universals, i.e. they specify how a given universal category is realized in the contrasted languages" (Fisiak et al. 1978, 10).

The authors, being contrastive linguists, also higlight the notions 'congruence', 'equivalence' and 'correspondence'. I don't consider them so important from the point of view of typology, but as a contrastive linguist I think they must be considered. The reference to universal categories is not sufficient and must be complemented with the rules of types. After such specification I can accept the following statement: "theoretical contrastive studies are language-independent. They do not investigate how a given category present in language A is represented in language B. Instead they look for the realization of a universal category X in both A and B. Thus, theoretical contrastive studies do not have a direction from A to B or vice versa." (Fisiak et al. 1978, 10.). So, the definition of theoretical contrastive studies is correct if it is made more specific, completed from the typological point of view.

The Polish scholars define applied contrastive studies in the following way: "Applied contrastive studies are preoccupied with the problem of how a universal category X, realized in language A as Y, is rendered in language B and what may be the possible consequences of this for the given field of application. Another task of applied contrastive studies is the identification of probable areas of difficulty in another language where, e.g., a given category is not represented in the surface and interference is likely to occur" (Fisiak et al. 1978, 107). It can be accepted if the comments made above are taken into consideration.

A minor part of contrastive research belongs to the theoretical contrastive studies as far as they compare two languages on equal or nearly equal footing. Most of the theoretical studies, however, do not satisfy the requirements formulated above because they do not take into consideration the universals and types, or their account is not satisfactory. The volumes of the Serbo-Croatian-Hungarian project belong to theoretical contrastive studies. The typological aspect, however, is manifested in them in a particular way. In the analysis of a sub-system, one of the two languages which represents a type more clearly, explicitly and with overt categories is in the foreground. In Hungarian, for example, the expression of definiteness is more explicit, therefore, it is highlighted in the second volume (Mikeš, M., Dezső, L., Vuković, G.). Serbo-Croatian clearly represents a type of aspect and only a "less developed" sub-type of the same type of aspectuality is to be found in Hungarian, therefore, the analysis of Serbo-Croatian will be in the focus of attention. The case systems of these two languages belong to different types. The characteristics of these types of case systems explain that the more differentiated "adverbial" cases of Hungarian are in the foreground (Cf. Vajda 1976). The "objective" cases are more explicit and reflect the universal categories better in Serbo-Croatian, they will, therefore, be in the focus in the contrastive study.

The bulk of the Yugoslavian investigation can be classified as applied contrastive studies. Most of them, however, do not meet the typological requirement, they cannot demonstrate, how a universal category X is reflected in langugae A because of the lack of integrated typological studies. But they are able to show very well, how a category in language A can be related to that or those of language B or is reflected in "covert" phenomena of B, i.e. how the semantic content of the categories of English, Russian, German etc. is expressed in Serbo-Croatian.

One of the crucial problems of applied contrastive studies all over the world is that they can be applied in their given form only on a very high level of instruction, in the training of teachers. For their application in programmes, in school textbooks supplementary applied investigations are needed considering the specific features of the programmes or textbooks. This is not a fault of contrastive studies, on the contrary, the fact that they reflect the problems of acquisition in general makes their application in various situations possible. At the same time, one must be aware of the necessity of the studies directed towards the concrete forms of foreign language education. A second cycle of applied studies is required, otherwise volumes of contrastive studies will woulder away and the teaching of foreign languages will go on in the old way. If a country has a system of research connected with education, as the socialist countries have, this can be avoided. There has been considerable progress in Yugoslavia in this direction.

3.4.6. THEORETICAL CONTRASTIVE STUDIES
FROM THE VIEWPOINT OF THE SYSTEM OF FOREIGN
AND SECOND LANGUAGE EDUCATION IN A COUNTRY

Typology is implied in the definitions of both theoretical and applied contrastive studies, moreover, universals and, I add, types play a major role in them. In theoretical studies languages A and B must be characterized separately, in applied studies language A is described and B is related to it. Both theoretical and applied contrastive studies can use the results of typology in an optimum way if they are based on the typological characteristics of the languages to be contrasted. This also holds for applied studies. If the typologically characterized system of A is related to that of B, the results will be more reliable. At present this is important because many researchers aim at a systematic description of language A but use unsystematic and unprecise information concerning language B.

The analysis of the application of contrastive linguistics cannot be limited to one language only, isolated from that of other languages taught in the country as it happens today. In many countries there are more than one languages taught as a foreign language or as a second language. Their relationship in the system of foreign language education must also be accounted for. This is not simple even in a country with one major language like Hungary. In Yugoslavia, there are major languages: Serbo-Croatian, Slovenian, Macedonian, and secondary languages: Albanian, Hungarian, Slovak and others which are major languages in other countries. Therefore, the relationship between the teaching of the major and the minority languages is very complex. All major languages must be contrasted with the minority languages, and Serbo-Croatian should be compared to other major languages. From the point of view of the application in the system of education their sequence must also be taken into consideration, e.g. a Hungarian pupil studies Serbo-Croatian before Russian and this is a source of both positive and negative interference. A jungle of contrastive studies will be the result of uncoordinated investigations. The contrastive studies will be useful to a great degree even then, but they might analyze questions which had been clarified, on the one hand, and, on the other, the results obtained in the various studies cannot be transferred without an underlying basis for reference. This fact will have an impact on the quality of studies in general. I can give an example. There is no article in Serbo-Croatian, but Macedonian, Hungarian, English, German, French have articles. Their use differs from language to language, but these systems of articles have common properties as well, and the typological information concerning them can be transferred and accounted for in contrasting these languages with Serbo-Croatian.

A system of contrastive research in a country requires both a high level theory and methodology as well as an isomorphic approach to the comparison of languages. Typology will contribute to this to a great degree in the future. The unordered set of contrastive studies can be turned into a system, if the typological characterizations of the given languages will be written. They serve as a basis for contrastive studies. In Yugoslavia the typological characterization of Serbo-Croatian is the first task which can be fulfilled only by Yugoslavian scholars. Many details are clear, some of them must be clarified, but these parts will be integrated into a whole if there will be a theoretical, typological approach underlying them. The same holds for other languages, too.

A system of contrastive studies based on the typological characteristics of the languages to be compared will not only make the research work more transparent, reliable from methodological point of view, but gives the opportunity for extension and variation. New studies can be joined to the existing ones, e.g. the questions of acquisition of Russian and English by Hungarian pupils who have some competence in Serbo-Croatian.

The theoretical and methodological problems, of course, must be solved first. The approach and the formulation of the typological characterization of Serbo-Croatian must be identical or isomorphic with that of Hungarian or Russian etc. to a degree admitting the comparison of these languages. This problem is not new, however, it is relevant to comparative studies in general.

The reader may have the impression that I am right in highlighting the systematization of contrastive studies, but may think that my requirements are too strong and cannot be met. I admit that these requirements are strong, at least at present. But the way towards such a system can be divided into stages. The typological characterization is a theoretical task but it considers the application and the latter can limit its scope. At present I am writing a typological characteristics of Russian for Hungarian students and teachers. Such a book must contain the major characteristics of Russian, but may disregard the types not relevant for Hungarian. A second variant written for students and teachers without regard to their mother tongues must be more complete from a typological point of view and take the major languages of the world into consideration. This will be a very hard task, requiring a complex team. The typological characterization of Serbo-Croatian can also be written in subsequent stages. Even in the first stage it will be complex because more than one language is to be accounted for. A typological characterization of Serbo-Croatian only for the Yugoslavian students with a variety of mother tongues (Slovenian, Macedonian, Slovak, Albanian, Hungarian, Turkish) extends the scope of the presentation of types and sub-types. It will result from the team work of scholars familiar with these languages.

References

Adamec, P. (1976). *Porjadok slov v sovremennom russkom jazyke* (Word order in contemporary Russian). Rozpravy ČAV Řada Společenskych Věd 76. Roĉn. 15. Prague.

Akĉurjan, I. A. and Mamcur, Je. A. (1972). Logika otkrytija ili psichologija issledovanija (The logic of discovery or the psychology of research). *Voprosy Filosofii* 8: 159—162.

Altmann, G. and Lehfeldt, W. (1973) *Allgemeine Sprachtypologie*. Uni-Taschenbücher 250. Munich.

Anderson, J. M. (1971). *The Grammar of Case: towards a Localistic Theory*. Cambridge:Cambridge University Press.

Antinucci, F. (1977). *Fondamenti di una teoria tipologica del linguaggio*. Bologna:Mulino.

Austerlitz. R. (1970). Agglutination in Northern Eurasia in perspective. In R. Jakobson and Sh. Kawamoto (eds.) *Studies in General and Oriental Linguistics Presented to Shirô Hattori on the Occasion of his Sixtieth Birthday*. Tokyo.

Bach, E. and Harms, R. T. (eds.) (1967). *Universals in Linguistic Theory*. New York:Holt, Rinehart and Winston.

Bazell, C. E. (1949). Syntactic relations and linguistic typology. *Cahiers Ferdinand de Saussure* 8:5—20.

Bell, A. (1971). Acquisition-significant and transmission-significant universals. *WPLU* 5:U1—U9.

Benveniste, E. (1966). La classification des langues. *Problèmes de linguistique générale* Paris: Gallimard. pp. 99—118.

Bertalanffy, L. von (1951). Problems of general systems theory. *Human Biology* 23:302—312.

Bertalanffy, L. von (1968). *General Systems Theory. Foundations, Development, Applications*. New York:Brazziler.

Bese, L., Dezső, L., and Gulya, L. (1970). On the syntactic typology of the Uralic and Altaic languages. In L. Dezső and P. Hajdú (eds.) *Theoretical problems of typology and the Northern Eurasian languages*. Budapest: Akadémiai Kiadó pp. 113—128.

Bihari, J. and Tyihonov, A. N. (1968). *Az orosz igeszemlélet* (The Russian aspect). Budapest:Tankönyvkiadó.

Birnbaum, H. (1970). *Problems of Typological and Genetic Linguistics Viewed in a Generative Framework*. The Hague:Mouton Publishers.

Birnbaum, H. (1974). Typology, geneology and linguistic universals. *Linguistics* 144:5—26.

Bogdanov, J. A. (1964). Dialektičeskij put' poznanija (The dialectical path of cognition). In
    P. V. Kopnin and M. V. Vil'nickij (eds.) *Problemy myšlenija v sovremennoj nauke.*
    Moscow: Nauka. pp. 106—123.
Bondarko, A. V. (1976). *Teorija morfologičeskich kategorij* (A theory of morphological
    categories). Leningrad: Nauka.
Buttke, K. (1969). *Gesetzmäßigkeiten der Wortfolge im Russischen.* Halle: N. Niemeyer.
Byrne, J. (1885). *General Principles of the Structure of Language.* London: Trübner.

Cholodovič, A. A. (1966). K tipologii porjadka slov (On the typology of word order).
    Filologičeskije Nauki 3:3—13.
Cholodovič, A. A. (ed.) (1969). *Tipologija kauzativnych konstrukcij. Morfologičeskij kauzativ*
    (A typology of causative constructions. The morphological causative).
    Leningrad: Nauka.
Cholodovič, A. A. (ed.) (1974). *Tipologija passivnych konstrukcij. Diatezy i zalogi* (A
    typology of passive constructions. Diatheses and voices). Leningrad: Nauka.
Chomsky, N. (1965). *Aspects of the Theory of Syntax.* Cambridge, Mass.: M.I.T. Press.
Chomsky, N. (1968). *Language and Mind.* New York: Harcourt-Brace.
Chomsky, N. (1976). *Reflections on Language.* London: Tempel Smith.
Chomsky, N. and Lasnik, H. (1977). Filters and control. *Linguistic Inquiry.* 8:425—504.
Členy predloženija v jazykach različných tipov (1972). (Parts of the sentence in languages of
    different types). Leningrad: Nauka.
Cole, P. and Sadock, J. M. (eds.) (1977). *Grammatical Relations.* New York: Academic Press.
Comrie, B. (1976). *Aspect. An Introduction to the Study of Verbal Aspect and Related
    Problems.* Cambridge: Cambridge University Press.
Corder, S. P. (1973). Linguistic theory and applied linguistics. *3rd AIMAV Seminar in
    collaboration with AILA, CILA and the Council of Europe* (Neuchâtel, 5th—6th May
    1972). Brussels. pp. 11—19.
Coseriu, E. (1968). Sincronía, diacronía y tipología. *Actas XI. Congr. Intern. de Lingüística y
    Filol. Romanicas.* Madrid. pp. 269—283.
Coseriu, E. (1970). Über Leistung und Grenzen der kontrastiven Grammatik. *Probleme der
    kontrastiven Grammatik.* Düsseldorf. pp. 9—30.
Coseriu, E. (1972). Über die Sprachtypologie Wilhelm von Humboldts. *Festschrift für Kurt
    Wais zum 65. Geburtstag.* Tübingen: Narr. pp. 107—235.
Coseriu, E. (1975). *Leistung und Grenzen der transformationellen Grammatik.*
    Tübingen: Narr.

Dahl, Ö. (1969). *Topic and Comment: A Study in Russian and General Transformational
    Grammar.* Stockholm: Almquist-Wiksell.
Daneš, Fr. (1957). *Intonace a věta ve spisovne čestině* (Intonation and sentence in literary
    Czech). ČSAV Ústav pro Jazyk Český. Studie a prace linguistické 2. Prague.
Deže, L. (1968). K voprosu ob istoričeskoj tipologii slavjanskogo porjadka slov (On the
    problem of the historical typology of Slavic word order). *Studia Slavica* 14:101—117.
Deže, L. (1982a). *Tipologičeskaja charakteristika russkoj grammatiki v sravnenii s vengerskoj*
    (Typological characteristics of Russian grammar). Budapest: Tankönyvkiadó.
Deže, L. (1982b). *Tipološka karakteristika hrvatsko-srpske gramatike u sporedivanju sa
    madarskom* (Typological characterization of Croato-Serbian grammar contrasted with
    Hungarian). Budapest: Tankönyvkiadó.

Dezső, L. (1970). A word order typology of three-member sentences (S, V, O). *Actes du X-e Congrès International des Linguistes*. II. Bucharest. pp. 551—555.

Dezső, L. (1974). Topics in syntactic typology. *Linguistica Generalia 1. Studies in Linguistic Typology*. Prague. pp. 191—210.

Dezső, L. (1979). Questions of system and structure in language from the viewpoint of typology. *Linguistica Silesiana* 3:41—54.

Dezső, L. (1980). Word order, theme and rheme in Hungarian, and the problems of word-order acquisition. In L. Dezső and W. Nemser (eds.) *Studies in English—Hungarian Contrastive Linguistics*. Budapest. pp. 245—298.

Dezső, L. (1981). *Studies in Old Serbo-Croatian Syntax*. Budapest-Munich:Akadémiai Kiadó-Böhlau.

Dezső, L. (1983). *Typological Characterization of Hungarian Grammar*. Budapest: Akadémiai Kiadó.

Dezső, L. and Hajdú, P. (eds.) (1970). *Theoretical Problems of Typology and the Northern Eurasian Languages*. Budapest:Akadémiai Kiadó.

Dezső, L. and Nemser, W. (1973). Language typology and contrastive linguistics. *Four papers of the Pécs Conference on Contrastive Linguistics. The Hungarian—English Contrastive Linguistics Project. Working Papers*. 4:3—26.

Dezső, L. and Szépe, Gy. (1974). Contribution to the topic comment problem. In Ö. Dahl (ed.) *Topic and Comment, Contextual Boundness and Focus*. Hamburg:H. Buske. pp. 65—93.

Diatezy i zalogi (1975). (Diatheses and voices). Leningrad:Nauka.

Dressler, W. (1967). Wege der Sprachtypologie. *Sprache* 13:1—19.

Ergativnaja konstrukcija predloženija v jazykach različných tipov (1967) (The ergative construction of sentences in languages of different types). Moscow:Nauka.

Enkvist, N. E. and Kohonen, V. (eds.) (1976). *Reports on Text-linguistics: Approaches to Word Order*. Abo.

Ferguson, Ch. A. (1970). Grammatical categories in data collection. *WPLU* 4:F1—F14.

Ferguson, Ch. A. (1971). A sample research strategy in language universals. *WPLU* 6:1—22.

Fillmore, Ch. J. (1968). The case for case. In E. Bach and R. T. Harms (eds.) *Universals in Linguistic Theory*. New York:Holt, Rinehart and Winston, pp. 1—90.

Fillmore, Ch. J. (1977). The case for case reopened. In P. Cole and J. M. Sadock (eds.) *Grammatical Relations*. New York:Academic Press. p. 59—81.

Finck, F. (1910). *Die Haupttypen des Sprachbaues*. Leipzig:Teubner.

Firbas, J. (1964). From comparative word order studies. *Brno Studies in English* 4:111—128.

Fisiak, J., Lipińska-Grzegorek, M., and Zabrocki, T. (1978). *An Introductory English—Polish Contrastive Grammar*. Warsaw: PWN.

Fraenkel, E. (1928). *Syntax der lituanischen Kasus*. Kaunas.

Gabelentz, G. von der (1891). *Die Sprachwissenschaft, ihre Aufgaben, Methoden und bisherigen Ergebnisse*. Leipzig:Weigel.

Gorodeckij, B. Ju. (1965). *K probleme semantičeskoj tipologii* (On the problem of semantic typology). Moscow:Moskovskij Universitet.

Gortan-Premk, D. (1971). *Akuzativne sintagme bez predloga u srpskohrvatskom jeziku* (Syntagms with the accusative without a preposition in Serbo-Croatian). Belgrade:Institut za Srpskohrvatski Jezik.

Grammatika russkogo jazyka II. 1. (1954) (A grammar of Russian). Moscow: Nauka.

Grasserie, R. de la (1888). *Des divisions de la linguistique.* Paris: Maisonneuve.

Grasserie, R. de la (1888, 1890). De la classification des langues. *Internationale Zeitschrift für allgemeine Schprachwissenschaft* 4:374—387, 5:296—338.

Greenberg, J. H. (1957). The nature and uses of linguistic typologies. *IJAL* 23:68—77.

Greenberg, J. H. (1960). A quantitative approach to the morphological typology of language. *IJAL* 26:178—194.

Greenberg, J. H. (ed.) (1963). *Universals of Language.* Cambridge, Mass.: M.I.T. Press.

Greenberg, J. H. (1963, paperback ed. 1966, 1968). Some universals of grammar with particular reference to the order of meaningful elements. In J. H. Greenberg (ed.) *Universals of Language.* Cambridge, Mass.: M.I.T. Press. pp. 58—90.

Greenberg, J. H. (1966). *Language Universals.* The Hague: Mouton Publishers.

Greenberg, J. H. (1969). Some methods of dynamic comparison in linguistics. In Jaan Puhvel (ed.) *Substance and Structure of Language.* Berkeley and Los Angeles: University of California Press. pp. 147—204.

Greenberg, J. H. (1970a). The role of typology in the development of scientific linguistics. In L. Dezső and P. Hajdú (eds.) *Theoretical Problems of Typology and Northern Eurasian Languages.* Budapest: Akadémiai Kiadó. pp. 11—24.

Greenberg, J. H. (1970b). On the language of observation in linguistics. *WPLU* 4:G1—G15.

Greenberg, J. H. (1972). Numeral classifiers and substantival number: problems in the genesis of a linguistic type. *WPLU* 9:1—39.

Greenberg, J. H. (1973). The typological method. In Th. A. Sebeok (ed.) *Methods in Linguistics.* The Hague: Mouton Publishers. pp. 149—193.

Halliday, M. A. K. (1967, 1968). Notes on transitivity and theme in English. *Journal of Linguistics* 3:37—87, 199—244.

Harries, H. (1973). Contrastive emphasis and cleft sentences. *WPLU* 12:85—144.

Hartmann, P. (1966). Satzstrukturen typologisch und logisch gesehen. *Kratylos* 11:1—32.

Hempel, C. G. (1951). General systems theory and the unity of science. *Human Biology* 23:313—322.

Hempel, C. G. (1965). Typological methods in the natural and the social sciences. *Aspects of Scientific Explanation and Other Essays in the Philosophy of Science.* New York. pp. 155—171.

Hempel, C. G. and Oppenheim, P. (1936). *Der Typusbegriff im Lichte der neuen Logik.* Leiden: Sijthoff.

Hetzron, R. (1970). Nonverbal sentences and degrees of definiteness in Hungarian. *Language* 46:899—927.

Hjelmslev, L. (1928). *Principes de grammaire générale.* Copenhagen: Munksgaard.

Hjelmslev, L. (1935, 1937). La catégorie des cas. Étude de grammaire générale. *Acta Jutlandica. Aarsskrift.* Vol. 7, facs. 1; Vol. 9. facs. 2.

Hockett, C. F. (1963). The problem of universals in language. In J. H. Greenberg (ed.) *Universals of Language.* Cambridge, Mass.: M.I.T. Press. pp. 1—22.

Holenstein, E. (1973). Jakobson und Husserl. Ein Beitrag zur Genealogie des Strukturalismus. *Tijdschrift voor Filosofie* 35:560—607.

Horne, K. M. (1966). *Language Typology: 19th and 20th Century Views.* Washington: Georgetown University.

Householder, F. W. (1960). First thoughts of syntactic indices. *IJAL* 26:195—197.

Humboldt, W. von (1836). *Über die Kawi-Sprache auf der Insel Java, nebst einer Einleitung über die Verschiedenheit des menschlichen Sprachbaues.* Berlin:Königliche Akademie der Wissenschaften.

Ingram, D. (1971). Typology and universals of personal pronouns. *WPLU* 5:P1—P35.

Isačenko, A. V. (1954, 1960). *Grammatičeskij stroj russkogo jazyka v sopostavlenii s slovackim* (The grammatical structure of Russian confronted with that of Slovak). I. and II. Bratislava:Izdatelstvo Slovackoj Akademii Nauk.

Ivič, M. (1953—54). O problemu padežne sisteme u vezi sa savremennim shvátanjima o lingvističnoj nauki (On the problems of case systems in connection with the modern approaches in linguistics). *Južnoslovenski Filolog* 20:191—211.

Ivič, M. (1957—58). Sistem predloških konstrukcija u srpskohrvatskom jeziku (The system of constructions with prepositions in Serbo-Croatian). *Južnoslovenski Filolog* 22:141—166.

Ivič, M. (1971). Leksema *jedan* i problem neodredjenog člana (The lexeme *jedan* and the problem of the indefinite article). *Zbornik za Filologiju i Lingvistiku* 14:103—120.

Jakobson, R. (1936). Beitrag zur allgemeinen Kasuslehre. *TCLP* 6:240—288.

Jakobson, R. (1941). *Kindersprache, Aphasie und allgemeine Lautgesetze.* Frankfurt am Main: Suhrkamp (2nd. ed. 1969).

Jakobson, R. (1953). Patterns in linguistics (Contribution to debates with anthropologists). *Selected Writings* 2. The Hague:Mouton Publishers. pp. 223—228.

Jakobson, R. (1958a). Typological studies and their contribution to historical comparative linguistics. *Proceedings of the 8th International Congress of Linguists.* Oslo:Oslo University Press. pp. 17—25.

Jakobson, R. (1958b). Morfologičeskije nabljudenija nad slavjanskim sklonenijem (Morphological observations on Slavic declension). *American contributions to the IVth International Congress of Slavists.* The Hague:Mouton Publishers. pp. 127—158.

Jakobson, R. (1962). Parts and wholes in language. *Selected Writings* 2. The Hague:Mouton Publishers. pp. 280—284.

Jakobson, R. (1970). Linguistics. *Main Trends of Research in the Social and Human Sciences.* Paris. pp. 419—463.

Jakobson, R. (1972). Verbal communication. *Scientific American* 227/3/:73—78.

Jarceva, V. N. (1975). Sopostavitel'no-tipologičeskoje izučenije jazykov i jego rol' v izučenii jazykov (The contrastive and typological study of language and its role in the study of languages). In Zs. Telegdi (ed.) *Modern Linguistics and Language Teaching.* Budapest:Akadémiai Kiadó. pp. 61—75.

Jarceva, V. N. (1976). Tipologija jazykov i problema univerzalij (Typology of languages and the problem of universals). *Voprosy Jazykoznanija* 2:6—16.

Jarceva, V. N. and Serebrennikov, B. A. (eds.) (1976). *Principy opisanija jazykov mira.* Principles of the description of the languages of the world. Moscow:Nauka.

Johnson, D. E. (1977). On relational constraints in grammar. In P. Cole, J. M. Sadock (eds.) *Grammatical Relations.* New York:Academic Press. pp. 151—178.

Kacnel'son, S. D. (1972). *Tipologija jazyka i rečevoje myšlenije* (Typology of language and speech related to thinking). Leningrad:Nauka.

Kálmán, B. Logische und grammatische Kongruenz. *Journal de la Société Finno-Ougrienne* (forthcoming).

Keenan, E. L. (1976). Towards a universal definition of "subject". In Ch. N. Li (ed.) *Subject and Topic*. New York: Academic Press. pp. 303—333.

Keenan, E. L. (1978). Language variation and the logical structure of universal grammar. In H. Seiler (ed.) *Language Universals*. Tübingen: Narr. pp. 89—123.

Keresztes, K. (1975). Hungarian Postpositions vs. English Prepositions: A Contrastive Study. *Working Papers 7. The Hungarian—English Linguistics Project*. Budapest.

Khrakovsky, V. S. (1970). Some theoretical problems of syntactic typology. In L. Dezső and P. Hajdú (eds.) *Theoretical Problems of Typology and the Northern Eurasian Languages*. Budapest: Akadémiai Kiadó. pp. 75—94.

Khrakovsky, V. S. (1973). Passive constructions (Definition, calculus, typology, meaning). In F. Kiefer (ed.) *Trends in Soviet Theoretical Linguistics*. Dordrecht: Reidel. pp. 59—75.

Khrakovsky, V. S. (1975). *Isčislenije diatez. Diatezi i zalogi* (Calculi of diathesis. Diathesis and voices). Leningrad. pp. 34—51.

Khrakovsky, V. S. (ed.) (1978). *Problemy teorii grammatičeskogo zaloga.* (Problems in the theory of grammatical voices). Leningrad: Nauka.

Khrakovsky, V. S. (ed.) (1981). *Zalogovyje konstrukcii v raznostrukturnych jazykach* (Constructions with voice in languages with different structures). Leningrad: Nauka.

Khrakovsky, V. S. Diathesis. *Acta Linguistica* (forthcoming).

Kibrik, A. E. (1979). Canonical ergativity and Daghestan languages. In F. Plank (ed.) *Ergativity*. New York: Academic Press. pp. 61—77.

Kiparsky, P. (1968). Linguistic universals and linguistic change. In E. Bach and R. T. Harms (eds.) *Universals in Linguistic Theory*. New York: Holt, Rinehart and Winston. pp. 171—202.

Kiss, E. K. Hungarian and English: a topic-focus prominent and a subject prominent language. In L. Dezső (ed.) *Contrasting Hungarian with English*. Budapest: Akadémiai Kiadó. (forthcoming).

Klimov, G. A. (1973). *Očerk obščej teorii ergativnosti* (An outline of a general theory of ergativity). Moscow: Nauka.

Klimov, G. A. (1976). Voprosy kontensivno-tipologičeskogo opisanija jazykov (Questions of contentive typological description of languages). In V. N. Jarceva and B. A. Serebrennikov (eds.) *Principy opisanija jazykov mira*. Moscow: Nauka. pp. 122—146.

Klimov, G. A. (1977). *Tipologija aktivnogo stroja* (A typology of active structure). Moscow: Nauka.

Kondakov, N. I. (1975). *Logičeskij slovar'-spravočnik* (A dictionary of logics). Moscow: Nauka.

Konferencija po problemam izučenija universal'nych i areal'nych svojstv jazykov. (1968). (Conference on problems of the study of universal and areal properties of languages). Moscow: Nauka.

Kont, K. (1963). *Käändsõnaline objekt läänemeresome keeltes* (Nominal object in Balto-Finnish). Eesti NEV Teaduste Akademia. Keele ja Kirjanduse Instituudi Uurimused 9. Tallinn.

Korš, F. (1877). *Sposoby otnositel'nogo podčinenija. Glava iz sravnitel'nogo sintaksisa* (Relative subordination. A chapter of comparative syntax). Moscow: Univ. Tipografii.

Koschmieder, E. (1965). *Beiträge zur allgemeinen Syntax*. Heidlelberg: Winter.

Kovács, F. (1971). *Linguistic Structures and Linguistic Laws*. Budapest: Akadémiai Kiadó.

Krámský, J. (1972). *The Article and the Concept of Definiteness in Language.* The Hague: Mouton Publishers.

Kroeber, A. L. (1960). On typological indices. I. Ranking of languages. *IJAL* 26:171—177.

Kuhn, Th. S. (1970). *The Structure of Scientific Revolutions.* (2nd ed.) Chicago: The University of Chicago Press.

Kuriłowicz, J. (1960). Le problème du classement des cas. *Esquisses linguistiques.* Wroclaw-Cracow. pp. 131—150.

Kurjajev, V. I. (1971). Vzaimootnošenije soderžatel'nych i formal'nych komponentov v postrojenii i razvertyvanii naučnych teorij (The relationship of components of content and form in the construction and development of scientific theories). *Voprosy Filosofii* 11:57—68.

Kuroda, S. Y. (1973). Edmund Husserl, grammaire générale et raisonnée and Anton Marty. *Foundations of Language* 10:169—196.

Lakatos, I. (1970). History of science and its rational reconstruction. *Boston Studies in the Philosophy of Science* VIII. Dordrecht. pp. 91—136.

Lehmann, W. P. (1972a). Converging theories in linguistics. *Language* 48:266—275.

Lehmann, W. P. (1972b). Contemporary linguistics and Indo-European studies. *Publications of the Modern Language Association of America.* 87:976—993.

Lehmann, W. P. (1974). *Proto-Indo-European Syntax.* Austin: University of Texas Press.

Lektorovskij , V. A. and Švyrev, V. S. (1971). Aktual'nye filosofsko-metodologičeskije problemy sistemnogo podchoda (Current philosophical and methodological problems of the systems approach). *Voprosy Filosofii* 1:146—152.

Li, Ch. N. (ed.) (1975). *Word Order and Word Order Change.* Austin: University of Texas Press.

Li, Ch. N. and Thompson, S. A. (1975). Subject and topic: a new typology of language. In Ch. N. Li (ed.) *Subject and Topic.* New York: Academic Press. pp. 457—489.

Lingvističeskaja tipologija i vostočnyje jazyki. (1965). (Linguistic typology and Oriental languages). Moscow: Nauka.

Lingvističeskije issledovanija po obščej i slavjanskoj tipologii. (1966). (Linguistic studies in general and Slavic typology). Moscow: Nauka.

Lötzsch, R. and Růžička, R. (eds.) (1976). *Satzstruktur und Genus verbi.* Berlin: Akademie Verlag.

Lyons, J. (1968). *Introduction to Theoretical Linguistics.* Cambridge: Cambridge University Press.

Magometov, A. A. (1965). *Tabasaranskij jazyk* (The Tabasaran language). Tbilisi: Mecniereba.

Majtinskaja, K. E. (1969). *Mestoimenija v jazykach raznych system* (Pronouns in languages of different systems). Moscow: Nauka.

Malošnaja, T. N. (ed.) (1963). *Issledovanija po strukturnoj tipologii* (Studies in structural typology). Moscow: Nauka.

Mamčur, Je. A. (1971). Kriterii naučnosti teoretičeskich koncepcij (Criteria for the scientificity of theoretical concepts.) *Voprosy Filosofii* 7:69—81.

Martinet, A. (1962). *A Functional View of Language.* Oxford: Clarendon Press.

Masayoshi, Shibatani (ed.) (1976). *The Grammar of Causative Constructions.* New York: Academic Press.

Maslov, Ju. S. (1978). K osnovanijam sopostavitel'noj aspektologii (On fundamentals of contrastive aspectology). In Ju.S. Maslov (ed.) *Voprosy sopostavitel'noj aspektologii.* (Questions of contrastive aspectology). Leningrad: Nauka. pp. 21—31.

Mathesius, V. (1975). *A Functional Analysis of Present-day English on a General Linguistic Basis.* Prague: Academia.

Menac, A. (1978). *Padež prjamogo dopolnenija s otricanijem v sovremennom russkom i chorvatskoserbskom jazykach* (The case of direct object with negation in Russian and Serbo-Croatian). Chorvatskoserbsko—russkije kontrastivnyje issledovanija 1. R. Filipović (ed.) Zagreb.

Meščaninov, I. I. (1963). *Struktura predloženija* (The structure of the sentence). Moscow: Nauka.

Meščaninov, I. I. (1967). *Ergativnaja konstrukcija v jazykach različnych tipov* (The ergative structure in different types of languages). Leningrad: Nauka.

Mikes, M., Dezső, L. and Vuković, G. (1972). *A főnévi csoport alapkérdései* (Fundamentals of the noun phrase). Novi Sad: Hungarológiai Intézet.

Milewski, T. (1950a). La structure de la phrase dans les langues indigènes de l'Amérique du Nord. *Lingua Poznaniensis* 2:162—207.

Milewski, T. (1950b). Podstawy teoretyczne typologii języków (Foundations of a theoretical typology of languages). *Biuletyn Polskiego Towarzystwa Językoznawczego* 10:122—140.

Misteli, F. (1893). *Charakteristik der hauptsächlichsten Typen des Sprachbaues.* Berlin: Dümmler.

Moravcsik, E. A. (1969). Determination. *WPLU* 1:64—98.

Moravcsik, E. A. (1971a). Agreement. *WPLU* 5:A1—A69.

Moravcsik, E. A. (1971b). Some cross-linguistic generalizations about yes—no questions and their answers. *WPLU* 7:45—193.

Nemser, W., Slamă-Cazacu, T. (1970). A contribution to contrastive linguistics. *Revue Romaine de Linguistique* 15:101—128.

Palek, B. (1971). Hyper-syntax as a potential typological parameter. *TLP* 4:97—106.

Palmatier, R. A. (1969). *A Descriptive Syntax of the Ormulum.* The Hague: Mouton Publishers.

Panfilov, V. (1977a). Linguistic universals and sentence typology. *Theoretical Aspects of Linguistics.* Moscow: Nauka. pp. 64—98.

Panfilov, V. (1977b). *Filosofskije problemy jazykoznanija* (Philosophical problems of linguistics). Moscow: Nauka.

Paul, H. (1880). *Prinzipien der Sprachgeschichte.* (5th ed., Halle, 1920.)

Peranteau, P. M., Levi, J. and Phares, G. (eds.) (1972). *The Chicago Witch-hunt.* Chicago: Chicago Linguistic Society.

Pete, I. (1973). *Sposoby vyraženija prostranstvennych otnošenij v russkom jazyke* (Expression of space relations in Russian). Szeged.

Pete, I. (1976). *Sposoby vyraženija vremennych otnošenij v russkom jazyke v zerkale vengerskogo jazyka* (Expression of temporal relations in Russian in the mirror of Hungarian). Budapest: Tankönyvkiadó.

Pike, K. (1967). *Language in Relation to a Unified Theory of the Structure of Human Behavior.* The Hague: Mouton Publishers.

Pilipenko, N. V. (1965). *Neobchodimost' i slučajnost'* (Necessity and chance). Moscow: Vysšaja Škola.

Pjall', E., Totsel, E., Tukumcev, G. (1962). *Sopostavitel'naja grammatika estonskogo i russkogo jazyka* (A contrastive grammar of Estonian and Russian). Tallinn: Eesti Riiklik Kirjastus.

Postal, P. M. (1970). The method of universal grammar. In P. L. Garvin (ed.) *Method and Theory in Linguistics.* The Hague: Mouton Publishers. pp. 113—131.

Ramat, P. (1973). Del problema della tipologia linguistica in Wilhelm von Humboldt e d'altro ancora. *Lingua e stile* 8:37—59.

Ramat, P. (1976). Introduzione. In P. Ramat (ed.) *La tipologia linguistica.* Bologna: Mulino. pp. 7—46.

Renzi, L. (1976). Storia e obiettivi della tipologia linguistica. In P. Ramat (ed.) *La tipologia linguistica.* Bologna: Mulino. pp. 47—77.

Ross, J. R. (1967). Gapping and the order of constituents. *PEGS Paper* 8. Washington.

Roždestvenskij, Ju. V. (1969). *Tipologija slova* (Typology of the word). Moscow: Vysšaja Skola.

Sadovskij, V. N. (1972). Obščaja teorija sistem kak metateorija (General systems theory as a metatheory). *Voprosy Filosofii* 4:78—89.

Sanders, G. A. (1972). Adverbial constructions. *WPLU* 10:93—129.

Sapir, E. (1921). *Language.* New York: Harcourt.

Šaumjan, S. K. (1971). *Filosofskije voprosy teoretičeskoj lingvistiki* (Philosophical problems of theoretical linguistics). Moscow: Nauka.

Schwartz, A. (1971). General aspects of relative clause formation. *WPLU* 6:139—171.

Schwartz, A. (1972). The VP-constituent of SVO languages. *WPLU* 8:21—54.

Sebeok, T. A. (1946). Finnish and Hungarian Case Systems: Their Form and Function. *Acta Instituti Hungarici Universitatis Holmiensis,* Series B. Linguistica 3. Stockholm.

Seiler, H. (1960). *Relativsatz, Attribut und Apposition.* Wiesbaden: Harrassowitz.

Seiler, H. (ed.) (1978). *Language Universals.* Tübingen: Narr.

Seiler, H. (1980). Determination: A functional dimension for interlanguage comparison. In H. Seiler (ed.) *Language Universals.* Tübingen: Narr. pp. 301—328.

Seiler, H. Language universal research, language typology and individual grammar. *Acta Linguistica.* (forthcoming).

Seiler, H., Brettschneider, G. et al. (1976). Materials for a research conference on language universals. (Mimeo.) Cologne.

Serebrennikov, B. A. (1974). *Verojatnostnyje obosnovanija v komparativistike* (Proof of probability in comparative studies). Moscow: Nauka.

Serov, N. K. (1970). O diachroničeskoj strukture processov (On the diachronic structure of processes). *Voprosy Filosofii* 772—80.

Sgall, P. (1967). Functional sentence perspective in a generative description. *Prague Studies in Mathematical Linguistics.* Prague. pp. 203—225.

Sgall, P. (1971). On the notion type of language. *TLP* 4:75—87.

Shannon, A. (1964). *A Descriptive Syntax of the Parker Manuscript of the Anglo-Saxon Chronicle from 734 to 891.* The Hague: Mouton Publishers.

Sharadzenidze, T. (1970). Language typology, synchrony and diachrony. In L. Dezső and P. Hajdú (eds.) *Theoretical Problems of Typology and the Northern Eurasian Languages.* Budapest: Akadémiai Kiadó. pp. 35—43.

Skalička, V. (1935). *Zur ungarischen Grammatik.* Prague: Filosofička Fakulta Univ. Karlovy.

Skalička, V. (1944). Über die Typologie der Bantusprachen. *Archiv Orientálni* 15:93—127.

Skalička, V. (1958). O současnem stavu typologie (On the present state of typology). *Slovo a Slovesnost* 19:224—232.

Skalička, V. (1968). Problem syntaktické typologie (The problem of syntactic typology). *Slavica Pragiensa* 10:137—142.

Skalička, V. (1974). Konstrukt-orientierte Typologie. *Linguistica Generalia 1. Studies in Linguistic Typology.* Prague. pp. 17—23.

Skorik, P. Ja. (1948). *Očerki po sintaksisu čukotskogo jazyka. Inkorporacija* (Studies on the syntax of Chukchee. Incorporation). Moscow:Nauka.

Skorik, P. Ja. (1965). O sootnošenii agglutinacii i inkorporacii (na materiale čukotskogo-kamčatskich jazykov) (On the relationship between agglutination and incorporation based on Chukchee and Kamchadal). In B. A. Serebrennikov and O. P. Sudnik (eds.) *Morfologičeskaja tipologija i problema klassifikacii jazykov.* Moscow:Nauka.

Slobin, D. (1970). Suggested Universals in the Ontogenesis of Grammar. *Working Papers 32.* Berkeley:Language-Behaviour Research Laboratory.

Solncev, V. M. (1971). *Jazyk kak sistemno-strukturnoje obrazovanije* (Language as a systemic and structural entity). Moscow:Nauka.

Staal, J. F. (1967). *Word Order in Sanskrit and Universal Grammar.* Dodrecht:Leiden.

Stankiewitz, E. (1966). Slavic morphophonemics in its typological and diachronic aspects. *Current Trends in Linguistics* 3. The Hague:Mouton Publishers. pp. 495—520.

Steinthal, H. (1860). *Characteristik der hauptsächlichsten Typen des Sprachbaues.* Berlin:Dümmler.

Stepanov, Ju. S. (1975). *Metody i principy sovremennoj lingvistiki* (Methods and principles of present-day linguistics). Moscow:Nauka.

Sviderskij, V. I. (1962). *O sootnošenii elementov i struktur v objektivnom mire i v poznanii* (On the relationship of elements and structures in the objective world and in cognition). Moscow:Izd. Soc.-ekon. Literatury.

Sviderskij, V. I. (1965). *Nekotoryje voprosy dialektiki izmenenija i razvitija* (Some problems of the dialectics of change and development). Moscow:Mysl.

Švyrev, V. S. (1971). Analiz naučnogo pòznanija v sovremennej filosofii nauk (The analysis of scientific cognition in current philosophy of science). *Voprosy Filosofii* 2:100—111.

Talmy, L. (1972, 1973). The basis for a cross-linguistic typology of motion location 1. *WPLU* 9:41—116, 2. *WPLU* 10:23—83.

Telegdi, Zs. (1970). A nyelvelmélet és a nyelvtipológia humboldti egysége (The unity of linguistic theory and language typology by Humboldt). *Általános Nyelvészeti Tanulmányok* VII. pp. 229—237.

Typologija grammatičeskich kategorij. (1975). (A typology of grammatical categories). Moscow:Nauka.

Ullmann, St. (1963). Semantic Universals. In J. H. Greenberg (ed.) *Universals of Language.* Cambridge, Mass.:M.I.T. Press.

Ultan, R. (1969). Some general characteristics of interrogative systems. *WPLU* 1:41—63.

Ultan, R. (1972a). The nature of future tenses. *WPLU* 8:35—100.

Ultan, R. (1972b). Some features of basic comparative constructions. *WPLU* 9:117—162.

Uspensky, V. A. (1968). *Principles of Structural Typology.* The Hague:Mouton Publishers.

Vajda, J. (1976). *Padežne mesne i vremenske konstrukcije* (Local and temporal constructions expressed by cases). Novi Sad: Institut za Hungarologiju.

Vědecká synchronní mluvnice spisovné češtiny. (Zakladni koncepce a problemy.) (1974). (Scientific synchronic grammar of Czech) (Basic conception and problems). Prague: Česki Komitet Slavistů.

Velten, H. V. (1932). The accusative case and its substitutes in various types of languages. *Language* 8:255—270.

Vennemann, Th. (1974). Topics, subjects, and word order: from SXV to SVX via TVX. In J. M. Anderson and Ch. Jones (eds.) *Historical Linguistics*. Amsterdam: North-Holland. pp. 339—376.

Voegelin, C. F. (1956). Subsystems within systems in cultural and linguistic typologies. In *For Roman Jakobson*. The Hague: Mouton Publishers. pp. 597—599.

Voegelin, C. F., Raumanujan, R. A., Voegelin. R. A. (1960). Typology of density ranges I: Introduction. *IJAL* 26:198—205.

Whiteley, W. H. (1966). *A Study of Yao Sentence Structure*. Oxford: Oxford University Press.

Winkler, H. (1887). *Zur Sprachgeschichte, Nomen, Verb und Satz. Antikritik.* Berlin: Dümmler.

Winkler, H. (1889). *Weiteres zur Sprachgeschichte*. Berlin: Dümmler.

WPLU = Working Papers on Language Universals. Stanford University.

Wundt, W. M. (1900). *Völkerpsychologie I. Die Sprache*. Leipzig: Engelmann.

Zvegincev, V. A. (1973). *Jazyk i lingvističeskaja teorija* (Language and linguistic theory). Moscow: Izd. Mosk. Univ.